History of the Bolshevik Party
– a popular outline

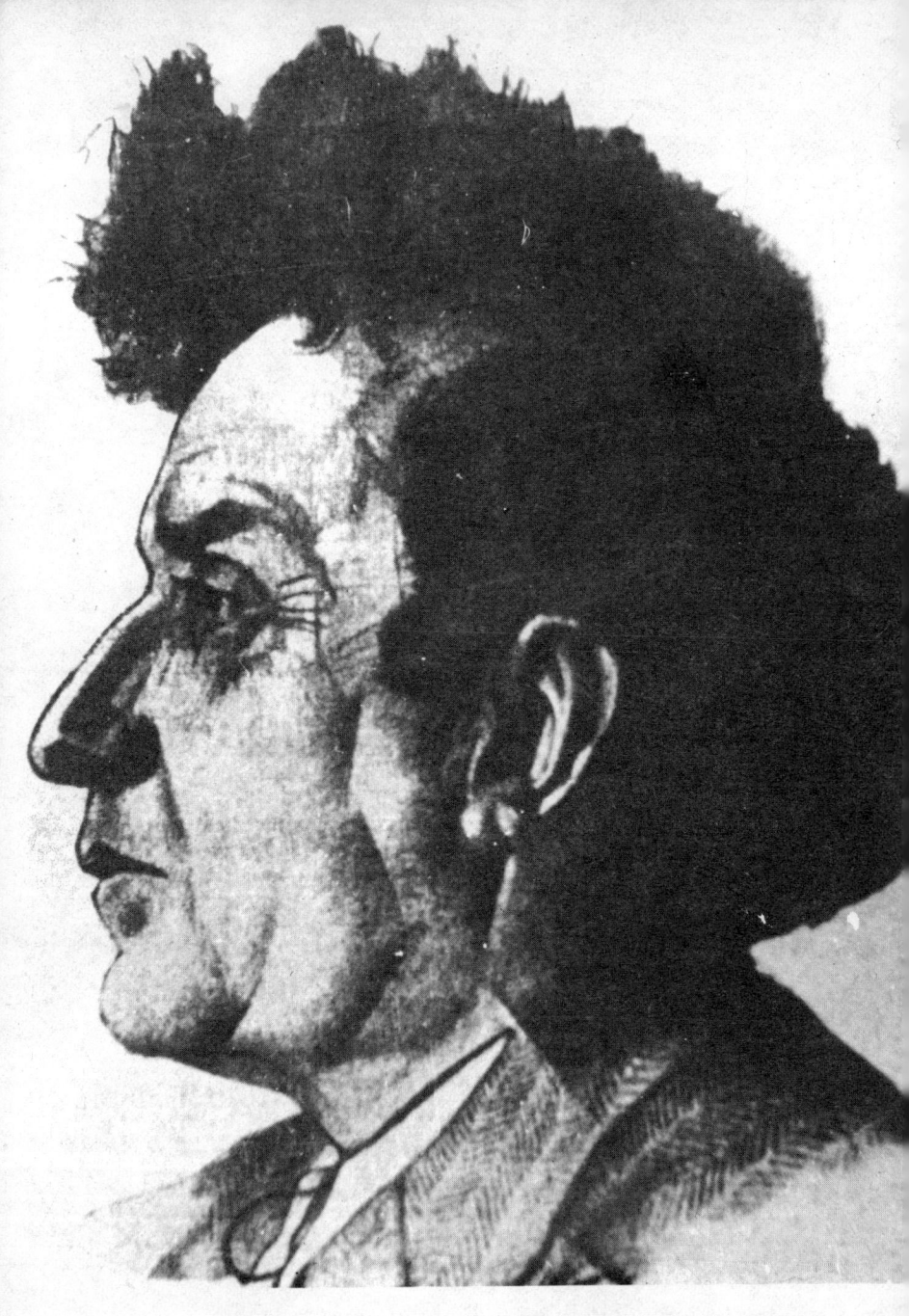

Grigorii Zinoviev

Grigorii Zinoviev

History of the Bolshevik Party
— *a popular outline*

translated by
R. *Chappell*

New Park Publications

First published in 1923 as
*Istoriya Rossiiskoi Kommunisticheskoi Partii
(Bolshevikov)—Populyarny Ocherk*
by State Publishing House
Moscow and Petrograd.

*Second Edition: 1924
This Edition: 1973*

Translation, Foreword and Glossary
Copyright © New Park Publications Ltd.
1973

Published by New Park Publications Ltd.
186a Clapham High Street, London, SW4 7UG.

**Set up, Printed and Bound
by Trade Union Labour**

Distributed in the United States by:
Labor Publications Inc.,
135 West 14 Street, New York,
New York 10011.

ISBN 0-902030-44-2

Printed in Great Britain by
Plough Press Ltd. (T.U.)
r/o 180 Clapham High Street, London, SW4 7UG.

Contents

Foreword	vii
Biographical Note	xii
From the Author	xxi

LECTURE ONE   1
[*Bourgeois Revolutionaries and the Russian Working Class before 1880*]

LECTURE TWO   27
[*Marxism versus Populism and Economism 1880-1900*]

LECTURE THREE   63
[*'Iskra' and the Fight for Bolshevism 1900-1903*]

LECTURE FOUR   97
[*The War with Japan and the First Russian Revolution 1904-1905*]

LECTURE FIVE   131
[*Lessons of the Revolution and the Years of Reaction 1906-1909*]

LECTURE SIX   165
[*The Bolshevik Party, Imperialist War and the Overthrow of Tsarism 1910-1917*]

APPENDIX I   201
Manifesto of the Russian Social-Democratic Labour Party (1898)

APPENDIX II   204
The War and Russian Social-Democracy (1914)

APPENDIX III   211
To the Workers of the USSR (1923)

APPENDIX IV   216
The Bolsheviks and the Hegemony of the Proletariat (1923)

APPENDIX V   222
Trotskyism (1924)

Glossary: Names and Organizations   225

Foreword

The book which follows consists of a series of lectures which Zinoviev gave to mark the 25th anniversary of the foundation of what was eventually to become the Russian Communist Party. It is an account of the history of the Party through its various stages down to February 1917, where the narrative ends.

Before dealing with the undoubted qualities of the work a word of warning must be issued to the reader. Zinoviev's work was published in 1923 when the struggle within the Russian Communist Party was beginning to assume intense proportions, and when the alliance between Zinoviev, Kamenev and Stalin against Trotsky was starting to take shape.

When the lectures were given, the triumvirate had not yet assumed power. The references to Trotsky are therefore cautious. But the implications of the lectures are clear, particularly in the footnote (Appendix 5) which Zinoviev inserted in the 1924 reprint.

Zinoviev's attack on Trotsky centres on the theory of Permanent Revolution. His account of this theory, developed by Trotsky in 1905, represents a complete distortion, particularly his allegations of Trotsky's 'underestimation' of the peasantry, which was to become one of the most important of the lies with which Stalin and his faction sought to discredit Trotsky after 1924.

In dealing with the controversies which dominated the preparations for the 1917 Revolution we must always bear in mind that at the beginning of the century, Russia was a country quite unlike Britain. Economically it lagged way behind western Europe; the vast majority of the population earned their living as peasants on the land while the working class, although concentrated in a few powerful and decisive centres, constituted only a small proportion of the population. Politically, Russia was still in the grip of a feudal, despotic Tsar; the capitalist class, having only developed in the relatively recent past, had not won the basic bourgeois rights — freely elected Parliaments, a free press etc. — which their fellow capitalists had achieved in Europe many generations before.

This, briefly, was the background against which the disputes, which Zinoviev describes in a distorted way, took place. The fundamental question of the revolution was this: what was to be the relationship between the working class and the capitalist class, both struggling against the Tsarist autocracy? On this issue there was a basic, irreconcilable difference. The Mensheviks (Zinoviev explains the origin of this term), while using Marxist terminology, in fact argued that the working class must subordinate itself politically to the capitalist class. The role of the working class was to support and assist the bourgeoisie to win its political freedoms. This would in turn pave the way for a period of capitalist development which would see the emergence of the working class and eventually, in the long-term future, the struggle for the socialist revolution.

It was against this conception that Lenin and the Bolsheviks were to fight at every stage in the preparation for 1917. As against Menshevism, Lenin insisted that the working class must be organized as an independent force to take the lead on *all* political questions. For Lenin understood, particularly after the experiences of 1905, that the capitalist class was too weak to fight for its own, bourgeois-democratic, revolution. Because of the lateness of capitalist development within Russia, the working class, although numerically small, was a decisive political force with a 'specific weight' far greater than mere numbers would have suggested. As against the peasantry which was a scattered and diffused class, the working class was highly concentrated in a few decisive centres. The great task of Marxism, said Lenin, was to establish the independence and leadership of this growing working class.

Here he was at one with Trotsky, on this most vital question of the revolution. But another question still remained unanswered: if the working class had to lead the struggle for the demands of the bourgeois revolution, what would happen after these had been won? The main point of Trotsky's theory of Permanent

Revolution* which Zinoviev so wilfully distorts, was that the revolution would be unable to stop at this point. Because of the international context in which the revolution would take place (imperialism) the working class would have to move over directly to the implementation of socialist measures. Thus the revolution would not come about through the establishment of the 'democratic dictatorship of the proletariat and the peasantry', as Lenin said it would. Instead Trotsky saw the proletariat as the leading force realizing an alliance with the poorer peasantry.

In the course of 1917, Lenin was to revise his position and accept the essence of Trotsky's theory. In his famous 'April Theses' issued on his return to Russia, Lenin demanded that the Bolsheviks cease their support for the Kerensky government and make plans for a second, proletarian revolution. Thus at the supreme moment of revolutionary crisis, the positions of Lenin and Trotsky were to come together against those of the majority of the old leaders of Bolshevism, amongst them Zinoviev.

Thus in no way did Trotsky 'underestimate' the peasantry; he saw them always as necessary allies of the working class. But he grasped with great clarity (more so than Lenin in this case) the *international* nature and consequences of the revolution in Russia. The fate of the Revolution would not be settled in Russia, but above all in Europe, through the struggle of the European working class to extend (make 'permanent') the gains of October 1917.

Zinoviev is unable to deal with these questions objectively in his account of the development of the Party. While he makes some mildly complimentary remarks about Trotsky's position in 1905 when he says in connection with Trotsky's editorship of the paper *Nachalo* that Trotsky 'gave it a considerably Bolshevik flavour', at the same time he fails entirely to deal with Trotsky's role in the 1905 Revolution as Chairman of the Petrograd Soviet.

Equally serious is Zinoviev's silence on the actual events of 1917. For good reason his narrative closes with the first, bourgeois-democratic revolution of February of that year. Zinoviev was amongst those who led the resistance to Lenin's 'April Theses' when it became clear that a large section of the Bolshevik Party leadership found themselves in the most conservative

---

* See L. D. Trotsky, *The Permanent Revolution*. New Park Publications.

position, having ended up adopting the outlook of Menshevism. For it was the Mensheviks who had always argued, as we have seen, that the revolution would take place in two distinct stages: first there would be the bourgeois revolution (which took place in February) and only much later would the working class be called upon to lead the socialist revolution.

Yet in continuing to support the bourgeois Kerensky government which was placed in power by the February revolution, the majority of the 'Old Guard' Bolsheviks, including Zinoviev, took precisely this line.

Even more serious is Zinoviev's failure to deal with the events of the October revolution. For he and Kamenev were the two leaders of the Bolshevik central committee who not merely opposed Lenin's plans for the insurrection but actually leaked the news of the plans to the non-Party paper, *Novaya Zhizn*. Lenin denounced these actions as 'strike-breaking' and 'a crime' calling for the expulsion of both Zinoviev and Kamenev from the Party, a demand which he later dropped.

Thus Zinoviev's lectures represent perhaps the first attempt to 'rewrite' the Party's history to meet the needs of immediate factional struggles, in particular the struggle against Trotsky and his supporters. Of course, in no way does he come anywhere near to the grotesque distortions which were to characterize Party histories under Stalin.

Trotsky replied to the mounting attacks on him in his famous *Lessons of October* (1924) which also answered the charges levelled against him by Zinoviev in these lectures. Trotsky shows that his conception of a Party history is quite different from that here presented by Zinoviev. Trotsky insists that a Party history must fall into three phases; it must deal with the history of the movement prior to the revolution; it must deal with the actual events of the revolution as they were reflected in the life and struggles of the party; finally it must deal with the Party's history after the revolution. For Trotsky the second period was the decisive one. For it was in the Revolution that the Party and all its individual leaders and members were faced with their supreme task. It was not so much a question of who had been 'orthodox' in the long years before the Revolution when it was not always possible to resolve many of the disputes and differences within the Party. A leader was to be judged by what he actually did during the Revolution. *Lessons of October* therefore concentrated on the actual events of 1917; on Lenin's struggle against the 'Old Guard', for the 'April Theses' and again on the very eve of the insurrection. In doing so he exposed Zinoviev's capitulatory position on both decisive occasions.

Despite these serious weaknesses, which the reader must keep constantly in mind, Zinoviev's lectures are nonetheless of great value and interest.

For they reveal the enormous struggle for *political principle* which underlay the history of the Bolshevik Party in Russia. At no stage of that history, from 1898 right through to 1917, was Lenin in the slightest degree willing to sacrifice the principles of the movement for immediate short-term 'unity'. It was this insistence on the theoretical foundations of the Party and the need, at all times, to protect them, which led to the split with the Mensheviks. Although only apparently on a matter of the wording of Party Rules, as Zinoviev makes clear, it was a split which went to the very heart of the problems of the Revolution: was the Party to abandon the independence of the working class in order to form an alliance with the 'progressive' elements of the bourgeoisie?

This is by no means a matter of purely historical significance. For it was Stalin and his followers, once they had defeated Trotsky and his supporters, who reverted to precisely this Menshevik position. For the 'theory' of Socialism in One Country which Stalin 'discovered' in 1924 substituted the struggle to establish the independence of the working class in every country in favour of an alliance between the Parties of the Communist International and the 'democratic' wing of the capitalist class. It was this Popular Front policy which was to produce such tragic defeats in France and Spain in the 1930s and most recently in Chile.

Zinoviev's lectures are also interesting in that they demonstrate clearly the important role which Plekhanov played in the foundation of the Marxist movement in Russia. Despite the fact that he later split from Lenin when the movement had to make a decisive turn to the working class in the early years of the century, his earlier role had been of inestimable significance. For it was Plekhanov who was the first to take up the fight against the Narodniks with their conception that the peasantry and not the working class was the decisive revolutionary force, which went along with their advocacy of terrorism as the principal means of revolutionary struggle.

These struggles of Plekhanov raise 'old' questions which are also extremely 'new'. For the last twenty years has seen a revival of precisely this theory within the Trotskyist movement. For the Pabloites (later joined by the American Socialist Workers Party) held that the working class was no longer the force to carry out the socialist revolution; at the same time these revisionist groups turned to 'guerrilla warfare' and individual terrorism as substitutes for building the Party. Zinoviev's lectures bring out absolutely clearly that these ex-Trotskyists can find nothing in Lenin and his fight for Bolshevism which in the slightest supports their petty-bourgeois conceptions.

It was also ironical that Zinoviev, who all his life fought against the idea of individual terrorism as the instrument for the liberation of the working class, should eventually be murdered by Stalin in the Moscow Trials after being falsely and fraudulently accused of terrorism against the Soviet Republic.

Zinoviev's lectures also bring out in detail a point which Lenin deals with in his *Left Wing Communism*: the fact that the Party was trained and steeled through its ability to work under the most varied and rapidly changing conditions. Zinoviev establishes with great clarity the fact that the movement had to endure periods of enormous difficulty, when it was reduced to small numbers often living in exile and having little contact with the working class. At other times, it worked in conditions of legality, sending its representatives to the Parliament (Duma) and having a much larger following in the working class. And because it was so firmly based on the theory and principles of Marxism it was a movement which was able to adopt the most *flexible* tactics in dealing with all the concrete questions which emerged in the course of preparing for the revolution.

It is this lesson which must above all be grasped by the movement today. The transformation of the Socialist Labour League into the Workers Revolutionary Party has been possible only on the basis of an unrelenting struggle over many decades, and often in most difficult circumstances, for principles against all brands of revisionism, reformism and Stalinism.

It is a decisive step forward, not simply for the movement in Britain, but for the International Committee of the Fourth International. It is an advance for the Trotskyist movement, equally as decisive as any of the events related in Zinoviev's lectures.

Biographical Note

GRIGORII EVSEYEVICH ZINOVIEV, whose real name was Radomyslsky, was born in 1883 at Elizavetgrad (later re-named Zinovievsk) in the Kherson province of Russia. The son of a Jewish petty bourgeois family, he had no formal education but was taught at home, and started work as a teacher at the age of 15. He soon took an active part in the strike struggles which broke out in 1900-1901, and joined the Russian Social-Democratic Labour Party in 1901.

During 1902 he went abroad to Berlin and Paris, then studied for a time in the University of Berne: while in Switzerland he met Lenin and Plekhanov early in 1903. During August of that year he attended the historic second Social Democratic Labour Party Congress in London, when the split between the Bolsheviks and Mensheviks took place. Zinoviev immediately supported the Bolsheviks and joined their faction; after the congress he was sent back to Russia as a party worker, but his health was poor and he had to return abroad.

In 1905 he went again to Russia and took a leading part in the St. Petersburg party organization, publishing the newspaper *Proletarii*. Throughout 1906 he carried out agitation among the St. Petersburg metal workers, who sent him as their delegate to the Fifth Party Congress of May 1907 in London, where he was elected for the first time to the Central Committee. The next year he was arrested for his revolutionary activities, but was released on the grounds of his ill-health; he then went to Switzerland and became Lenin's closest collaborator from that time until 1917. He was the only Bolshevik to support Lenin in 1910 against those who advocated compromising with the Mensheviks and retaining the joint central committee (during this period the Bolsheviks and Mensheviks were formally in the same organization). In 1911 he lectured at Lenin's party school for Bolshevik underground workers, held at Longjumeau, near Paris.

At the Sixth Party Conference in Prague during January 1912 he was elected to the new all-Bolshevik Central Committee. During the First World War he took a clear internationalist stand, representing the Bolshevik party at the 1915 Zimmerwald conference against the war, and the Kienthal conference of 1916; he helped to organize the 'Zimmerwald Left' which called for the imperialist war to be turned into a civil war. Together with Lenin he wrote the pamphlet *Socialism and the War* (1915) and a collection of articles, *Against the Current* (1916) which attacked the social-patriotic betrayal of the reformist parties in the Second International.

After the February revolution of 1917 he returned to Russia with Lenin, but, like the other leading Bolsheviks, initially opposed Lenin's 'April Theses' which called for the overthrow of the bourgeois Provisional Government. He went underground with Lenin during the 'July Days', when the Provisional Government clamped down on the Bolsheviks; they were both forced to hide in Finland, and returned to Petrograd only in October.

At this point, faced with the immediate necessity of taking power, Zinoviev, along with Kamenev, came out openly against the insurrection. He and Kamenev published an article in the non-party press which exposed the Bolshevik's plans for the insurrection; for this Lenin denounced them as 'strike breakers' and proposed their expulsion from the party, a demand which was later dropped.

After the October revolution, Zinoviev advocated a coalition government to include the Mensheviks and SRs and resigned from the Central Committee in protest against Lenin's resolution excluding these parties, but returned within a few days. Nevertheless he became one of the Soviet regime's principal figures; at first the chief party spokesman in the Trade Union Central Council, he presided at all the early trade union congresses, and was later elected president of the Petrograd Soviet. Petrograd was the centre of the metal-working industries where the core of Bolshevik trade union cadres were concentrated, and where Zinoviev had considerable support within the party.

When the government was transferred to Moscow during the Civil War, he was appointed chairman of the Northern Commune: at this time he was also a member of the Military Revolutionary Committee of the 7th Army and president of the Committee for the Defence of the Republic. At the Eighth Party

Congress in March 1919 he was elected a candidate member of the Politbureau, and a full member at the Tenth Congress in 1921.

At the Comintern's foundation in 1919, on Lenin's motion he was elected chairman of the Executive Committee. One of his biggest achievements was to win the majority of the German Independent Social-Democratic Party for fusion with the new German Communist Party (KPD) in 1920, after a four-hour speech in German! However, against Trotsky's opposition to an adventure, he and Bela Kun instigated the abortive rising in Germany in 1921, believing that this would 'electrify' and spur to action the masses; in fact its defeat led to a great crisis in the German Communist Party and increased the isolation of the USSR.

At the plenum of the ECCI prior to the Third Congress of the Comintern, he bitterly opposed the introduction of the tactic of the 'United Front', the policy designed to win the mass of workers away from their reformist leaders. However he eventually agreed that this tactic should be presented to the Congress as the official policy of the Executive, and delivered the main report to the Congress himself.

A decisive turning point in the international situation was the defeat of the 1923 German revolution. As president of the Commintern, Zinoviev urged on the KPD with left phrases, but only half-heartedly supported Trotsky's proposal for a definite plan of action. When the irresoluteness of the KPD leadership led to the failure of the plan, he sanctioned the cancelling of the insurrection at the decisive moment and made the KPD secretary, Brandler, the scapegoat for its failure. When Trotsky protested against this bureaucratic evasion of responsibility, Zinoviev used his influence within the foreign Communist Parties to have Trotsky denounced at the fifth Comintern Congress (the so-called 'Congress of Bolshevization')

Zinoviev had opposed Trotsky at almost every crucial turn of Bolshevik policy in government; after the onset of Lenin's illness in 1922 he had come together with Kamenev and Stalin to form the *troika* which was eventually to wield virtually all state power. Despite Lenin's serious doubts, he led the Petrograd delegation in pushing through Stalin's appointment to General Secretary at the 11th Party Congress in 1922.

At the 12th Party Congress which took place in the vacuum of leadership left by Lenin's illness, the *troika* covered up their intrigue with a whispering campaign against Trotsky ('he imagines himself a Bonaparte') and a glorification of Lenin.

Zinoviev in fact took the initiative in the struggle against

Trotsky, answering the crisis of leadership with the suppression of all discussion of policy: 'Every criticism of the party line, even a so-called 'left' criticism, is now objectively a Menshevik criticism.'

However, when in the summer of 1923 wildcat strikes broke out in the industrial centres, threatening the base of the régime, the triumvirs found many party cadres in sympathy with the strikers' demands. Within the party, 46 prominent Bolsheviks signed a declaration in October calling for the restoration of party democracy and the right to form factions, and severely criticizing the economic policies of the ruling clique. This was close to the policies fought for by Trotsky.

Adapting to this opposition, Zinoviev made a speech in November promising to restore party democracy — but once begun, the discussion revealed enormous hostility to the triumvirate within the party, and it was hastily suppressed.

Trotsky then openly broke with the 'Old Guard', writing an Open Letter attacking their handling of the 'New Course'. Zinoviev's reply, at the 13th Congress the next year, was to demand that Trotsky should publicly recant his views — an unheard-of demand at that time which many of Zinoviev's own supporters would not back, and which he had to drop. 'It is now a thousand times more necessary than ever that the party should be monolithic', he declaimed.

In autumn 1924 Trotsky wrote 'The Lessons of October' as a preface to an edition of his speeches in 1917. Zinoviev used this as an excuse to launch the 'Literary debate' — a massive campaign in the party press in which the slogan of Trotsky's 'underestimation of the peasantry' was invented and proclaimed, while the writings of Trotsky and his comrades in the Left Opposition were suppressed. It was implied that Trotsky's non-Bolshevik past meant he was hostile to Bolshevism — i.e. that he was basically a Menshevik at heart.

At the end of 1924 Zinoviev demanded in the Politbureau that the Central Committee be asked to expel Trotsky from its ranks; Stalin, sensing the crisis this would provoke within the party, refused to comply. Instead Trotsky was dismissed as Commissar of War. Once Trotsky had been removed from any position of power, the chief force holding the triumvirate together was gone. Zinoviev intrigued with Kamenev to oust Stalin from the General Secretaryship, and proposed that he replace Trotsky as Commissar of War; they found it was too late to dislodge Stalin from his position in the apparatus.

The increasing isolation of Russia following the defeat of the German revolution in 1923 and the temporary stabilization of conditions in Western Europe had strengthened the position of the bureaucracy, and during late 1924 brought Stalin to the fore as the dominant force in the *troika*. When Bukharin abandoned the perspective of revolution in Europe and in autumn 1924 advocated making wholesale concessions to the peasantry so as gradually to build 'socialism in one country', Stalin seized on this theory as an ideological justification for the growing power of the apparatus and in April 1925 attempted to make it official party policy.

Both Zinoviev and Kamenev strongly opposed this move, but the breach was hushed up in order to avoid scandalizing the party. Zinoviev did not come out openly against 'socialism in one country' until September 1925, in his book *Leninism,* where he argued that on its own the backward Soviet economy could never raise its productive technique to a level high enough for socialism, and that to abandon the perspective of revolution abroad was a break with Leninist internationalism. At the October session of the Central Committee he demanded a free debate on this question at the forthcoming 14th Party Congress, but was outvoted by the supporters of Stalin and Bukharin, who at the same time prohibited any public criticism of official policy.

A tremendous clash between the opposing factions took place at the 14th congress, but the outcome was that Stalin and Bukharin increased their majority on the CC. The new CC immediately set about destroying the strength of the 'Leningrad opposition': Zinoviev was replaced by Kirov as Leningrad party secretary and his supporters were removed from positions of authority.

In April 1926 the Leningrad and Left Oppositions finally began to collaborate; Zinoviev then revealed to Trotsky the methods by which the triumvirate had excluded him from power. At the July session of the CC Zinoviev declared that 'On the question of apparatus-bureaucratic repression, Trotsky was right as against us'; and Trotsky read out a joint statement attacking Stalin's policies.

Stalin hit back with a charge that they had violated party discipline by forming a faction, and the CC voted by a massive majority to dismiss Zinoviev as president of the Comintern. The Opposition turned to the party rank-and-file, only to find an organized heckling campaign to prevent them being heard at meetings: Zinoviev was driven from the platform at the 15th conference of the party. However, he shrank back from an all-out conflict with the apparatus, vowing not to bring matters to the point of expulsion from the party — which meant accepting in advance the limits laid down by Stalin.

Ideologically, Zinoviev remained hostile to the theory of permanent revolution and clung to the shibboleth of the 'democratic dictatorship of the proletariat and peasantry', even within the Joint Opposition, and insisted that their *Platform* (1927) should specifically deny its validity.

The Platform was drawn up in May as a balance-sheet of the position reached by the revolution, and a campaign for signatures to it was launched in preparation for the 15th Congress due at the end of the year. Zinoviev optimistically expected 20-30,000 signatures; they got 6,000. Although their perspectives had been proved correct, the effect of the international defeats of the proletariat was a greater force, producing demoralization throughout the party, and the bureaucracy prepared to expel the opposition before the congress even took place.

On 14th November the CC expelled Trotsky and Zinoviev from the party, together with virtually the entire Opposition. By December Zinoviev had parted company from Trotsky and capitulated to Stalin; on 18th December he appeared at the Congress to condemn his own views as 'wrong and anti-Leninist'. Zinoviev was readmitted to the party in 1928 and appointed to an unimportant post in the Consumer Cooperatives, then to the Collegium of the Peoples Commissariat of Food. From then on he and Kamenev, who had capitulated with him, issued denunciations of the Left Opposition to the order of the bureaucracy. They had ceased to live politically.

However, during the period 1930-32 when the country was convulsed by the consequences of the forced collectivization begun in 1928, they began anxiously to discuss the dangers of the new policy. The development of the economic crisis led to a revival of opposition to Stalin within the apparatus itself; because of this weakening of its position the bureaucracy had to eliminate any candidates for leadership of any opposition group. For being in possession of a document emanating from the Right Opposition which bitterly attacked Stalin and collectivization, they were expelled from the party and exiled to Siberia. In 1933 they again recanted and prostrated themselves before Stalin; they were finally allowed to return to Moscow in May, broken men.

Stalin hoped to use Zinoviev as a means of striking against 'Trotskyism' and thereby consolidate the ranks of the bureaucracy. In December 1934 Zinoviev and Kamenev were arrested and brought before a military tribunal 'in connection' with the GPU-engineered assassination of Kirov (this was part of a campaign of harassment to force them to indict Trotsky); they were sentenced to 10 years imprisonment as the leaders of a mythical counter-revolutionary group.

Finally in August 1936 they were brought from the jails to be framed in the first of the Moscow show trials. After making a public 'confession', Zinoviev was sentenced to death for 'organizing the joint Trotskyite-Zinovievite Terrorist Centre for the assassination of Soviet government and CPSU leaders', and shot on August 21st, 1936.

From the Author

The Russian Communist Party is not just any party. History decreed that the R.C.P was to become a mighty instrument of human progress and a major instrument of the world revolution. Its importance is great and immeasurable in the history not only of Russia but also in that of the whole world. So it is not accidental that the course of development of the R.C.P is studied today by the best minds of the international workers' movement. And so, the more is it the duty of each one of us who has to live and fight in the ranks of the R.C.P. to know its history and to study each of the steps along its difficult road to victory and the smallest episodes of its heroic struggle for the cause of the liberation of the proletariat.

The following six lectures which I read on the eve of the 25th anniversary of our party afford only a most cursory sketch of its history. The five years after 1917 on their own would require several books. My lectures are but preliminary drafts which only serve as a brief introduction to the history of our party. I am presenting them here upon the insistence of comrades and only because the literature of the history of the R.C.P. is as yet very poor. In view of this paucity, my sketches might possibly be of some use.

LECTURE ONE

WHAT is a party? This question would appear to be very simple. Amongst those present there will be without doubt many party members, and it is even possible that this question will seem to them an idle one. But this is not so at all.

When we are dealing with scientific definitions in those fields where masses of people are involved in a living way—this is entirely applicable to social organizations—then you will nearly always see that the representatives of different classes and world-outlooks define differently the essence of this or that social organization. Let us take as the nearest example to the present case, that of the trade union in which millions of people participate. Everyone knows what such an organization consists of. And yet, at the same time, the representatives of different classes give it different definitions. While Karl Marx used four words to express the essence of a trade union as 'a school of socialism' the representatives of the bourgeois world of science define it quite differently. The Webbs, the well-known British writers of reformist and Menshevik persuasion, maintain that a trade union is nothing other than an organization of mutual aid and in fact, benevolence. And if in addition you wish to know how, let's say, some German professor supporting the Catholic Centre party defines a trade union you will find that in his opinion it is virtually a religious institution or a charitable foundation. And this is understandable, for in questions where the interests of hundreds of thousands of people are directly involved you will search in vain for any impartiality in the definition of the most ordinary things. Therefore our wish to define a party, from the very beginning, is far from idle.

Marxist and bourgeois definitions of the word 'party'

The word 'party' comes from the Latin *pars*, that is, a part. Today we Marxists say that a party is a part of a particular class. The representatives of the bourgeois world of course think otherwise. So for example the distinguished German conservative journalist Stahl who classified parties by the appearance of their degree of revolutionary or constitutional basis in relation to the old regime came to the conclusion that the struggle of parties is the struggle between the divine and the human order, between the precepts of divine providence and institutions created as a result of the transient needs and fancies of man, or to put it more briefly, between good and evil. And the no less distinguished Zurich political figure, Rohmer, attempts to place psychology at the basis of the definition of parties. He says approximately the following: 'Human society is born, develops and dies. Consequently it can be young or old. In accordance with its age this or that political outlook holds sway. In man's childhood the passive forces of the spirit prevail; sensibility and living fantasy develop during this stage but there is no creative force or rational criticism. Radicalism above all corresponds to this state. (Hence radical parties). In youth and maturity the creative forces of the spirit and healthy criticism move to the fore, in youth a striving for creativity plays the major role while in maturity it becomes one to conserve what has been acquired. Liberalism and conservatism correspond to these states. (According to this theory the majority of those present in this hall filled with communists ought to be either liberals or conservatives.) Finally in old age the passive forces of the spirit take the upper hand; a fear of everything new and an addiction to the old; this corresponds to absolutism. Thus in any society young, mature and senile elements are simultaneously in existence and we can see corresponding to this co-existence radical, liberal, conservative and absolutist parties out of which those which most closely match the temperament and spirit of the people predominate. The existence of all these parties is inevitable; political life must proceed through equally active forces which have developed in society and the wise politician must even when fighting against them never aim to destroy any one of them completely because such an aim is unattainable, and to accomplish it would only drive the infection inside the organism. The temperament of a given individual will primarily determine his adherence to one or another party. Thus Alcibiades* was a boy all his life, Pericles† remained a youth until his grave, Scipio‡ was a man and Augustus§ was born an old man. And peoples also are in just the same way distinguished by different characters: the Germans are conservative by temperament but liberal by their cast of mind; the Russians are radical but inclined towards absolutism.' (All this was of course written before 1917).

*General in Ancient Greece, switched sides from Athens to Sparta to thwart Athens' imperial power and support Sparta's right to national independence.

†Statesman who broke rule of aristocratic party in Athens and extended democracy to all Athenian citizens, but suppressed weaker states to construct Athenian empire.

‡Roman General, crushed major tenants' revolt to save the government of the day.

§Emperor who re-organized Roman government to give himself supreme power.

Why cannot bourgeois science provide a correct definition of the word 'party'?

So you can see that in bourgeois science the definitions of the concept of 'party' are extremely diverse. And it is a rare thing when one of its representatives decides to take the bull by the horns and says straight out that a party is the militant organization of this or that class. This simple truth which is absolutely plain to you and me, bourgeois scientists will not and cannot admit for the same reason that they avoid calling parliamentarianism or the church by their proper names. The bourgeois system is by its very nature compelled to depict a whole number of institutions designed for the class oppression of the proletariat as organs of class harmony and reconciliation; it has to present them to public opinion and even to itself in just this form and not as organs of class struggle.

To clarify even more I will give you a definition of the word 'party' belonging to one of the comparatively inoffensive Russian journalists, the half-Cadet, half-Narodnik and fairly talented journalist, Vodovozov. In a particular essay devoted to the definition of the word 'party' he writes 'What is a party? This word refers to more or less sizeable groups of people having common political ideals and striving for one and the same political reforms and organized for the defence of these ideals or for the struggle to realize them'. This definition appears to be innocuous and close to the truth. But in fact the author consciously and carefully avoids the words 'class' and 'class struggle'. In his opinion a party is purely and simply an organization of like-minded people sympathizing with a specific 'ideal'. To put it another way the very essence is lacking from this definition, it lacks flesh and blood, suffers from anaemia and has no real content.

Milyukov's Definition

Let us take an even more recent example: Milyukov's definition. You will see that this too is dictated by a particular class interest. We all know that the Cadet Party which Milyukov led called itself 'non-class'. We fought it on this ground and demonstrated that non-class parties do not exist and that the Cadet Party was a class one representing a definite class of landowners and the bourgeoisie. For if today you cast a glance in retrospect, that is, look back, then you will understand why Milyukov, in the event, emerged simultaneously as a bourgeois scholar and as a militant politician. For him as a militant politician it was necessary that the class, landowner character of his party was not clear to the people: the Cadets could not openly tell the masses that they were defending the interests of the landowners and the upper bourgeoisie, that is, of the small propertied minority of the population. As a militant politician he sensed and understood that at every mass meeting it was necessary to keep his party under a veil, to bring it onto the stage as a beautiful unknown and to conceal its features carefully. And in this task Milyukov the militant politician was faithfully served by that pillar of learning, Professor Milyukov, who proved with the aid of his bourgeois erudition that it is not at all obligatory for a party to be a class one and that his party was a group of like-minded people having definite 'ideals' irrespective of what layer of the population they might be connected with. This example clearly shows you how easy it is to throw a bridge across from the academic definition

P.N. Milyukov

of Vodovozov to the wholly concrete active bourgeois policy of Milyukov. Vodovozov's latter formula was very useful as it could easily shield the Cadet party and thus smuggle in a class party under a non-party yoke.

The S.R. party's formula

Let us now take some closer neighbours of ours, the Socialist-Revolutionaries. You know that they did not call their party non-class but inter-class. This definition flowed from their programme. And in fact the classic formula of the Socialist-Revolutionaries stated that they represent in the first place the proletariat, in the second, the peasantry, and in the third, the intelligentsia: that is, three major social layers at one and the same time. For this reason the very first theoretical battles waged between the Marxists and the S.R.s revolved around the assertion that inter-class parties do not exist. Every party is connected with a definite class and must therefore defend definite interests. We have linked our fate with the proletariat, we said. This still does not mean that we will have an inimical relationship with the peasantry, particularly in this predominantly peasant country. The task of the proletariat in such a country consists in creating a certain co-operation and collaboration with a second and numerically vast class. We have come from the proletariat. We are *its* party. While being a party of the proletariat, we will, however, lead the peasantry in struggle too, for we have many interests in common.

After the events of the recent years the practice of the S.R. party has become sufficiently clear and only now is it transparently clear why they latched on to that definition of the concept of the party which they gave in the 1900s, for example, when their party was still only being born. It seemed to many young comrades at that time that Plekhanov — then the generally acknowledged leader of our party — paid too much attention to this controversy; it seemed that he had embarked upon a struggle without any real point. Many people then supposed that the polemic between Plekhanov and Chernov was purely academic, and others reproached them for starting a row over the

V.M. Chernov

concept of 'party and class' instead of waging a joint struggle against autocracy. But now you can see that this dispute was not academic but political and highly important.

That is why it is necessary above all to specify what you and I will understand by the word 'party' and define it clearly and exactly. We understand by this word a political organization forming a part of any class. To put it another way parties are proletarian and bourgeois. For us, a party is not simply a group of like-minded people or a collection of people sharing a common ideology which, irrespective of their connection with this or that class, they can preach wherever they wish. For us a party is, I repeat, a part of a particular class, which has arisen from its depths and has linked its fate with it. And the circumstance of the class from which a given party arises places upon it an ineffaceable imprint, determines the whole of its future life and its role in relation to a given state.

Class and Party

Today we use the words 'working class' and 'class' which are clear, comprehensible and beyond the realm of debate for any of us. For you and I the concept of 'class' has entered our flesh and blood and our everyday life: we have seen a class acting in two revolutions and have studied it well; for us it is an elementary basic concept. But previously it was not so. From my exposition you will see that the whole struggle between the Marxists and the Narodniks took shape, at least in its first period, over the formula of 'class' or simply 'people' as it was then expressed. There was a time when the entire struggle in Russian socialism turned around the questions: what is a class and should the revolutionary have in mind a particular class or is he obliged to fight for the whole 'people'?

As you know the theory of the class struggle was discovered by none other than Marx. This does not mean that he discovered the class struggle. This struggle is not a theory but a living fact. But formulating, generalizing and providing us with a conception of the whole history of mankind as a struggle of different classes was Marx's work. And the whole struggle of the founders of our

LECTURE ONE

Marxist party against the first generation of revolutionaries, the Narodniks, could essentially be to explaining the class struggle by the Russian experience and to providing a conception of what the working class in Russia was. That is why this simple concept which today forms the property of each one of us, the concept that our party is a part of the working class, has been forged over decades of theoretical and practical struggle. And if we wish to understand the history of our party then we must before all else be quite clear on this first point.

In finishing the examination of this question I must say the following as well. I may be reminded that frequently one class has several parties. This is of course true. The bourgeoisie as a whole for example can count several parties: republicans, democrats, radical-socialists, simple radicals, independent liberals, conservatives etc. 'Doesn't this fact contradict the definition I have given?' I will be asked. I don't think so. It is necessary to bear in mind that bourgeois parties often in practice form not separate self-contained parties but merely factions of a single bourgeois party. These factions fight amongst themselves like game-cocks at this or that moment (especially when it is a question of elections) and rattle pasteboard swords at each other generally. Often it is even advantageous to them to put things over to the people as if they had serious disagreements. But in actual fact on the basic questions embracing millions of people they share a complete unanimity. They quarrel only over secondary questions while on the fundamental questions over which people fight on the barricades, plan revolutions and suffer from civil war and famine — on all these questions, and above all on the question of private property, all bourgeois parties are unanimous. And in the final count we have every right to say that in relation to the main questions there exists only one big bourgeois party, the party of the slave-owners and supporters of private property.

In history there are plenty of examples of this. At one time in America the northern and the southern states came to blows over disagreements on the question of slavery. But this did not prevent the young bourgeois country which was only then taking shape, from emerging a short time later before the whole world in the role of a strong bourgeois state based firmly upon the principle of private property and in no way denying modern capitalist slavery. And you can in general point to as many such collisions between different bourgeois parties as you like but they only confirm our position that a party forms a part of a definite class.

Now I shall direct your attention to yet another circumstance. It should not be thought that every class immediately puts forward as it were a ready-made party corresponding to its interests as a whole. It would be a mistake to think that things are just as simple as follows: class no. 1 with party no. 1; class no. 2 with party no. 2. In social life and conflict things develop in a much more complex way. Individual people can make mistakes. It sometimes seems to them that they belong heart and soul to one class but when put to the test and a decisive moment arrives it can turn out that in fact they are in their whole being of another class. Their road follows a zigzag path. In certain periods of their development they put forward definite policies. In the course of time and under the influence of the turmoils of the class struggle and whirlwind of great events; when hidden layers of the particular class heave up and sharply pose new questions, deep down inside these people regroupings, shifts and crystallizations take place. And it is only a long while afterwards in the critical years that the basic questions powerfully emerge and divisions are finally created which really correspond to the given class. That is why if you approach this question too schematically and too simplistically you will meet many contradictions in your way. This basic question of our life has to be approached scientifically as befits Marxists — that is by rejecting from the outset an excessively mechanical approach to social phenomena. One has to understand that a party is not born overnight, that it takes shape over years, that inside its ranks definite social regroupings occur and that individual groups and people will sometimes fall accidentally into this or that party, will then leave it and others will take their place. And only in the process of struggle when we are confronted with a more or less completed cycle of developments can it be said that a particular party fully corresponds to a given class.

All the above also gives us an answer to the question, what is the relation between the Communist, Bolshevik Party and the working class? It can be said: if a party is a part of a class, if our party is a part of the working class, its representative body, vanguard and leader then how is it that there are still other workers' parties? How is it that there is the party of the Mensheviks calling itself a workers' party and the party of the Socialist-Revolutionaries which also declares that it defends the working class? And speaking on an international scale how is it that there exist Social-Democracy and the Second International, both connected with the working class? Doesn't all this contradict our definition?

This question is not academic either because it brings us right to the crux of the matter. What I said about bourgeois parties relates to a considerable degree to workers' parties too. Neither the working class nor a workers' party is born all at once. The working class takes shape gradually over decades: the rural population overflows into the cities, in part returning home and in part settling there; it simmers over and over again in the cauldrons of the industrial cities creating the working class with its characteristic psychology. In a similar way a party of the working class also takes shape over years and decades. Certain groups considered subjectively that they were defending the workers, as for example the Mensheviks did in the first revolution. And only gradually when history raises all those questions which I have attempted to outline to you, those basic questions which separate people into different sides, make enemies of friends and place them on opposing sides of the barricades and produce civil war — only then does stratification, crystallization, splitting and re-unification begin and only then does a definite party finally take shape. And this process which is closely tied up with people's lives will terminate in a complete form only with the era of the complete victory of socialism, that is when classes and parties disappear. It is not a chemical process which can be observed through to the end in a flask. In social phenomena one has to learn how to generalize and to probe more deeply into events and facts which embrace in their radius of action millions and tens of millions of people.

At the present moment the Second International still has considerable links with working class groups while being, as it is clear to all of us, in essence nothing but a faction of the bourgeoisie, its left wing. Many honest workers are members of the Second International. We have several workers' parties while there exists only one working class. At the same time it is necessary to note that although there are several workers' parties there is only one proletarian party. A party can be a workers' one in its composition and yet not be proletarian in its orientation, programme and policy. This is clear from the examples of the capitalist countries of Europe and America where there are several workers' parties but only a single proletarian one, the Communist Party. There you have not only Social-Democratic parties but Catholic, i.e. church, trade unions and all sorts of other unions. All of them are parts of the working class but in their policies they are merely a faction of the bourgeoisie.

Anniversary dates

All we have said above is necessary for a conscious attitude towards the history of our party. Its creation, its 'process of formation'; or to use philosophical terms, all its prehistory and its first chapters which occupied many many years is nothing but a gradual crystallization of a workers' party in the depths of the working class. And therefore when we speak of the twenty-fifth anniversary of our party this must be taken with certain qualifications. You will see this from a number of examples.

The 'North Russian Workers' League' founded with the assistance of Plekhanov and set up under the leadership of Khalturin, a joiner and Obnorsky a fitter must be regarded as the first cell of a workers' party. It was born at the end of 1877 (you could even say 1878) in St. Petersburg and was first to advocate the idea of the political struggle of the working class. This organization was of course not yet Marxist. Exactly 45 years have passed since

S.I. Khalturin

V.P. Obnorsky

P.B. Axelrod

1878 and it would not of course be stretching matters too far to count the chronology of our party from the formation of the 'North Russian Workers' League'.

The 'Emancipation of Labour Group' was founded in 1883. It was formed at a time when a generation of revolutionaries, headed by Plekhanov and Axelrod, which had survived the Narodnik affliction, broke from populism and recognized the necessity of building a party on the basis of the working class. This group first put forward, in 1885, a draft programme of the Social-Democratic Party and forming therefore the first Marxist organization in the history of our revolutionary movement has therefore every right to be the chronological point of departure of our party. In this instance we would say that we are celebrating its 40th anniversary.

We could consider as a third date our First Party Congress which was held at Minsk on 14th March 1898 and if we take this as our starting point then we can celebrate our 25th anniversary. But it must be noted that this date is accidental. This congress passed leaving relatively no traces. The organizations formed in Minsk were broken up almost 24 hours after the congress, its participants were nearly all arrested while the Central Committee of our party fell almost wholly into the clutches of the gendarmes and could not carry out even a hundredth of the party's programme of work.

Later followed our Second Congress which was held in 1903 and began in Brussels and ended in London. In essence it was this congress which was the first and we could say with just as much right in this case that we are celebrating the 20th anniversary of our party. Then in 1905 in London the third and genuine congress of our party was held, a congress of a party of Bolsheviks as there were no Mensheviks there. (This was at the point of the split with them). This congress can also be considered as the first one for it drew up the basis for the tactics of the Bolsheviks on the eve of the first, 1905, revolution. So, in this case, we could celebrate the 18th anniversary of our party's foundation. And finally we could say that we should count the history of our party from the moment of the complete rupture from the Mensheviks which occurred in 1912 when we began to resurrect our party after the lengthy period of the counter-revolution upon the basis of the upsurge precipitated by the Lena strike and the events following it.*

* Lena Strike — See Lecture Six.

This was at the All-Russian conference at Prague where there were no Mensheviks present either and at which we said: the old Central Committee no longer exists, we are building the party afresh. Strictly speaking it was then that the foundations of our party were laid after the defeat of 1905 and after the phase of counter-revolution which it had passed through.

Following this road further we could say that a complete break from the Mensheviks came not in 1912 but in 1917. And this is correct because after the February revolution and after the overthrow of Tsarism, in this very hall, an attempt was made to convene a united congress of social-democracy where everyone was invited and to which Lenin addressed his celebrated theses which have entered the history of international socialism, the theses on Soviet power. Up till that minute everyone thought that after the fall of Tsarism social-democracy would manage to unite itself, and that the Bolsheviks would merge with the Mensheviks.

And as a final point it might be said that not until our Seventh Congress in 1918 after the Brest peace*, when we decided to rename the party the Russian Communist Party, was it finally formed.

* Brest-Litovsk Peace — See Glossary.

The process of formation of a party

I have deliberately included a whole series of dates as I wish to show that the formal and secondary question of whether it should be 20 or 25 years is not important, but rather the fact that a party takes shape in living reality. This does not at all occur so that on one fine day, as Vodovozov expressed it, the supporters of definite 'ideals' get together and say to each other: 'Well then, come on, let's form a party!' No, a party is not formed quite so simply! It is a living organism connected by millions of threads with the class from which it emerges. A party takes shape over years and even decades. If you calculate for example from the moment when Khalturin formed the 'North Russian Workers' League' then the result is 45 years; if you start your calculation from the moment when our party was called 'Communist' then you have 5 years; if you count from the first congress of our party then you have 25 years and finally if you calculate from the moment of the birth of the 'Emancipation of Labour Group' then you have 40 years. Hence it is clear that the living dialectical formation of a party is a very complex, lengthy and difficult process. It is born amid sharp pangs and it is subject to perpetual crystallizations, regroupings, splits and trials in the heat of the struggle before it finally takes shape as a party of the proletariat, as the party of a given class and then only with the reservation which I have already made, namely that the process is still not finally completed since the departure of some groups and the adherence of others continues for a long time to follow. All this we can observe in the fate of our party as well. If you make a close examination of our party's social composition then you will see that even in its current shape when it has managed over 45 years to have finally formed itself there still occur definite shifts and a relentless renewal of its elements; you will see how after the revolution the number of peasants in it increased with enormous speed and how afterwards their specific gravity became less; you will see how once again the number of the urban proletariat grew and how the intelligentsia at first entered it in whole groups and then began to leave in dense crowds. That is why only by pondering the peculiarities of this movement, only by examining the party as a dialectical concept, only by juxtaposing it with the living struggle of the masses which stretches over years and decades, can you understand the party as you should.

Populism ('Narodnikism')

I have already said that the first phase of the history of the Russian revolutionary movement was occupied by the struggle between Marxism and populism: a movement which in one of its wings was undoubtedly revolutionary and which reached its particular high point in the 1870s.

Populism has inscribed many glorious pages in the history of our struggle and has provided a number of unforgettable examples of personal courage. The heroism of individual Narodniks who left their families, their class and their class privileges and went off, as was then said 'to the people', was amazing and we have an admiration for it. But at the same time populism as a whole was not a proletarian movement. If it was said at that time: 'we must go to the people' then this expression was not used accidentally. The concept of 'class' did not exist for the Russia of those days and the revolutionaries of that era only knew the concept 'people'. All of us of course stand for the people and it is self-evident that there is nothing but good in this concept. But if we take a look at it from the point of view of scientific definitions then we will see that in those days a confused idea was purposely incorporated in the word. In those days the 'people' meant in most cases the peasantry, for the working class as such did not then exist: it was only being born. By dint of this the Narodnik movement, though revolutionary, was still petty-bourgeois. From this, however, it does not follow that we renounce this heritage and reject the models of heroism and remarkable courage displayed by the revolutionaries of the Narodnik period.

Attitude of Communists towards the French Revolution

Let us recall how we communists approach, let us say, the great bourgeois revolutionaries of the French Revolution of 1789, when the working class also was still only in embryo. We approach them with the greatest respect and especially those of them who proved their unusual dedication to their people. We study the history of the French Revolution and we urge our youth to learn from the example of the materialists of that time.* And as a matter of fact anyone who is interested in philosophy can learn far more from any prominent materialist of the era of the bourgeois revolution than from certain newly-fledged revisionist 'Marxists'. For this very reason our party regards it as absolutely necessary to re-issue especially the classics of materialism as every one of us will extract far more benefit

* **French Materialism:** The best starting point for a study of French materialist philosophy and its connection with Marxism is to be found in Plekhanov's *The Development of the Monist View of History.*

J.P. Marat

M. Robespierre

from them than from the hastily worked out 'theories' served up to us which, though at times outwardly well-intentioned, have nothing in common with Marxism. Let me repeat: we are bringing our youth up in the spirit of the deepest respect for the outstanding representatives of the French bourgeois revolution. We understand its class nature. We know that it sent the monarch to the guillotine but we remember also that it promulgated a law against workers' associations. And at the same time the pleiad of the great bourgeois revolutionaries was the strike force of humanity; it was the first to breach the front of feudalism and thereby to give a clear passage to the floodwaters of the then swelling proletarian revolution. This did not stop the epigones of the French revolutionaries from being despicable, petty little men and the agents of capital in the fullest sense of the word. And we know very well the difference between Marat and even Robespierre and their epigones, the present-day Poincaré, Briand and Viviani. It is well-known to us that the then representatives of the bourgeoisie, acting under the conditions of feudal oppression, drove a breach through feudalism while today's representatives of the bourgeoisie who, readily attiring themselves, like Poincaré and his associates, in the robes of the heirs of the French Revolution form in actual fact only the contemptible tools of bourgeois reaction. We know the difference between them. And such is our attitude towards the Narodniks too.

Attitude of Communists towards Populism

We know the worth of Zhelyabov, Sofia Perovskaya and all those who, in the days of the Tsarism which hung upon the feet of Russia like a ball and chain, in the days when an unprecedentedly barbaric oppression raged through the country, knew how to level their weapons up against autocracy, how to lead the first groups of revolutionaries into battle and how to walk firmly towards the gallows. Granted that this 'going out to the people' was not a proletarian movement, granted that this was a revolutionary movement painted only in a misty socialist hue; granted all this, yet it was a great movement just as the

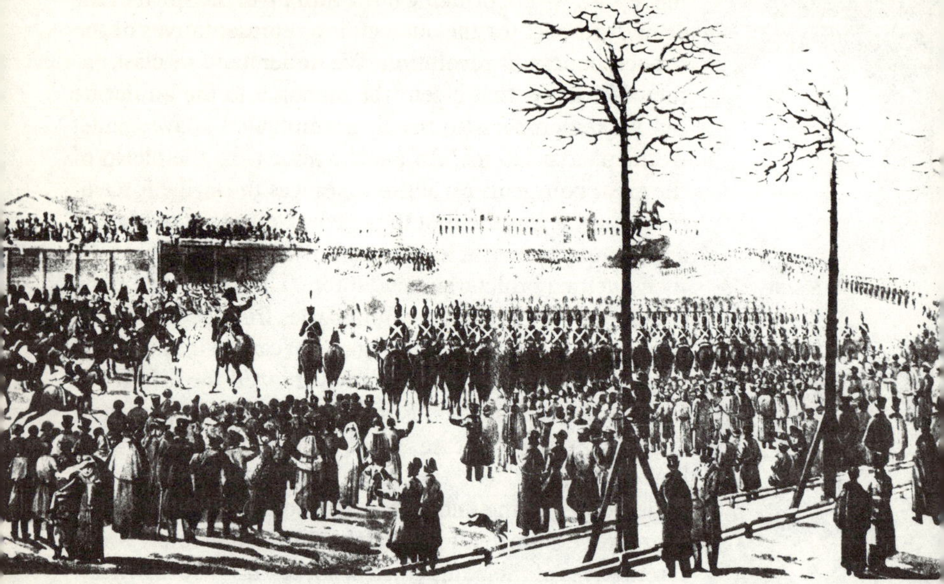

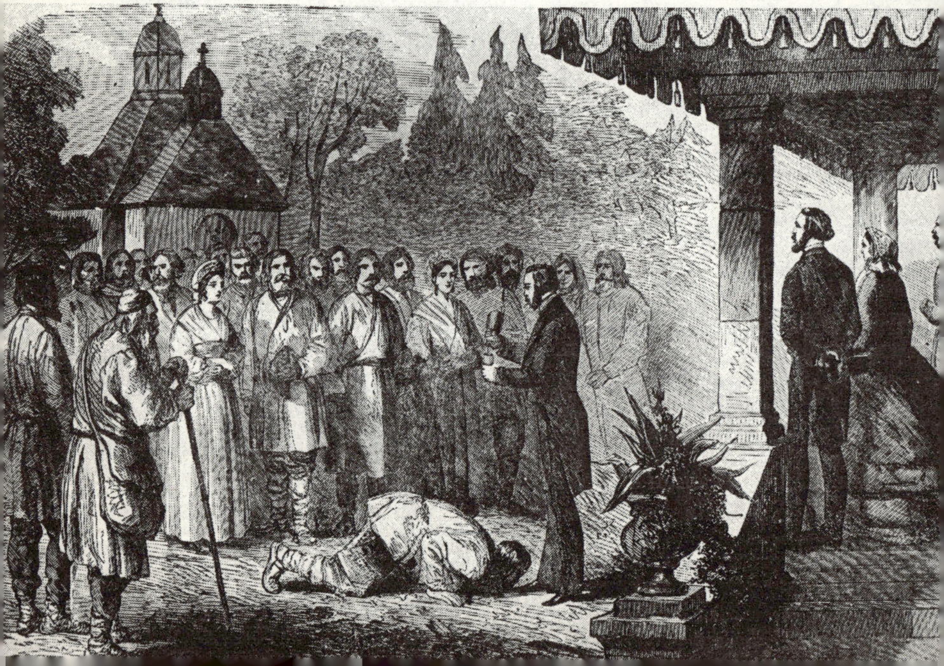

start of the French Revolution was. These Narodniks made a breach in the Tsarist wall and in the autocratic stronghold. They were heroes, they broke from prejudices, they burst the chains shackling them to the privileged class, they renounced everything and went into the struggle for political freedom. While they sometimes embellished their struggle with socialist phrases without having a definite socialist programme, they could not have one, as they marched into battle with a slogan which did not transcend the bounds of bourgeois democracy. It is not accidental that the executive committee of 'Narodnaya Volya', the leading Narodnik organization, addressed in its day an open letter to Lincoln.

We are even ready to take our hats off to the Decembrists as well, that earlier generation of bourgeois revolutionaries which also entered the struggle against Tsarism. These men who formed, in the literal sense of the word, the cream of the aristocracy, nobility and the officer caste, detached themselves from their class, broke from their families, abandoned their privileges and joined battle with autocracy. Although they did not have a socialist programme and although they were only bourgeois revolutionaries our generation does not renounce this heritage. On the contrary, we say that this is a glorious past and we bow low before the first representatives of revolutionary populism, who knew how to die for the people in the days when the working class was still only being born, when there was no proletariat and there could not be a proletarian class party. But at the same time we know that between Zhelyabov and Perovskaya on the one hand and Gotz and Chernov on the other, there exists just as great a difference as between Robespierre and Marat on the one hand and Poincaré and Briand on the other. Gotz and Chernov said that they were pursuing the casse of populism. But we said to them: 'You are pursuing it in the same way as Briand and Poincaré are pursuing the cause of Marat and Robespierre'.

Let me repeat, if we are speaking about individual people then among the Narodniks of the first period who were stars of the first magnitude, people who will for ever remain for us ineffaceable examples of self-sacrifice,

A.I. Zhelyabov

S.L. Perovskaya

The Decembrist Rising Emancipation of the Serfs

heroism and enormous dedication to their people. But if we put this movement under a magnifying glass and examine it in the proper way we will find that, while remaining in general a great step forward, it was not a proletarian movement.

Prehistory of the Russian Proletariat

Our proletariat was born in the course of long decades: one could even say over the course of a century. In Martov's book *The History of Russian Social-Democracy* which despite its Menshevik standpoint I recommend you to read, you can find side by side with erroneous Menshevik views many interesting facts. The Russian working class began to be born in the eighteenth century. The first large-scale factories and the first substantial workshops arose in Russia in precisely this era. At the same time the first bondsmen, semi-bondsmen and afterwards the so-called free workers separated themselves out from the class of peasant, handicraft and artisan serfs.

If you take a look at a work such as Tugan-Baranovsky's well-known study, which does not stand up to a Marxist critique but does provide a multitude of facts, and, if you study Comrade Lenin's book *The Development of Capitalism in Russia* and become familiar with Struve's works, you will see that the first workers' movements can be attested in the eighteenth century and the subsequent years. [Lenin's *Collected Works* Vol. 3, pp. 23-607.]

In 1796 disturbances of factory workers occurred in Kazan, in Moscow Province in 1797, in Kazan again in 1798 and 1800 and in Moscow Province and in Yaroslavl in 1806, in Tambov Province in 1811, in Kaluga Province in 1814, in Yaroslavl in 1815, in St. Petersburg Province in 1816, again in Yaroslavl and Kazan in 1817, in Yaroslavl in 1818, in Kazan in 1819, in Voronezh and Kaluga provinces in 1821, in Vladimir and Moscow provinces and in Yaroslavl in 1823, in Kazan in 1829, in Kazan and Moscow Province in 1834, in Kazan in 1836, in Tula Province in 1837, in Moscow Province in 1844 and in Voronezh Province in 1851.

Besides, scholars who have researched into the Decembrist rising can prove by pointing to authentic documents that, at the moment of the emergence of the movement of 1825 (a hundred years ago), standing in the crowds on the Senate Square were St. Petersburg factory operatives who in small numbers then worked in St. Petersburg and who openly expressed their sympathy with the insurgents when the troops turned out against Nikolai I.

In 1845 Nikolai's government was compelled to issue the first law instituting criminal penalties for striking. In 1848 the storm of the bourgeois revolution rolled across the whole of Europe. This movement did not directly affect Russia except inasmuch as the Tsarist government sent feudal forces to quell the Hungarian revolution; nevertheless it was of course obliquely reflected in our country too. So a fresh breeze blew through Russia as well.

Another basic date is 1861, the year of the emancipation of the serfs — and the incipient movement of the liberal bourgeoisie. Gradually a fairly considerable working class began to appear in Russia which acquired the character of a mass phenomenon as early as the 1870s. Yet despite this the first circles of revolutionaries which arose after the Decembrists were not composed of workers.

Chaikovsky's Circle

Formed in 1869, Chaikovsky's circle can be considered the first revolutionary group. Perovskaya, Natanson, Volkhovsky, Shishko, Kropotkin and Kravchinsky became members of it. These names are in themselves distinguished to the highest degree. Chaikovsky has lived on until our day although politically he has been long since dead. He took part in the bourgeois revolution of 1917, was a member of the first Executive Committee (of the Congress of Soviets) and then occupied a place on the extreme right (even further to the right than the Mensheviks and the S.R.s). During the unprecedented campaign of slander against Comrade Lenin when the latter was declared to be a spy, Chaikovsky was half the instigator of that affair. After this he was appointed governor by the British in Archangel, kept company with Kolchak and today finds himself in Paris, tossed into the dustbin of history.

N.V. Chaikovsky
P.A. Kropotkin
S.M. Kravchinsky

Perovskaya as you know perished in 1881. She took part in preparing the assassination of Alexander II and entered the history of the revolutionary movement as one of its most brilliant names. M. Natanson died very recently as a Left S.R. who came very close to us, especially after the famous and absurd uprising that the Left S.R.s mounted against us. He had split away from the Right S.R.s at the start of the revolution, was together with us at Zimmerwald and represents to a certain measure a founder of the Third International. The remaining members of Chaikovsky's organization have died either physically — or politically, as they stayed in the S.R. party.

M.A. Natanson

This little circle shows distinctly how populism developed and how it provided ideologists for various groups. Kropotkin ended up an anarchist while Natanson was an internationalist and very close to the communists. Chaikovsky revealed himself to be a definite representative of the bourgeoisie and nobody will nowadays dispute the fact that he was merely a bourgeois revolutionary and at that a mediocre and poor democrat, not being even able to defend genuine bourgeois democracy; he did not achieve a hundredth part of what the real bourgeois revolutionaries accomplished when they made their bourgeois revolution.

The first *workers'* circle was formed approximately in the middle of the 1870s, in about 1875. Its most notable participants were Petr Alexeev, the weaver, Malinovsky, Agapov, Alexandrov, Krylov and Gerasimov. Those are the principal names. Petr Alexeev's celebrated speech is well-known and also some of his contemporaries are still alive — if I am not mistaken we recently met Moiseenko.

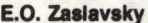
E.O. Zaslavsky

The 'South Russian Worker's League'

In 1875 Zaslavsky founded the 'South Russian Workers' League' in Odessa. But its programme was not as clear as the programme of the 'North Russian Workers' League' founded some three years later. Expressed from the very start in this situation was perhaps that enormous difference which existed between the north and south and which you can trace through the subsequent course of the

whole of our revolution as well. Today it cannot be doubted that the north will enter the history of our revolution as a revolutionary section of the Russian proletariat, while all of the counter-revolution was fledged chiefly in the south where it continually bred and accumulated its forces.

This disparity of social stratification evidently left a certain imprint on the first workers' organisations: the South Russian and the North Russian. If we compare the programmes of the former and the latter then we will see that the 'North Russian Workers' League' was without doubt far closer to us and revolutionary truth, and it will become clear to us that it was more advanced in its estimation of the importance of political struggle and its approach to the mass revolutionary workers' movement.

Marxism and Populism

To gain a clearer understanding of the inter-relation between populism and Marxism it is necessary to bear in mind the canvas upon which it appeared: in the first place, the absence of a substantial working class which then consisted of only tiny streams, whose sources, it is true, rose before the end of the eighteenth century, but which thereafter lay under the heavy oppressive weight of autocracy at a time when all cats were grey, so to speak. The ultimate threads of this canvas consisted of the journey out to the people—which meant a journey out to the peasantry with a very confused programme, the courage of the revolutionaries of that time coupled with a lack of a proletarian viewpoint, the formation of the first circles made up of intellectuals, and only in 1875 the appearance of the first workers' circles which were in all their ideology still closely connected with populism.

I have already spoken about Chaikovsky. This man, as it were, personifies the finger and thumb of populism. The Chaikovsky of the end of the 1860s and beginning of the 1870s was the standard-bearer of the best part of the revolutionary intelligentsia, a political leader who laid the basis of the revolutionary movement. But the Chaikovsky of the 1920s represents quite definitely a tool, and a miser-

able little one at that, in the hands of Kolchak and the British bourgeoisie. Thus you can see in the figure of one man both sides of populism. And in reality right from its beginning to its end two trends, two currents and two tendencies clearly revealed themselves in this movement. One of them brought forward Zhelyabov and Perovskaya and created heroes: the Sazonovs and the Balmashevs. The second current especially observable in the 1880s formed the right wing of populism, i.e. those Narodniks who both in their practical activity and in their writings were little distinguishable from the liberals.

The populism of the 1870s taken as a whole represents a tendency of bourgeois revolutionaries which had however important merits. The victorious proletariat will always pay homage to these revolutionaries. But it will say at the same time: 'Don't imitate their weaknesses, don't repeat their nebulous phrases about the people but speak about a class, go to the proletariat and know that the industrial proletariat is the fundamental class which will liberate all humanity.' The Narodniks could not help being weak, unclear and vague for lived at a time when the working class was only just being born and still lay in diapers. From them we must take not the fog which enshrouded them but what was their strength: be dedicated to one's people, serve it as selflessly as they did; be courageous and self-sacrificing; break as they did from class prejudices and privileges; know how to go against the current at a difficult moment, as they knew how to. The darker the night the brighter the stars. The darker the Tsarist night was, the brighter shone the stars that were Zhelyabov and Perovskaya. And the Russian working class which has been victorious in struggle and workers of all the world respect them for this.

Bourgeois and Proletarian Revolutionaries

We know moreover that within populism, which began in the 1870s and continued into the 1880s, there was a liberal, functionary-class current which animated a number of literary tendencies which were close to the ideas of liberalism and which subsequently drew the S.R.

party towards the evolution which we have observed. Into precisely this framework were born the first groups of proletarian revolutionaries who laid the foundation of our party. You must bear in mind and you must clearly remember that there are both bourgeois revolutionaries and proletarian ones. Only when we are clear on this fact can we understand the Ovid-like metamorphosis of the S.R. party. For it was just when it was a question of a victory over Tsarism and the bourgeois revolution that these revolutionaries had sweep, energy, enthusiasm and gusto; they knew what they were fighting for and what they made sacrifices for and produced great men like Gershuni. But when the bourgeois revolution had been finished in the rough, and the job of the proletarian revolution started, everything which the day before had been their strength became the next day their weakness. They had become more dangerous to us than the usual bourgeois counter-revolutionaries because they immediately turned their energy, dexterity, conspiratorial talent and their certain rapport with the masses through 90 degrees to oppose the revolutionary class. And here lies the solution to the whole riddle.

In all the evolution of the S.R.s and in all the metamorphoses of populism we must distinguish two factors. For a certain period they were bourgeois revolutionaries. They were a progressive force and we had to support them and to proceed in a united front together with them over many years against autocracy. But they were a progressive force only until the moment that the working class, having toppled the privileged property-based class, the class of landowners and bourgeois, reached for power. From this moment as soon as we passed on to the urgent questions regardless of the landowners and the bourgeoisie, the S.R.s immediately swung their whole front against the workers and against the proletarian revolution.

Struggle between proletarian and bourgeois revolutionaries

All the first phase of the history of our party is nothing other than at first a semi-conscious and then a fully-conscious struggle of proletarian revolutionaries against bourgeois revolutionaries. In so far as it was a case of a struggle against Tsarism we had, I repeat, a united front. But as soon as the struggle to win the masses and the soul of the working class was unleashed, our paths diverged. From this moment the proletarian revolutionaries grappled with the bourgeois revolutionaries, and this struggle filled a number of years which proved to be decisive for the future of Russia.

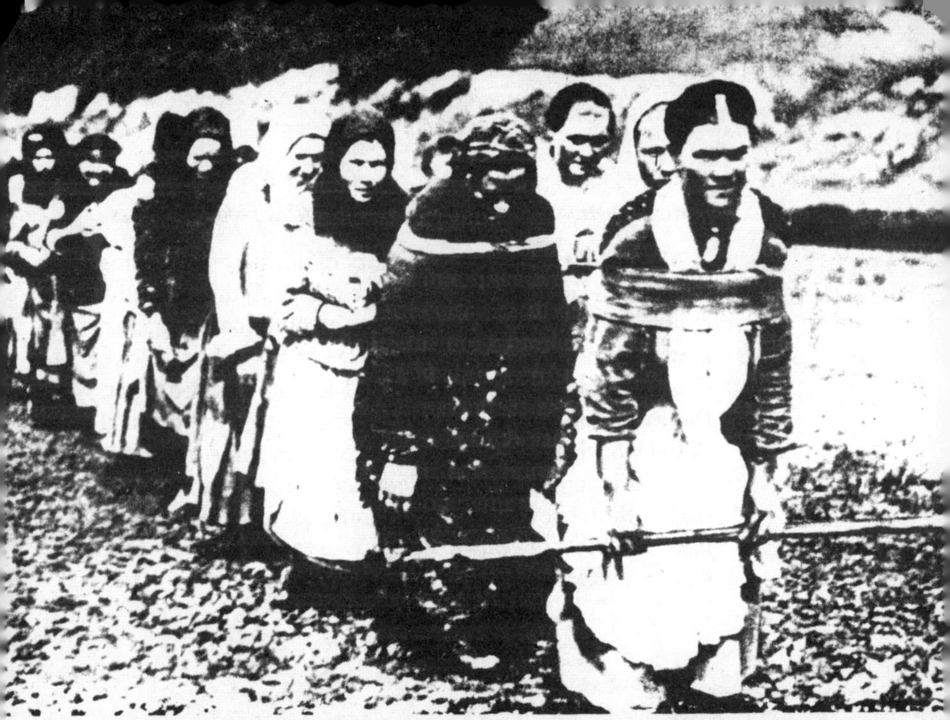

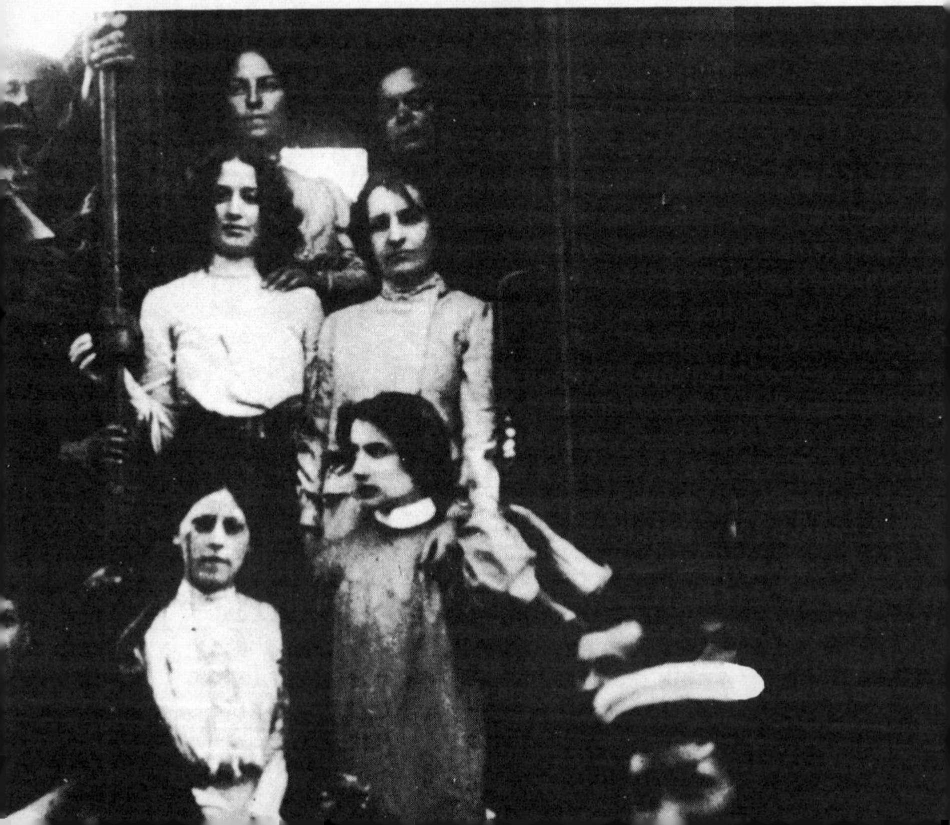

LECTURE TWO

Controversy between Populism and Marxism

Yesterday I said that the whole polemic between populism and Marxism turned upon the formulae; 'people' and 'class'. But the historical argument between them was not of course so simple and monothematic. In order to understand it we must go into it more deeply and seriously.

Populism took issue with Marxism over the question of Russia's future and, above all, over the role of capitalism in our country. In the 1870s, and even in the 1880s, one could still attempt to prove (as the Narodniks in fact did) that Russia, as distinct from other states, would not pass through capitalism. Starting from the premise that at that time capitalism was still very weak in our country while large-scale industry was still only just being born, a whole school which considered itself to be socialist — the Narodnik school — argued that the development of Russia would not proceed like everywhere else but along quite different paths, and that we would manage to leap directly across from the then highly primitive relations of small-scale production to socialism.

It was in connexion with this that the enormously important question arose of the attitude towards the peasant commune. A number of Narodniks maintained that our rural commune was nothing other than a cell of communism, that Russia would by-pass the path of factory production, large-scale urban industry, the accumulation of great wealth and the creation of a proletariat as a class, and that it would pass over these intermediate phases and go directly to a new socialist system based on the small, supposedly communist cells which they considered the rural communes to be.

With regard to the workers, revolutionary populists held the view that they would also probably be of help to the struggle against capitalism. It is true that with the passage of time the Narodniks were to become convinced that workers were far more receptive than all the other layers of the population and that they energetically began to recruit them into their circles. But despite this the basic force upon which they built their tactics was not the workers but the so-called 'people' or, put more concretely, the peasantry.

The misconception of the Narodniks

Little by little, with the development of social relations in our country, the populists' misconception became more plain. The number of factories and plants increased yearly, the quantity of workers in the cities grew and the role of the peasant commune, which was becoming more and more clearly defined, proved that the latter had nothing in common with socialism or communism. In short the course of development ran against populism, and it was for precisely this reason that the Marxists, allying themselves with the reality of life, comparatively quickly broke their opponents' necks.

I will not dwell in detail on this controversy as it would take us too far off course. We must merely keep in mind that when they argued over the role of the commune, over whether or not there would be capitalism in Russia, over whether our country would proceed along peculiar and unprecedented paths by-passing the pit of industrial development, then in actual fact they were, in so doing, arguing over the *role of the proletariat*, over the role of the working class and over which class would be the basic force of the coming revolution. The implicit prerequisite of all these disputes, which took various different forms in the theoretical struggle, was the question of whether a working class would take shape in Russia, and if so what role would fall to it. That is why, in summing up all these controversies, it could be said that the conflict between

Marxism and populism reduced itself essentially to the question of the role of the working class in Russia, whether we would have a class of industrial workers, and if we did, what its role in the revolution would amount to.

Mixed character of Populism

Populism was by no means a uniform phenomenon; on the contrary, it was marked by an unusually diverse and mixed character. In its broadest aspect we can see tendencies of every kind starting from an extremely well-defined anarchism and finishing with an equally well-defined bourgeois liberalism. It is not accidental that, as regards individuals, prominent leaders emerged from the ranks of populism who later became leaders of distinct tendencies and differing political groups, as I pointed out in the last lecture. Nevertheless, despite this mixture, one can and must distinguish two basic currents in populism: on the one hand the revolutionary-democratic and on the other the bourgeois-liberal. If we speak chronologically we have to distinguish between the 1870 Narodniks and the 1880 Narodniks, that is, the two generations which were active predominantly in the 1870s and in the 1880s. In fact it can be said that the Narodniks of the 1870s consisted for the most part of supporters of the first current, which I called the revolutionary-democratic, and was frequently tinged with anarchism, while the populism of the 1880s formed itself mainly out of supporters of the current which could be called with all fairness bourgeois-liberal and which subsequently merged largely with Russian liberalism itself, the Cadet party and other groups.

Narodniks of the 1870s and of the 1880s

The revolutionary Narodniks of the 1870s created a number of organizations which have gone down in the history of the revolutionary movement as major gains. In this category above all are 'Zemlya i Volya' and 'Narodnaya Volya'. The Narodniks of this type brought forward a number of figures who displayed great heroism and courage and who although not numbering among pro-

G.V. Plekhanov

letarian revolutionaries were none the less revolutionaries, democrats as they might have been. The second generation of Narodniks bore an entirely different character and in the 1880s it frequently played a directly reactionary role. You can find interesting details on this question in the fine and in no way outdated work of Plekhanov, as for example in his book *An Analysis of Populism* which he published under the pseudonym of 'Volgin', and also in a whole number of other works which I have still to speak about.

Krivenko

To illustrate my point it is sufficient to give two or three examples. One of the greatest Narodnik writers, Kablits-Yuzov, argued very cogently that the small proprietor, and in the first instance the peasant, represented by virtue of their 'economic independence', as he put it, a type of citizen of a superior rank. The position of the small peasant crushed down by the money lender and by bondage was styled by the worthy Narodnik 'economic independence'. Krivenko went as far as to demand that the peasant should not renounce his 'economic independence' even in favour of political freedom. It is clear that such an ideology can only be called reactionary. We know very well that nowhere in the world is the small proprietor economically independent but that almost always he finds himself in close dependence upon the big proprietors and upon the whole system of government. Consequently Krivenko and company definitely dragged revolutionary thinking backwards as opposed to those revolutionaries who saw that, with the working class springing up, they should go to these workers and who began to understand that the issue was one of the formation of the new revolutionary class which lacked property and was thus not bound by any shackles.

Mikhailovsky

However, not only writers standing clearly on the right wing of populism but even such a master of thought as Mikhailovsky carried the argument so far as to declare with glee in the controversy with the Marxists that in Russia there could not be a Labour movement in the western European sense of the word because, you see, there was no working class; because the Russian worker was linked with the countryside, being a landowner who could always go back home and who thus had no fear of unemployment.

Korolenko

Mikhailovsky as you know headed the *Russkoe Bogatstvo* group to which Korolenko also belonged. And it is perhaps in the example of the latter that we can best show how from the beginning of the 1880s a certain section of populism more or less openly merged with the bourgeois-liberal camp. I have mentioned Korolenko intentionally because as a personality he enjoyed and still enjoys the deserved sympathies of all those who have read his literary works. And therefore it is the harder to reconcile oneself at first with the idea that he was not a revolutionary but belonged to the bourgeois-liberal camp of populism. Nonetheless, this is doubtless the case. As an artist he unquestionably represented one of the greatest magnitudes of our time and we shall still engross ourselves in his excellent books for many decades to come. But as a politician Korolenko was nothing but a liberal. At the start of the imperialist war he came out with a pamphlet in its defence. Moreover, today after his death, his correspondence has been published from which it becomes evident that within the *Russkoe Bogatstvo* circle itself he occupied the right wing of this already right wing Narodnik group. As is now known from Korolenko's letters, a fierce debate arose in this circle as to whether or not to collaborate on the Cadet party's *Rech*, Milyukov's organ; heatedly arguing in favour of this, Korolenko would not submit to the majority decision of his sympathizers but worked on this newspaper, such was the solidarity he felt with this liberal group.

N.K. Mikhailovsky

Two wings of Populism

And so we must always bear in mind that populism was in the highest degree a heterogeneous and diverse

LECTURE TWO

phenomenon ranging from anarchism to liberalism (amongst the Narodniks were people with an anarchist veneer who declared against the political struggle and defended this view with the very arguments of anarchism); we must also always bear in mind that there were two wings in the Narodnik camp: the one, revolutionary, and the other, non-revolutionary, opportunist and liberal. But the revolutionary wing of populism was neither proletarian nor communist, nor did it conceive of the proletarian revolution: it was revolutionary in the sense that it wished for the revolutionary overthrow of autocracy.

The question of terrorism likewise played no small role in the controversies between Marxists and populists. From the second half of the 1870s the revolutionary wing of populism came to the conclusion that it was essential to adopt individual terrorism against representatives of autocratic Russia in order to unleash revolution and advance the cause of liberation. At first the Marxists only very diffidently dissociated themselves from the Narodniks' terrorism as for example in the first programme written by Plekhanov in 1885. But from the moment that the workers' party began to take shape they took a firm stand against individual terrorism. At the time the Narodniks, and later on the S.R.s, attempted to make out that we Marxists were against terrorism because we, in general, were not revolutionary, lacked such a temperament, were afraid of blood and so on. Today after our great revolution scarcely anyone will begin to accuse us of this. But at the time this argument had an effect on the best part of the youth, students and many of the more hot-headed of the workers, and lured revolutionary elements over to the Narodniks.

Marxist attitude to terrorism

In actual fact Marxists have never been against terrorism in principle. They never stood on the ground of the Christian precept: 'thou shalt not kill'. On the contrary it was none other than Plekhanov who asserted repeatedly that not every killing was a murder and that to kill a monster is not to commit a crime. He more than once quoted Pushkin's fiery lines written against the Tsars:

> O, despotic villain
> I hate you and your line
> I will see your ruin and your children's death
> With a wicked delight.

The Marxists stressed that they were the supporters of violence and regarded it as a revolutionary factor. There is too much in the world that can only be destroyed by arms, fire and the sword. The Marxists spoke out for mass terrorism. But they said: the assassination of this or that minister does not change things; we must raise up the *masses*, organise *millions* of people, and educate the *working class*. And only when it is organized and when the decisive hour strikes will we use terror, and then not retail but wholesale; then we shall resort to the armed uprising, which in Russia was to become a fact for the first time in 1905 and led to victory in 1917.

But at that time, the question of terror to some degree shuffled up the cards and gave a section of the Narodniks a more revolutionary aura than the Marxists. The Narodniks said: 'there you can see the one who kills a minister and the other who merely gathers circles of workers together to teach them their political ABC; isn't it plain that the one who kills the minister is the revolutionary, while the one who educates the workers is just a 'high-brow'?' For some time this state of affairs complicated the struggle between the Marxists and the populists. But today, in making an historical review of this controversy, we have to put on one side what played merely an episodic, more or less incidental role, and take the main point which separated us from the populists. And this main point consisted, in the final analysis, in the estimation of the role of the working class.

Here we must elucidate the question of the hegemony of the proletariat, as this fundamental and key question determined the whole of our party's subsequent history and the struggle between Bolshevism and Menshevism, the struggle between the Montagne and the Gironde.

LECTURE TWO

Question of the hegemony of the proletariat

The word 'hegemony' signifies supremacy, leading role or primacy. Thus the hegemony of the proletariat signifies the leading role of the proletariat and its primacy. It is self-evident that as long as there was practically no proletariat as a class in Russia there could not be a controversy over the hegemony of the proletariat. You cannot wrangle over the leading role of a non-existent class. But the perspicacity of the Marxists lay in the fact that, at a time when the proletariat was only just beginning to appear and when it still did not present a major force, they saw and understood that this incipient class would in the revolution be the leading, supreme and most advanced class and that it would be the basic force of the coming revolution and assume the leadership of the peasantry in all the struggles to come. Thus the whole dispute between the Marxists and the populists — especially in its second half, in the 1880s and 1890s — can be reduced essentially to the question of the hegemony of the proletariat.

The fathers of the idea of the hegemony of the proletariat were Plekhanov and Lenin. At the First Congress of the Second International, the International Congress at Paris in 1889, Plekhanov spoke literally the following words: 'The Russian revolution will either triumph as a revolution of the working class or it will not triumph at all'. Nowadays this truth may appear banal and commonplace to us. It is clear to everyone that the working class is the basic force in our revolution, which can only triumph finally as a workers' one. Otherwise it will not triumph at all. But take yourself back into the situation at the end of the 1880s when a workers' party did not exist as such, as the working class was only just being born, and when the Narodniks stood in the forefront of the Russian revolutionary movement, when even such a far-sighted man as Mikhailovsky rejoiced over the fact that a workers' movement did not exist in Russia, and stated that here there would not be one in the western European sense of the word either. Take yourself back to that situation and you will understand why Plekhanov's words were, to some extent, a revelation. And if it can be said that, in a certain sense, Marx discovered the working class on a world scale, then it can also be said (with reservations of course) that Plekhanov discovered the working class in *Russia*. Let me repeat, with reservations. It wasn't Marx of course who discovered the working class. It was born in Europe in the process of the replacement of feudalism by capitalism; but Marx explained its great historical role, perceiving it as early as 1847 when the working class was only just being born in Europe and sketched out its great future role in the liberation of the peoples in the world revolution. Just such a role was played by Plekhanov in relation to Russia, when in 1889 and earlier he demonstrated that the working class was being born in Russia and that it would not be simply one among other classes, but the fundamental, leading class—the leader-class and the hegemonic class which would take the lever of revolution into its hands. The idea of the hegemony of the proletariat formed the basic watershed in all controversies that followed. We must return to this point more than once again when we expound the essence of the struggle between Bolshevism and Menshevism.

Plekhanov's polemic with Tikhomirov over the hegemony of the proletariat

Plekhanov advanced the same view very lucidly in another controversy with Lev Tikhomirov who was at one and the same time the most brilliant figure in 'Narodnaya Volya', one of the chief members of its Executive Committee, and that organization's best writer. Subsequently this same Lev Tikhomirov ended up by entering the service of Tsarism and became a colleague of Menshikov, one of the most intractable obscurantists. But let me repeat, Tikhomirov was in the years of the blossoming of his activity, the chief representative of 'Narodnaya Volya' and Plekhanov had to cross swords with him above all others. That was how it was. When, despite all the predictions of the Narodniks, workers began to appear in the cities and, in the first instance, in the St. Petersburg of those days, the Narodniks became convinced that these workers were nonetheless very receptive to revolutionary propaganda and that it was necessary to take account of them.

Tikhomirov put forward, as a compromise, this formula: we also (the Narodnaya Volyaists) are agreeable to carrying out propaganda among workers and we do not deny that they are *very important for the revolution*. Plekhanov seized upon these words, and with his characteristic brilliance turned them against his opponent. He wrote in this connection a brilliant article against the Narodniks and in them fired a few shots which very happily found their mark.[^1] He wrote that their very posing of the question as one of the benefit of the workers to the revolution indicated that they did not understand the historical role of the working class; that it was necessary to turn the formula inside out if one wanted to see it correctly posed; he wrote that to say that the workers are important 'for' the revolution is impossible, and that one must say: *the revolution is important for the workers*. 'You argue', he said, turning to the Narodniks, 'as if man was created for the Sabbath and not the Sabbath for man. But we declare that the working class is the basic class and the hegemonic class and that it and only it will succeed in toppling the capitalist system, in uniting the peasantry and opposition elements in general around itself. As long as you Narodniks look upon the working class as something subsidiary you will find that its leading role remains a book with seven seals and you will not be able to understand it.' Thus we must say, in all fairness, that Plekhanov was one of the first people in Russia to formulate the idea of the hegemony of the proletariat. And in subsequently supporting the Mensheviks he inflicted cruel blows upon his own past, thereby renouncing the teaching whose brilliant pages have gone down in the history of the Russian revolutionary movement.

[^1]: his reply to Tikhomirov in Plekhanov, *Selected Philosophical Works*, Vol. , pp. 411-450.

Lenin as a father of the idea of the hegemony of the proletariat

Another father of the idea of the hegemony of the proletariat was Lenin, who managed, over three decades, in diverse situations, in unprecedentedly difficult and complex circumstances, to carry forward this idea right up till the present day. Lenin first formulated it in one very interesting work which is only now, in two or three weeks' time, being published. In 1894 he wrote this first major revolutionary work entitled *What the 'Friends of the People' Are and How They Fight the Social-Democrats* (don't forget that then we were all called Social-Democrats). As I have said this work of Lenin's could not then be published. Only quite recently, a few weeks ago, did he succeed in tracing part of it in the archives of the Police Department and part in a foreign archive, in Berlin, actually. It forms a whole volume embracing nearly fifteen printed sheets. After dismantling stone by stone the Narodnik misconceptions, Lenin's book ends with some remarkable words. Having shown that a new star was rising, that of the working class, and that this would be the liberator class, the hegemonic class and the chief force and main spring of the revolution, Lenin said approximately the following: 'Today Russian workers do not yet understand the role of the working class as hegemonic, or only individual sections understand it; but the time will come when all advanced workers of Russia will understand it. And when this happens the Russian working class will, by leading the peasantry behind it, take Russia to the communist revolution.' This was said in 1894. You have to agree that now, thirty years later, you read these words with some amazement. Even the terminology—the proletariat which leads the peasantry behind it, even the nomenclature characterizing our revolution as communist—all this is wholly contained in the concluding lines of Lenin's historic work. And, as we shall see later, he was to defend this idea over a period of thirty years under all circumstances: the situation changed and changed again, but for Lenin and the Bolsheviks the basic appraisal of the proletariat as the leader of the future revolution was never to change.*

Lenin's *Collected Work* Vol. 1, pp. 129-326.

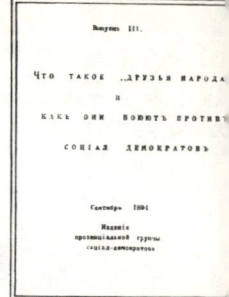

What the 'Friends of the People' Are

* In view of the enormous importance of the question of the hegemony of the proletariat we have included as Appendix an article by Zinoviev where this question elucidated in great detail.

Legal Marxism

It must also be said, however, that just as there were two tendencies in populism so also there were two tendencies in the Marxism of that time. An important place in our account must be taken up by a chapter on Legal Marxism.

In the middle of the 1890s, against the background of an

already definite revival of the labour movement and the political struggle generally in our country, a tendency called Legal Marxism first arose. If illegal Marxism was born in Russia in 1883 when the 'Emancipation of Labour' group appeared, then Legal Marxism was born some twelve years later. Only a little more than ten years after the formation of the above-mentioned group by Plekhanov the appearance of Legal Marxism became possible in Russia. And within this Legal Marxism there were, in turn, at least two basic tendencies.

One of these was headed by Plekhanov and Lenin and the other by Struve, Tugan-Baranovsky and others. Two literary works had a decisive character in this connection. On the one side there was Struve's well-known book *Critical Notes* which was published in 1894 and on the other the book by Lenin which I just now called: *What the 'Friends of the People' are*. (The latter, in spite of the fact that it had not been published until today and did not have a wide mass readership, did nevertheless penetrate into the circles of Marxists and the first revolutionary workers and play a historical role).

Struve then and now

What was Struve at that time? He was in those days a young but already promising writer who called himself a Marxist, waged a struggle against Mikhailovsky, regarded himself as a member of our party and became subsequently the author of the manifesto of its First Congress in 1898. In short he was then a Marxist star of the first magnitude. What is Struve today? This you know. Before 1905 he had become the editor of the illegal bourgeois liberal journal *Osvobozhdenie* published abroad in Stuttgart. After this he became one of the leaders of the Cadet party, taking up a position on its right wing alongside Milyukov. Still later he became an avowed monarchist and counter-revolutionary, and in the years of Stolypin's triumph became his bard. After the February revolution he at once took a place on the extreme right wing of the Cadet party and then played a role (and a very large one at that) among the White émigrés and in the governments of

P.B. Struve

LECTURE TWO

Denikin, Wrangel and others. Today Struve is abroad, and constitutes one of the most prominent ideologists of the counter-revolution. A transformation of rare distinction as you can see.

Let me say in passing that in the course of my account you can observe no small number of major personalities who traced a path from the left wing of the revolutionary movement to the right counter-revolutionary camp. It is sufficient to mention, besides Struve, Chaikovsky of whom I spoke in my last lecture; Tikhomirov who contrived to ascend from 'Narodnaya Volya' to the pedestal of the Tsar's throne; Plekhanov, who, starting with the foundation stone of the idea of the hegemony of the proletariat, finished his wretched days in the position of a right wing defencist Menshevik; and finally Breshkovskaya, who commenced her revolutionary activity on the left wing of the revolutionary Narodniks and likewise ended her days in the retinue of the bourgeois counter-revolution.

E. Breshkovskaya

All these metamorphoses and evolutions were not accidental. In the period of terrible upheavals which our country underwent when we had three revolutions in the space of twelve years it was inevitable that individual personalities suffered crises. Under the yoke of Tsarism, that heavy gravestone which pressed down on the whole country, it was inevitable that certain people considered their place not to be where they were situated in reality and fell accidentally into this or that party, but when the decisive moment came they frequently ended up in the other camp. And so it happened with Legal Marxism too. A whole wing of it turned out afterwards to be chieftains of the bourgeois counter-revolution in Russia.

Struve's Critical Notes

Struve's book *Critical Notes* was directed entirely against populism. It was in essence devoted to a single theme: will there be capitalism or not in Russia? Struve was right when he wrote in his critique of the Narodniks 'You will dream in vain of some self-sufficient Russia and the economic independence of the small proprietor. No, take off your Narodnik spectacles and have a look round: Russia is moving forward, factories and plants are going up and the urban industrial proletariat is making its appearance. Capitalism in Russia is inevitable. Russia will pass through it.' In this much Struve, like Tugan-Baranovsky, was right, and in agreement with Lenin and Plekhanov. For indeed the immediate task at that time consisted in demonstrating that the growth of the working class and of large factories and plants in Russia was inevitable; it had to be proved that capitalism existed, that it had a progressive side, for what we Marxists always had the audacity to assert, even up till the present day was that in comparison with serfdom and the antediluvian feudal system capitalism was a step forward. Capitalism breaks workers' bones, exploits them and in a certain sense deforms them; this is true, but capitalism creates mighty factories and plants, electrifies the country, raises the level of agriculture, creates means of communication, breaches the walls of feudalism and is thus progressive.

The task of revolutionary Marxists of that time was a double one. On the one hand they had finally to knock out the Narodniks who tried to demonstrate that there would not be capitalism and assured us that capitalism was merely a filthy stain, a sin, an evil and a hellish fiend, and that we must flee from it like the plague. On the other hand it was necessary for the revolutionary Marxists at the very first glimmers of capitalism to begin to organise the working class at its very birth and create a workers' party. And so we see Struve, who solved the first task very well, completely 'forgot' about the second one. He proved convincingly that capitalism was inevitable, had in fact arrived, existed and that it had its progressive side, but he lost sight of our basic task, that once capitalism had arrived and once the working class had appeared, then one must immediately begin to organize the workers, create their workers' party in what was still Tsarist Russia and prepare it for battles not only against the Tsar but also against the bourgeoisie. Struve's book *Critical Notes* ended with a significant phrase. He wrote: 'And thus we admit our lack of culture but we shall learn from capitalism'. Compare Struve's final chord in 1895 with the conclusion from Lenin's book: *What the 'Friends of the People' Are* of 1894. Lenin had also hit out at populism, proving that capitalism had arrived, was in existence, that this stage was unavoidable, and that capitalism prepared the victory of the working class; but he in addition gave at the end of his book a prognosis and a prediction, that has now been borne out, that the Russian workers would understand the role of the working class as the hegemonic class, and having understood this would lead the peasantry behind them and bring Russia to the communist revolution.

Such was the 'little' difference between Lenin and Struve in those days. And yet social relations were so confused under the rule of Tsarism that people so sharply divergent in essence were nonetheless considered in those days sympathizers, and were in one camp. Some issued the slogan: 'Let's learn from capitalism!' Others said: 'We shall raise up the working class, the vanguard proletariat, in order to lead Russia towards the proletarian revolution!' And they all went along together against populism in one phalanx and in one front. Let me repeat: this was inevitable at that time of extremely unclear and undifferentiated social relations. But this was to have an ineffaceable imprint upon all the subsequent development of our party.

Plekhanov as theoretician and Lenin as political leader

From the other literary works we must mention another book by Plekhanov (Beltov) which he produced in 1895: *On the Development of the Monist View of History*. In this work Plekhanov revealed his most brilliant side, giving battle to populism chiefly on another field, that of philosophy, and coming out in defence of materialism. It seems to me that many of our modern academics would act more wisely if instead of 'criticizing' Plekhanov with a dilettante's conceit, as they generally do, they were to expound and interpret to the rising generation this remarkable book which whole generations of Marxists studied, and from which they learnt to understand the principles of militant materialism. Plekhanov's political side was never especially strong. He was a theoretician. He was then the acknowledged ideological leader of the party,

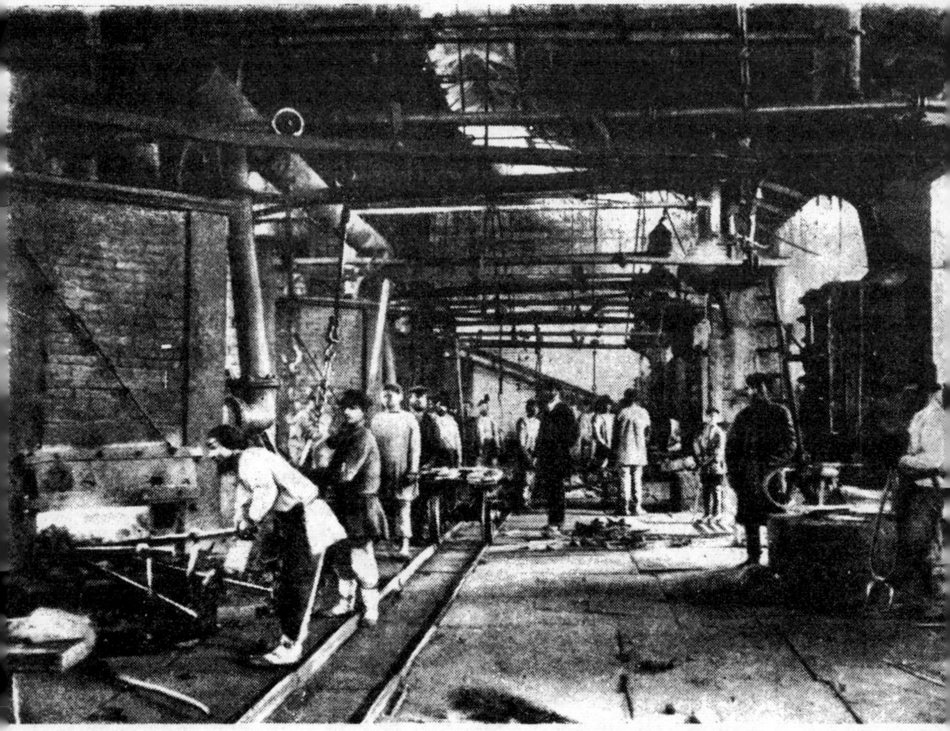

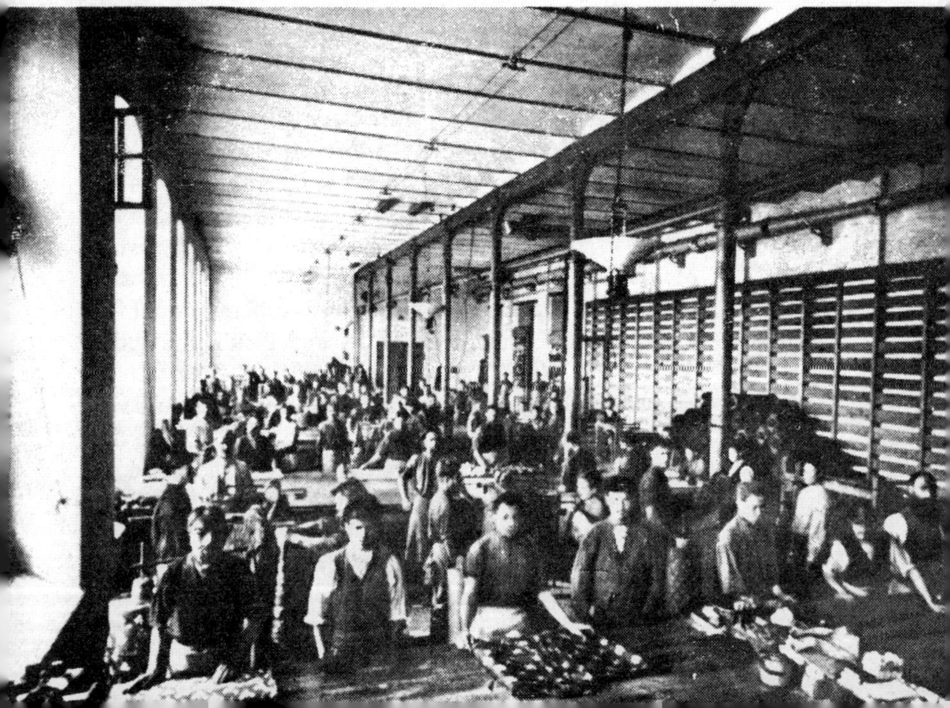

LECTURE TWO

if not of an entire generation of Marxist intellectuals and Marxist workers. Lenin was younger than him: he was only just beginning his activity then. Taking a glance in retrospect, we can now clearly see how from the second half of the 1890s a certain division of labour as it were was established between Plekhanov and Lenin from the outset. Neither ever came to an agreement about this but in fact it was so. Plekhanov's strong side was his theoretical side and he took on the philosophical battles with the enemy wherever he might be, and he will be remembered as an incomparable master of that craft. But the young Lenin concentrated all his attention from his very first works upon socio-political questions and the organization of the party and the working class. And in this sense they complemented each other.

We must mention another book of Lenin's which he wrote in exile: *On the Development of Capitalism in Russia* where he emerged for the first time as a major economist. In this work he analyses social relations in Russia and proves with a remarkable lucidity and scholarship the indisputable development of capitalism in Russia.

Lenin's struggle against Struve

In this way, two trends could be noted in Legal Marxism from the very beginning. Lenin subjected Struve's *Critical Notes* and his other writings and speeches in his *Marxist Anthology* (which was burnt and has also not been published) to criticism. (His articles written in this connexion which appeared under the pen-name of 'Tulin', have been included in his *Collected Works* and you can read them today). Lenin was one of the first who, while travelling hand in hand with Struve, nevertheless sensed that this ally was not altogether a firm one. In those years when Struve was one of the most brilliant representatives of Legal Marxism in Russia it was very difficult to go against him but Lenin did so all the same. As long ago as in the article we have mentioned he, under the pseudonym of 'Tulin', analysed Struve's legal works and even in those days reproached him for the most deadly sin. He said as it were to him: you see one side of the phenomenon; you see

The Development of Capitalism in Russia

Lenin's *Collected Works*, Vol. 3 pp. 23-607.

Lenin's *Collected Works*, Vol. 1, pp. 333-507.

Foundry at Rezha in the Urals 1880
Packing shop at an Ivanovo-Voznesensk factory, 1895

that capitalism exists and that it is striking at the peasant commune and serfdom but you don't see the other side of the phenomenon; you don't see that our task is not to learn from capitalism just because it has appeared but to organize right now our class, the working class, which will be able to smash the autocracy of the Tsar and will then move on against the autocracy of capital ...... In point of fact we can say here again that the fundamental controversy between these two groups within one and the same camp of Legal Marxism could be reduced to the controversy over the hegemony of the proletariat and over the question of whether the proletariat as a class would play a leading role in the revolution, whether it would actually lead a struggle that would end with the victory of the working class and the destruction of capitalism, or whether it would move only in harness alongside other opposition forces and halt at the victory over autocracy, that is, at the establishment of a bourgeois system in Russia.

It was against this background that the formation of the workers' party proceeded in Russia.

If you take a look at other countries, or even at Germany alone, and if you remember Lassalle's historic work then you will see that in that country the bourgeois parties succeeded in dominating a considerable section of the workers sooner than the latter created their own party. Lassalle began by liberating from the influence of the bourgeois parties those first layers of workers which the bourgeoisie had managed to win over, and by drawing them over to the side of the workers' socialist party. And what occurred in Germany was no chance happening. Everywhere the bourgeoisie took shape as a class earlier than the proletariat and everywhere it had its parties, its ideologists and its literature earlier than the proletariat and it attempted to attract a part of the workers to it and its party.

This phenomenon was also present in Russia but in a highly peculiar form. Despite the fact that the bourgeoisie began to take shape as an open political force later here, we can nevertheless see in Russia also that the first workers' circles and the first revolutionary workers were not drawn

F. Lassalle

towards the workers' parties but towards the Narodnik party, which in the final analysis was a bourgeois party, albeit a bourgeois-democratic one. Lenin too had to begin from the same point that Lassalle had to begin from in Germany. The setting was a different one of course, and the ideological struggle assumed different forms, but the essence of things was in many respects the same. He had to begin by winning over individual groups of workers who had been misled, finding themselves in the ranks not of the workers' parties but of the Narodnik parties, essentially bourgeois as they were, and once having won over these groups to begin to build together with them the workers' party. Consequently if we bear in mind the two tendencies in populism on the one hand and the two tendencies in Legal Marxism on the other, then we will have in front of us the ideological backcloth against which the workers' party began to be created in Russia.

And at this point after everything that has been said I can pass on to my immediate subject, the history of the party in the real sense of the word.

The Party's embryonic period

In his book *What is to be Done?* about which we shall have more to say later, Comrade Lenin wrote that our movement in the 1880s represented the embryo of our party. In this decade the working class was still so to speak carrying its future child, the workers' party, in its womb. As yet only the first circles were growing up and these were very shaky, now collapsing and now being reborn for the first major ideological battles for the independence of the working class and the idea of the hegemony of the proletariat were only just beginning.

<small>Lenin's *Collected Works*, Vol. 5, pp. 347-529.</small>

In the first half of the 1890s the party was already being built upon the basis of a mass movement of workers and this period can be regarded as its childhood and adolescence. Moreover a strike movement appeared which grew rapidly as is evident from the following figures.

From 1881 to 1886 there were in all 40 strikes in which eighty thousand workers took part. From 1895 to 1899 the strike movement already embraced almost half a million workers, four hundred and fifty thousand in fact—i.e. the number of strikers increased roughly six to sevenfold. In St. Petersburg the strike movement had been quite considerable in 1878. From the beginning of the 1880s it took on larger proportions and in the middle of the 1890s one strike alone involved up to thirty thousand workers engaged in textile production.

First St. Petersburg workers' Social-Democratic circles

On this basis, workers' *Social-Democratic* circles began to grow up. The first such circle was formed by Blagoev, a Bulgarian by origin. In 1887 he was a student in St. Petersburg where many Bulgarians were studying at that time. Together with other comrades whose names have been preserved, like Gerasimov and Kharitonov, he brought together around him a group of sympathizers and founded the first Social-Democratic circle in St. Petersburg, which was to play no lesser role than did the 'North Russian Workers' League' founded by Khalturin. Blagoev is alive to this day. He is the leader of the Bulgarian Communist Party and one of the founders of the Third International.

D.N. Blagoev

Leagues of Struggle for the Liberation of the Working Class

1895 proved to be exceptionally rich in events. I have already pointed out that in that year there appeared a whole number of books which were not simply books but landmarks on the road to the creation of a workers' party. This year was remarkable also for the fact that the 'League of Struggle for the Liberation of the Working Class' was founded in St. Petersburg. It could be said that this was really the first provincial committee of our party. Leagues of Struggle for the Liberation of the Working Class were subsequently created in a number of other cities too: in Ivanovo-Voznesensk in 1895 and in Moscow in 1896. These leagues were the first major social-democratic organizations which formed the foundation of our party and the first, St. Petersburg one, included in its ranks not a

St. Petersburg League of Struggle for the Liberation of the Working Class:
Front row seated: V.V. Starkov, G.M. Krzizhanovsky, V.I. Lenin, I.O. Martov
Back row standing: A.L. Malchenko, P.K. Zaporezhets, A.A. Vaneev

few remarkable people and above all Comrade Lenin himself, who organized it. Also belonging to it were: S. I. Radchenko, Krzhizhanovsky who is now working on the electrification of Soviet Russia, Vaneev, Starkov, Martov who as you know is now a Menshevik, Silvin (a Bolshevik), a worker from the Putilov works called B. Zinoviev, of whose fate I unfortunately know nothing, a worker from the Obukhov works called Shelgunov who was a member of our party and is alive to this day but has unfortunately gone blind, and finally a worker from the Alexandrov foundry, I. V. Babushkin who in 1905 was shot in Siberia by Rennenkampf's detachment: he was one of the first Bolsheviks and a man towards whom Comrade Lenin held a profound sympathy as one of the most prominent representatives of the first generation of Marxist workers.

I.V. Babushkin

Provincial workers' Social-Democratic circles

At the same time there were numerous circles scattered throughout which attempted to join together and which enjoyed a considerable influence in many cities. You will find in Martov's book (he has a wonderful memory for names) a long list of the leaders of the circles of that time. They deserve to be read out: Krasin in St. Petersburg, now our foremost technical specialist; Fedoseev in Vladimir; Melnitsky* in Kiev; Alabyshev in Rostov on Don; Goldendach (Ryazanov), Steklov and Tsyperovich in Oessa; Kremer, Eisenstadt, Kosovsky and others in Vilnius; Khinchuk in Tula. Comrade Khinchuk was in the beginning one of the founders of the party, but then he went over to the Mensheviks and was a member of their Central Committee, and afterwards the first chairman of the Moscow Menshevik Council after which he re-entered the ranks of our party; today he is a leader of the co-operative organizations. As regards Kremer, Eisenstadt and Kosovsky, they were founders of the Bund, about which I must say a few words.

* The Kiev Circle was in fact led by Melnikov

L.B. Krasin

LECTURE TWO

The 'Bund'

A.I. Kremer

These days the word 'Bund' is very little known to the workers of our major cities but it was at one time extremely popular in the revolutionary camp. Bund means in Yiddish 'league'—in this case the league of Jewish workers of Poland and Lithuania. It was founded in 1897, a year before the First Congress of our party. It brought a powerful if not stormy movement to life among Jewish craft workers in Poland and Lithuania: a movement which was several years in advance of the workers' movement in St. Petersburg and Moscow. And for this there were peculiar and entirely understandable reasons. The fact was that Jewish workers and craftsmen at that time had to suffer under the yoke not only of capitalism and economic exploitation but of national oppression too. By force of this circumstance the Jewish workers and craftsmen be-became revolutionized earlier than workers of other cities and were able earlier than others to create a mass workers' organization which united itself in a league which received the title of the 'Bund'.

From the bowels of this Jewish workers' organization there emerged no small number of individual heroes and major figures. It is sufficient to mention Lekert, the Jewish worker who killed Von Wahl the Vilnius police chief, and to recall a whole number of figures in the Jewish workers' movement who are in the ranks of our party to this day and participate in its organizations.*

Lekert, a shoemaker, in ct seriously wounded on Wahl, the governor-neral of Lithuania, who id sentenced 26 workers flogging.

Founded as I have said in 1897, the Bund was at one time, for a period of two to three years, the strongest and most numerous organization of our party. But then when our most important cities like St. Petersburg, Moscow, Ivanovo-Voznesensk and Orekhovo-Zuevo awoke and when lower depths of the Russian workers raised themselves up, then the lesser contingent of Jewish craft workers, which had previously in a certain sense occupied the front of the stage, had of course to move into the background. But be that as it may, in the second half of the 1890s the movement of Jewish workers was a very considerable one and the role of the Bund in the party was very great. It is sufficient to say that the main organizer of the

First Congress of our party in 1898 was the Bund. And it was not at all an accident that this congress was held at Minsk, a city of the Jewish Pale and on the territory of the Bund's activity. And incidentally, seeing that Jewish workers and craftsmen played for some time the role of shock troops, the Black Hundred press, as is not unknown to you, mounted a frantic slander campaign and over a long period attempted to prove that the instigators of the revolutionary movement in Russia were exclusively Jews.

Nowadays in reviewing the history of our party which has by now grown into a powerful organization, we are obliged, so it seems to me, to remember the brave Jewish craftsmen and workers who were the first to rise to the struggle and helped us lay the first bricks of the edifice of our party.

B.L. Eidelmann
N.A. Vigdorchik
A.A. Vannovsky

First Party Congress

But now let us return to the Leagues of Struggle for the Liberation of the Working Class. The First Congress of our party, at which there were eight representatives present, was convened at Minsk on 1st March 1898 out of representatives of those leagues which were located in St. Petersburg, Moscow, Ivanovo-Voznesensk, Kiev and other cities and also out of delegates from the Bund and individual groups which at that time published workers' newspapers. We can mention them by name. From *Rabochaya Gazeta* came Eidelmann and Vigdorchik. (Both of them are alive: the first a Bolshevik but the second—alas!—a right-wing Menshevik). From the St. Petersburg League of Struggle for the Liberation of the Working Class came S.I. Radchenko who died in 1912. (His brother, I.I. Radchenko is alive and is working in our party). From the Kiev League came Tuchapsky who, if I am not mistaken, is dead also. From the Moscow League, Vannovsky. From the Ekaterinoslav League, Petrusevich. From the Bund, Kremer, Kosovsky and Mutnik. As regards the last of these I can tell you nothing; Kremer and Kosovsky however I knew personally. (They are now — alas! — the rightest of right-wing Mensheviks).

Such was the composition of this First Congress which

LECTURE TWO 53

attempted to carry out the work of forming the party. The congress elected a Central Committee, appointed the editorial board of the central organ, and issued an appeal written, as I have said, by none other than P.B. Struve, the very same as the man who is now the most virulent enemy of the working class. I advise you to read this document which you can find in many books and also in the form of an appendix in *Sketches of the History of Social-Democracy in Russia* by N. Baturin.*

* See Appendix I.

**P.L. Tuchapsky
K.A. Petrusevich
A. Mutnik**

I cannot deny myself the pleasure of reading you a couple of passages from this appeal. In giving a characterization of the international situation Struve wrote, among other things, the following about the revolution of 1848, whose fiftieth anniversary fell precisely in 1898.

> Fifty years ago the life-giving storm of the revolution of 1848 swept over Europe. For the first time the modern working class came on to the stage as a major historical force. By using its efforts the bourgeoisie succeeded in sweeping away many obsolete feudal-monarchic institutions and laws. However, it quickly saw in its new ally its most avowed enemy and betrayed itself, the latter and the cause of freedom into the hands of reaction. But it was already too late: the working class which for a while was pacified, ten to fifteen years later re-appeared on the historical scene, but with redoubled force and an adult self-consciousness, as a wholly mature fighter for its own final liberation ......

Struve goes on to describe the role of the international bourgeoisie and passes on to an appraisal of the role of the Russian bourgeoisie. And what is particularly interesting is that he says literally the following:

> *The further to the east of Europe (and Russia as we know, is the east of Europe) the weaker, more cowardly and baser in its political attitude, is the bourgeoisie and the greater the cultural and political tasks that fall to the proletariat.*

I think that Peter Struve could be forgiven many things for these prophetic words. Of course it later became clear that he was writing about himself and his class. It remains for us only to repeat after him that 'the further east the weaker, more cowardly and baser the bourgeoisie becomes in its political attitude'. And no one demonstrated this as clearly as did P.B. Struve himself.

Economism

By the end of the 1890s and the time of the First Congress of the party two tendencies begin to emerge, now no longer merely on the literary field but inside the workers' movement itself, within the social-democratic party of that time poorly developed as it was. One of them acquired the title of Economism and I will briefly attempt to give a sketch of it. Let me say to begin with, that Economism was closely tied up with the struggle between the same trends which we have noted in Legal Marxism. And if we wish to express quite briefly the essence of this 'Economism' and the controversy which took place between the revolutionary Marxists of that time and the supporters of the *Iskra* men, the future Leninists, on the one hand and the Economists on the other, then it has to be said that here also, as previously, everything could be reduced to the question of the role of the proletariat in the revolution and to the question of the hegemony of the proletariat. This idea was to serve over the course of some thirty years as the basic watershed which arose before us in different situations and in different forms. In 1917 it put us on the opposite side of the barricades from the Mensheviks; in 1895 it took the form of a purely literary controversy, while in 1898-1900 it was decided in a struggle between tendencies . . . So when you examine the facts you will see that between the supporters of Economism and the representatives of the right wing of legal Marxism, the future builders of the Menshevik party, there is also a personal link. This was one and the same nucleus, from Legal Marxism via Economism to Menshevism and then to liquidationism and finally to what we have today with the Mensheviks having openly crossed over to the camp of the bourgeoisie. This is one logical chain. The question of the hegemonic proletariat was so important that it did not permit anyone who made a mistake over it to go unpunished. Anyone who stumbled over this question was compelled by the laws of gravity to sink lower and lower.

Sources of Economism

Economism arose in the second part of the 1890s when

LECTURE TWO

social-democracy started to move from discussion-group activity, as it was then called, to agitation and mass work. What does discussion-group activity mean? It is clear from this name that this was a period when the party comprised separate, very small propagandist groups. And at that time nothing else could be done since workers could only be brought together as individuals. But when the movement began to broaden against the background of the considerable strike movement of which I have spoken, the revolutionaries began to set themselves new and greater tasks. They said: we cannot be content with discussion-group activity, we must change over to mass work and agitation; we must make an attempt not only to gather together isolated workers but also to get the working class organized. And so at that point, at that very important moment, there was also born the tendency called 'Economism'. Why it was given this name I will now explain.

When we began to change over to the mass organization of workers, questions of the economic struggle and the immediate living conditions of the workers started, quite understandably, to play an enormous role. Moreover in the period of discussion-group activity only propaganda was undertaken, but with mass work this of course had to be replaced by agitation.

Let me note in passing that there is a difference between agitation and propaganda. Plekhanov grasped it very firmly. He said: 'If we give many ideas to a small number of people we have propaganda; if we give one idea to a large quantity of people we have agitation'. This definition is a classic one. In this, really, lies the distinction between agitation and propaganda.

In the period of discussion-group activity we had propaganda, that is, many ideas and a whole world-outlook were propounded to a small group of people; in the period of agitation, on the other hand, it was attempted to instil numerous workers with the one basic idea of the economic subjection of the working class.

Thus we had by then moved on to economic rails. And this was understandable. It was not at all an accidental occurrence that one of Lenin's first works was a pamphlet called *On Fines*, the fines which were in those days imposed upon working men and women in St. Petersburg for lateness, poor work and so on. These fines and deductions were then the evil of the hour, as sometimes a fifth or even a quarter of one's pay was taken off. Therefore anyone who wished to stir the rank and file to action had to talk fines. Nor was it an accident that the first leaflets of the 'League of Struggle for the Liberation of the Working Class', written by Comrade Lenin partly when at liberty and partly when he was sitting in the Kresti jail, were devoted to the question of a dispute, or this or that disorder in the factories. At that time workers had to be approached through elementary questions of pure ABC for only in this way could the rank-and-file worker, who was to a considerable extent an illiterate countryman unused to protest and organization, be roused from his deep slumber. Hence it is clear why Marxists of that time emphasized the economic aspect so greatly.

But here there occurred a dialectical twist frequently observable in the course of historical phenomena. While correctly stressing the economic aspect, a section of leading figures, who in point of fact were simply fellow-travellers and future Mensheviks, twisted the idea of Economism to mean that workers should by and large interest themselves in nothing other than mere narrow economic questions: everything else, they said, did not concern workers, they did not understand other things and we must talk to them only about things which directly affect them, that is, only about their economic demands. And so it was at this point that the word 'Economist' appeared. This name began to be given not to experts in economic science, but to those who began to assert that one must not discuss with a worker anything outside of disputes, fines and other such similar matters. The Economists went as far as to begin even to deny the necessity of the struggle against autocracy. They said that the worker would not understand that; we will frighten him away if we go up to him with the slogan of 'Down with Autocracy'. The Economists, developing and 'deepening' their views advocated in the end the following 'division of labour': politics should be the concern of the liberal

---

Lenin's *Collected Work* Vol. 2, pp. 29-72.

Contained in volumes 2-

LECTURE TWO 57

bourgeois and the struggle for economic advancement that of the workers.

Leaders of Economism

If I name to you some individuals who were among the leaders of this tendency, you will see some fairly old acquaintances before you. Such are Prokopovich and Kuskova; the very same people who the previous year had acquired the abbreviated nickname of 'prokukish'. At that time they were members of the Social-Democratic Party and participated in Legal Marxism. Nor is there anything accidental in this circumstance. Like Struve and also many figures from the radical intelligentsia out of which the bourgeois party was shaped, they had then entered the Social-Democratic Party and ranked among workers' leaders. Thus with Economism these self-same Prokopovich and Kuskova emerged with their own creed and symbol of faith and attempted to prove that workers ought not to be drawn into politics since that was the job of the liberals and the opposition within bourgeois society. The workers' interest, so they assured us, was but a very small one: economic demands. And not only that. In their struggle against Plekhanov and Lenin, Prokopovich and Kuskova even adopted the posture of genuine friends of the workers. They would say: we are the real friends of the workers. There you go considering the overthrow of autocracy and the revolutionary political struggle. But this is not the workers' business at all! You put forward tasks of a bourgeois-democratic character, but we, the true friends of the workers, say to them: autocracy does not affect you —you have to think about your dispute, your wages, and your working day.

So what was the issue here? Through and through a total misunderstanding of the hegemonic role of the working class. Marxists did not all propose that the working day and wages should be forgotten. Both Comrade Lenin and the Leagues of Struggle for the Liberation of Workers remembered these things. Of course we wanted to raise wages and improve workers' lives but for us this was not the whole story; we wanted the worker to govern the state, to be its master and its leader. And so we said that there was not a single question in which the working class ought not to be interested. Least of all the question of Tsarist autocracy which did affect him directly. We stood for the hegemony of the proletariat and we would not let the workers be driven into the kennel of petty economic demands. That was what the opponents of the 'Economists' said.

In Russia Prokopovich and Kuskova were supported by a few groups including the illegal newspaper *Rabochaya Mysl* which was published in St. Petersburg in 1896 under the editorship of Takhtarev, the author of valuable studies of the labour movement and one of its major figures in the 1890s. Alongside him on *Rabochaya Mysl,* which at that time enjoyed a considerable influence in St. Petersburg circles, Lokhov-Olkhin and the Finn, Kok, also participated. This organ and its leaders energetically defended the view of Prokopovich and Kuskova that the working class must concern itself solely with economic questions which directly affect it, and must not intrude into politics.

The first retorts to this were provided by Plekhanov and Lenin. The former did so in a booklet entitled *Vademecum* (that is, a guide book or a directory). In his *Vademecum* Plekhanov smashed the ideas of Prokopovich and Kuskova and dealt some heavy blows at *Rabochaya Mysl*. He showed that whoever wishes to leave the worker only the meagre scraps of 'economics' and does not wish them to be concerned with politics is not a workers' leader.

Another even better-aimed reply was given by Comrade Lenin. The latter was at this time in exile in Siberia and in a remote settlement there he wrote a remarkable reply to the Economists under which he brought together the signatures of a number of sympathizers in exile together with him. Comrade Lenin was always distinguished from Plekhanov in that he was, as it were, a 'collective' person striving on every occasion to present himself as an organization. This reply of Comrade Lenin's at that time went round all the workers circles. Comrade Lenin's pamphlet, *The Tasks of Russian Social-Democracy* went abroad with a foreword by the present-day Menshevik Axelrod who twenty years ago could not praise enough the pers-

Lenin's *Collected Works* Vol. 5, pp. 323-351.

LECTURE TWO

picacity that Lenin then showed. In this pamphlet, Comrade Lenin presented the question of the hegemony of the proletariat in a wholly concrete way and gave battle all along the line to the Economists, who opposed this idea.

The Economists were finally smashed at the beginning of the 1900s: by around 1902 their song was sung. But between 1898 and 1901 their ideas were predominant to some extent. At that time the workers' movement was, thanks to them, placed in the greatest danger, as the slogan of the Economists was outwardly very alluring for little experienced workers for whom it was easy to fall for this bait. And if in this period Lenin, Plekhanov, and then the actual practice of the Russian revolutionary movement had not given battle all along the line within the workers' movement, then who knows for how many years it might have been sidetracked up the path of Economism, that is, opportunism.

The Economist centre in exile

We have seen in the examples of legal and illegal Marxism (Economism was illegal: the Tsarist autocracy persecuted it and it was forced to publish illegal newspapers and leaflets) the paths of the influence of the liberal bourgeoisie, which sometimes then, given the relationship of forces, entered directly into the workers' party and attempted to infect it with the poison of adaptationism and the venom of bourgeois ideas. They did this first in the literary arena, as Struve (in *Critical Notes*) or Tugan-Baranovsky did, and then in the field of organization, like some Economists who founded in exile the 'League of Russian Social-Democrats Abroad' and published the journal *Rabochee Delo* which had a considerable circulation. Major figures in the workers' movement of that time, as for example Martynov who subsequently became a prominent Menshevik but recently came over to us, Akimov-Makhnovets, Ivanynin, Krichevsky and others participated in the editorial board of *Rabochee Delo*. They dug themselves in abroad, formed an exiles' centre there and had in Russia illegal newspapers, circles and committees which systematically worked to bend the whole of the workers' movement to the right, to push it in the direction of a moderate policy and to force the worker only to think about his narrow economic interests. Their ideology was extremely crude but highly dangerous: the worker must know his place, not concern himself with politics nor interest himself in the Tsarist autocracy; he must work only for the improvement of his shop-floor conditions and not aspire to higher things but leave this matter to the upper crust — the liberals. As was to be expected, all this was said not in quite such crude and open fashion but in a more skilful and very frequently wholly sincere way, because it seemed to people like Martynov, Teplov, Akimov-Makhnovets and Takhtarev that this is how it was and had to be. This idea was, let me repeat, dangerous in the highest degree, for it could enthuse little-experienced masses who found themselves in a desperate economic situation. But if this had happened then, the revolution would have been deferred for many years and the working class would not have succeeded in playing an independent part in it.

Role of the working class from the standpoints of Economism and Bolshevism

The advocates of 'Economism' did not acknowledge the hegemonic role of the proletariat. They would say: 'So what, in your opinion, is the working class, a Messiah?' To this we answered and answer now: Messiah and messianism are not our language and we do not like such words; but we accept the concept which is contained in them: yes, the working class is in a certain sense a Messiah and its role is a messianic one, for this is the class which will liberate the whole world. The workers have nothing to lose but their chains; they do not have property, they sell their labour, and this is the only class which has an interest in reconstructing the world along new lines and is capable of carrying the peasantry with it against the bourgeoisie. We avoid semi-mystical terms like Messiah and messianism and prefer the scientific one: the *hegemonic proletariat*, that is, the proletariat which is not content with increasing its wages by ten per cent or shortening its working day by half an hour but declares: I am master; I create the wealth for capitalism which has doomed me to my fate. For just so long I will work as capitalism's hired slave, but the hour will strike for the expropriation of the expropriators and the moment will arrive when the working class will take the power into its hands.

Hegemony of the Proletariat means power to the Soviets

The word 'hegemonic' is a foreign one. Today the workers have translated it into Russian: the hegemony of the proletariat signifies, speaking in modern language, *power to the Soviets*, power to the working class. This slogan was prepared over years and tested in a decades-old crucible; it withstood a cruel struggle not only against autocracy and the Cadet party (speaking from right to left), not only against the bourgeoisie and populism, but also against the right wing of Legal Marxism, Economism and subsequently against Menshevism too. That is why the idea of the hegemony of the proletariat is the basic ideological foundation of Bolshevism. It is one of the 'planks' upon which the Bolshevik Party stands. And every conscious partisan of communism must reflect on this if he wishes to understand the history of our party.

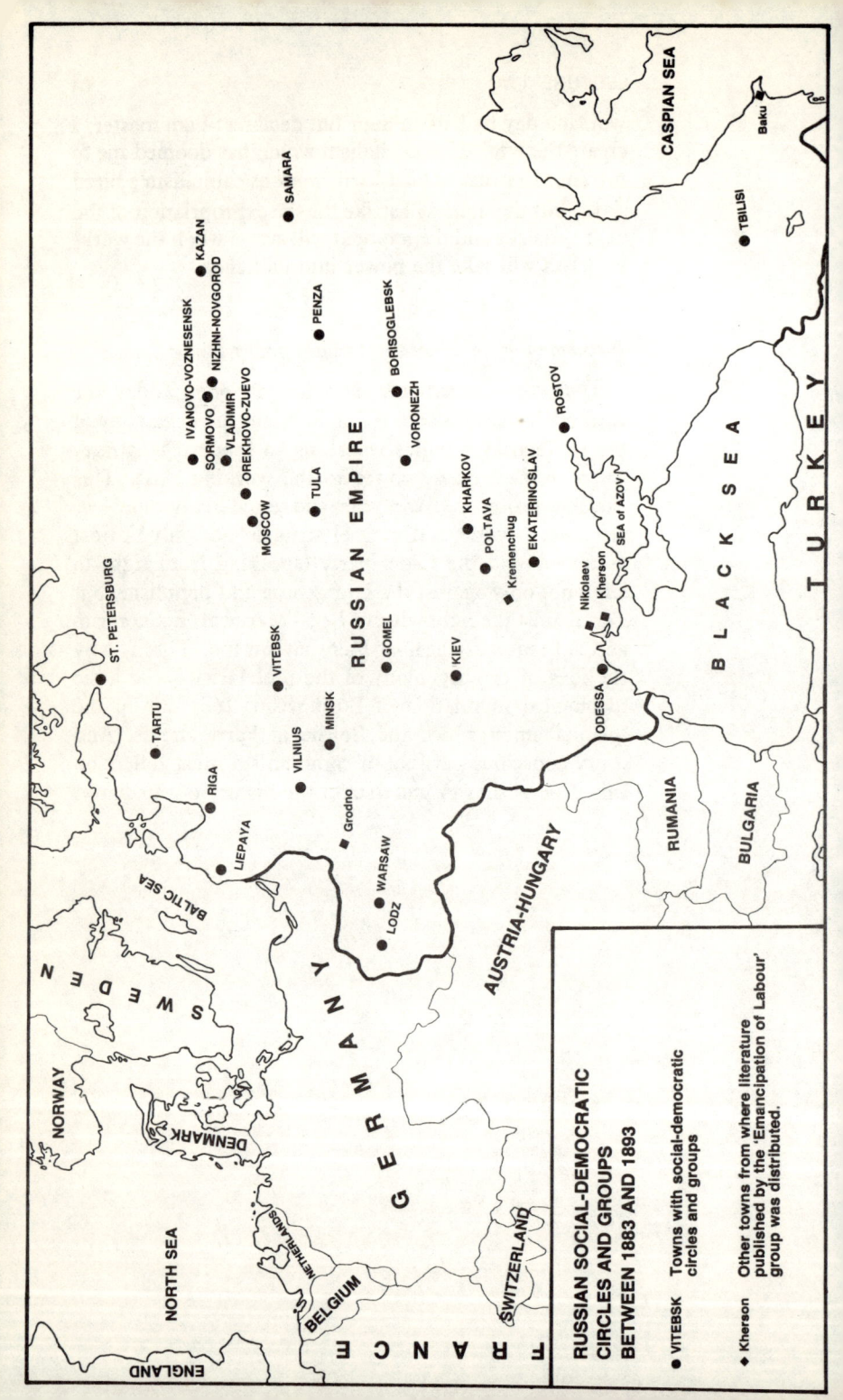

LECTURE THREE

In today's lecture I shall deal with the five years from 1898 to 1903: that is the period which lies between the first and second congresses of our party and can be regarded as the ante-chamber of the first 1905 revolution.

The Student Movement

Until now I have been speaking about the birth of the working class and the process which it undertook of defining its own party. Here it is essential to deal with certain other phenomena and above all the student movement of that time. The latter developed in broadly the following manner.

In the beginning the worker aroused the student but the latter subsequently gave his support to the worker. The workers' strike movement chronologically preceded the demonstrations and the general political student movement. Hence it is clear that it was precisely the workers' movement which brought the student movement to life and not the reverse. But the student movement too, in turn powerfully assisted the development of the workers' movement at a certain stage.

The students of today and yesterday are completely different people. There was a time (chiefly in the second half of the 1890s) when the term 'student' was synonymous with the term 'revolutionary', for in that period pupils in higher educational establishments were revolutionarily or radically minded and supported the workers' revolutionary movement. Nowadays we find this hard to imagine because over the latter years of the civil war we nearly always found the student on the opposite side of the barricade. By 1923 the position has changed somewhat, as we can without doubt witness a certain new evolution deep inside the student movement.

The evolution of the student movement

If you examine it closely you can say that the students developed 'à la Hegel'. At first we had students who were solidly revolutionary and assisted the working class in every way; then, from 1917 to 1920 we had as it were an antithesis when the student movement moved entirely against the working class and the revolution; and finally we can observe today something of a synthesis when a considerable section of the students seem to be beginning to ponder their obligations with respect to the labouring classes and are stepping into the camp of the revolution, even if only with one foot.

The first phase of the above-mentioned development occurred at the end of the 1890s when students wholly supported the workers' movement of the time. It was not for nothing that the autocracy considered the students, after the workers, to be its most dangerous enemies. And when the students deepened their movement and began to cross over gradually from academicism to open political activity, the Tsarist government began to act against them.

The academic movement of that time as distinct from today's had a revolutionary tenor. Today, *after* the overthrow of the bourgeoisie, academism has acquired quite a different meaning from what it had before the revolution. In the days of Vannovsky and Plehve, of course, the demand for the autonomy of the university was a revolutionary one and for this reason deserved support; *even* the academicism of that time was a movement aimed against Tsarist autocracy. The so-called academicism of our days takes on a completely different meaning when there are more or less White Guard professors and students attempting to sit snugly barricaded away from the proletarian revolution behind the walls of our educational institutions.

V.K. Plehve

The student youth of that time was closely connected with liberal and democratic society and sought a mass force which could smash autocracy. At every step the students became more convinced that the working class was this force and that only this class held in its hands the hammer which could be brought down on the head of Tsarism. And so the students in one way or another supported the workers' movement of the time.

Tsarism's struggle against the student movement

The Tsarist government, taking note of the students' efforts to draw closer to the workers, emptied a nest of scorpions on to the head of the students. The stupidest method then devised was to draft radically-minded students into the army. Tens and hundreds of them were seized during street demonstrations and tumultuous student gatherings and sent into the ranks. But this only poured oil on the fire. The movement broadened, grew and what is more the student youth who had been thrown into barracks lit sparks of discontent there as well, conducting propaganda inside the army. Upon this basis a terrorist movement began to grow up among students. Soon after, Karpovich shot at the Minister of Education, Bogolepov, and then Lagovsky shot Pobedonostsev. Bogolepov was replaced by General Vannovsky with his programme of 'tender care', which of course the students of that time laughed at.

K.P. Pobedonostsev

The students and the S.R. Party

Here it is important to note one circumstance: the terrorist students who subsequently became connected with the Socialist-Revolutionary party originally belonged to the social-democrats. The S.R.s attracted two groups of students to their side by their terrorist tactics: on the one hand people of great courage and unquestioned sincerity like Balmashev, Karpovich and Sazonov who were drawn towards their terrorism by their burning hearts, their insufficient confidence in the mass workers' movement and a desire to substitute for it their own personally dedicated activity; on the other hand people after the style of Savinkov also went off to the S.R.s, being dragged on to this path by an already embryonic adventurism and their own hostility to the workers' movement. (Savinkov had also once regarded himself as a social-democrat).

The Social-Democrats' attitude to the student movement

The question arose for the social-democracy of that time: what attitude should be taken towards the student movement? From what I have said about the 'Economists' it is clear that consistent supporters of that tendency would have had to ignore the student movement, which in fact they did, for the student movement, being purely political, had in their opinion nothing in common with the immediate economic demands of the workers. But the supporters of political struggle—the revolutionary wing of social-democracy of that time—headed by Comrade Lenin and the future *Iskra* men did not look at it like this but appraised the movement in an entirely different way. Of course both Comrade Lenin and his fellow-thinkers took account of the fact that the student movement of that time was not a proletarian one; they understood that it was a temporary phenomenon and that a time would come when the students would turn away from the workers; likewise they knew that the students of the day, being in their broad mass sons of property-owning parents, went out on to the streets and demonstrated not because they wanted socialism and communism but because they wanted to win political freedom and the establishment of the rule of bourgeois democracy in the country. But Comrade Lenin and his supporters in standing for the hegemony of the proletariat took the view that if the working class was the leading factor, and if it was the fundamental and basic force of the revolution, it had to take on as assistants and auxiliary forces all those who were to any degree inclined towards struggle against autocracy. As revolutionary Marxists standing for the viewpoint of the hegemony of the proletariat they said to themselves; in a large house everything can be of use: the student movement can benefit us in the struggle against Tsarism. We are obliged to make use of any opposition movement aimed against autocracy. The students are rebelling against the Tsar: excellent, let us take them in tow behind the working class, let us help them, let us attempt to lead them and direct their blows also against the bastion of autocracy ......

Revolutionary Marxists and the students

In this way the revolutionary Marxists of that time, the future Bolsheviks, not only did not ignore the student movement like the Economists, but in fact paid a great deal of attention to it. This circumstance must be borne well in mind if one wants to understand correctly certain principal and characteristic traits of Bolshevism. Bolshevism of the pre-revolutionary period up to 1905 was frequently reproached for being too interested in the bourgeois liberals and the bourgeois opposition: the students, the zemstvo* movement, the 'League of Liberation' and so on. The Mensheviks used this fact repeatedly to put on a pose and assert that they were greater friends of the working class than us. They would say: what do we want with some zemstvo members and students; ours is a workers' affair; we only think about the workers' movement. They frequently accused Comrade Lenin of supposedly seeking excessively close contacts with the bourgeois opposition: liberals, students and so on.

The Bolsheviks' tactics with regard to the students

But what was the real meaning of this Bolshevik tactic? Just this: if from its very birth Bolshevism was interested in the slightest glimmers of opposition and revolutionary movement directed against Tsarism; if it extended its hand to any group moving against autocracy then it was not in order to debase its programme to a liberal-bourgeois programme. No, for in this instance also it remained true to itself. While advancing a maximum programme (the overthrow of the bourgeoisie) Bolshevism in addition con-

---

* **Zemstvo**: Organs of local government set up by Alexander II in 1860s to run limited public services, dominated by 'liberal' landowners.

sidered that in order to realize this it was necessary to topple the Tsar and to this end it was essential to make use of any tendency which was trying to wash away the Tsarist dam. And so from the very beginning the Bolsheviks regarded the working class as the leading force and declared that the workers would not only overtake the student and liberal movements but, as Comrade Lenin put it, would also 'nudge it forward'. But at the same time the Bolsheviks warned the workers: 'Beware: today the students are supporting you and today the liberals are finding fault with the Tsar but tomorrow when the Tsar is overthrown they will go against you; once having won everything they need, that is, political liberty, they will move against you'.

Thus a double task stood before the Bolsheviks: to build on the one hand a class party which had to carry the struggle forward until the complete victory of socialism, and on the other hand to make use of any force directed against Tsarism, including the students, the liberals and the bourgeois opposition. Hence the divergent attitudes towards the students which were to become clearly discernible by the end of the 1890s between on the one hand the Economists, the future Mensheviks, and on the other the advocates of political struggle, the future *Iskra* men and subsequent Bolsheviks.

The 'League of Liberation' and the League of S.R.s

At this time, however, the beginnings of a liberal movement could be observed not only among students: the 'League of Liberation' was also being prepared, at whose head stood Milyukov, Kuskova, Struve, Prokopovich, Bogucharsky and other figures who at first had found themselves with one foot in the social-democratic camp and the other in the camp of the liberals. The League of Socialist-Revolutionaries took shape towards the end of the 1890s. In the first period of their existence both these groupings, the 'League of Liberation' and the League of S.R.s attracted supporters who prior to this had belonged to the general social-democratic mass.

The workers' movement and especially the strike movement grew simultaneously and quite rapidly too. From the middle of the 1890s the celebration of May Day began in a whole number of cities, and with each year this May Day holiday assumed ever greater proportions. And through this the movement developed in a certain sense against the Economists who had always marched at the tail of the workers' movement, forming not its head and its vanguard but its rearguard. It was not by chance that Comrade Lenin in his book *What is to be Done?* jokingly nicknamed them the 'tailists'; while Plekhanov in his *Vademecum* told the Economists, somewhat rudely, but quite correctly that they could not see the head of the workers' movement and its face, but only its backside ......

<small>Lenin's *Collected Works*, Vol. 5, pp. 347-529.</small>

Working class disturbances in St. Petersburg and other cities

Once it had begun, the workers' movement quickly moved forward drawing with it ever wider layers of workers. The most turbulent period of this movement was the beginning of 1901 and the whole of this year particularly in St. Petersburg. The revolutionary mood in the capital grew with great speed and with every day rolled further *beyond* the Economists' programme. Major disturbances flared up in the Vyborg district in 1901 in connection with May Day which led up to bloody clashes and veritable street battles. Similarly, disorders occurred following a demonstration of students supported by workers mainly from the Obukhov works, which ended in out-and-out skirmishing with the constables and soldiers. This so-called defence of Obukhov involved several thousand workers and provoked a tempestuous movement throughout St. Petersburg. When the students came out on to the streets not only in the capital but in Moscow and Kiev as well, and especially when on May Day demonstrating workers came out on to the streets of St. Petersburg, the struggle acquired a particularly clear-cut character.

The Rostov strike, 1902: mass meeting

LECTURE THREE

Letters from workers

In the literary sources of the history of the workers' movement extracts can be found from 'letters to the editor' which working men and women of that time sent in to illegal newspapers. This is what one working woman wrote after a conflict in the Vyborg district:

> You don't know what a shame it was for me and all of us. We didn't half want to go down the Nevsky Prospekt or into the city. It's really sickening to die in a hole like dogs where no one can even see you ......
> And another thing I want to tell you: though they captured lots and lots of us — perhaps there are no more left at all — all the same we will stand fast.'

The worker B. remarks:

> It's a pity we didn't have a banner. Another time we'll get hold of both a banner and pistols.

Comrade Lenin and his group obtained these letters which were worth their weight in gold and published them in the struggle against the Economists, wishing to show that advanced workers wanted not only to increase their wages but also recognised the necessity of going on to the streets, getting pistols and fighting the Tsarist police. Comrade Lenin published with great pleasure the following excerpts from a letter from a worker beyond the Nevsky Gate who wrote the following about the Economists:

> I showed it to many comrades and it became completely tattered to shreds.* But it is dear to me, much dearer than *Mysl*† although there is nothing of ours printed in it. There you have all about our cause and all the Russian cause which you cannot value in kopecks or measure in hours ...... Working people may now easily burst into flame; everything down below is rotting nowadays—it needs only a spark and there'll be a fire.‡ How truly it is said that a flame will flare up from a spark. Before, every strike was an event but now everyone can see one strike is nothing: now it is necessary to win freedom and to seize it with both hands. Now we don't need cash, or even books; just learn how to go to battle and how to fight a battle.

---

* The writer is referring to *Iskra*.
† Mysl, i.e. *Rabochaya Mysl*. See Glossary.

‡ *Iskra* carried on its masthead these words: 'From a spark a flame will flare up.' (From the Decembrists' reply to Pushkin).

The Rostov strike, 1902: Mass Meeting
Police break up May Day demonstration at the Obukhov works, St. Petersburg, 1901

The newspaper 'Iskra'

Supporters of Leninism of that time seized upon such statements by individual workers, as they wished to prove that the advanced worker no longer thought of limiting himself to a single economic struggle but asked to be taught how to go into battle and how to overthrow autocracy by armed force, that is, he wanted to create a real revolutionary party which would help him to play his role as the leading factor, and the basic force, in the revolutionary struggle. And it was in this way and against the background of all these facts and events that the newspaper *Iskra* was created.

Comrade Lenin had returned from exile at the beginning of the 1890s together with a group of his then sympathizers: Martov, Potresov and several others. They met in St. Petersburg Vera Ivanovna Zasulich, one of the founders of the 'Emancipation of Labour' group, through her establishing a link with this group, whose centre was located in Geneva in Switzerland. As I have already said, Comrade Lenin had already begun his struggle against Economism when he was in exile. Returning to St. Petersburg he began to gather together his sympathizers who were to be found in all the cities where the workers' movement had developed. Incidentally, he began as well to seek out those workers with whom in 1895 he formed the 'League of Struggle for the Liberation of the Working Class'; he also established links with Moscow workers and together with his supporters, Martov and Potresov became convinced that for the struggle against the 'Economists' and for the creation of a really revolutionary proletarian party it was essential to set up , as they then said an 'All-Russian' political newspaper.

V.I. Zasulich

Soon afterwards in 1900 an illegal meeting was held in the city of Pskov at which Lenin, Martov and Potresov were present and just two representatives of local revolutionary activity: Stepan and Lyubov Radchenko. (The latter is still alive today and many of us know her through her work in the Moscow area in 1905 and 1906 when she was — alas! a Menshevik.) It is curious to note that Struve and Tugan-Baranovsky also came to the Pskov meeting and at that time had contemplated setting up a bourgeois-liberal organ, *Osvobozhdenie;* as they did not wish to break off their connexion with the workers' movement they attempted to patch up some sort of coalition between the then illegal liberals and the illegal social-democrats.

At the meeting in Pskov it was decided to publish the newspaper *Iskra*. Comrade Lenin departed abroad with Potresov in order to implement this decision. In Munich in December 1900 the first issue of the newspaper *Iskra* appeared which was to play an enormous role in the history of the revolution in general and of the communist party in particular.* This was not just any newspaper: it was a published organ which succeeded in becoming the master of a whole generation of minds, fulfilling a great literary and political task and simultaneously accomplishing huge organizational political work in consolidating the party.

* The first issue was edited in Munich but printed in Leipzig.

Its role and significance

If *Iskra* is compared with other well-known newspapers then it can be said that it played in no way a lesser and possibly an even greater role than *Zvezda* and *Pravda* during 1910-1912. Like *Pravda*, which in the pre-revolutionary period raised up an enormous layer of workers, so *Iskra* in its time likewise raised up a definite stratum of workers and revolutionaries. Just as a whole generation of *Pravda* men came from *Pravda* so a whole generation of '*Iskra* men' or 'Iskryaks' as they were then called, came from *Iskra*. *Iskra* came out under the editorship of Plekhanov, Lenin, Martov, Axelrod, Potresov and Zasulich. Amongst these six people was one future Bolshevik and five future Mensheviks. But Comrade Lenin's role on it was so great that in only a short time this paper began to be called 'Lenin's' and so it was in actual fact.

Its tendency and ideas

The fundamental ideas of *Iskra* consisted of the following. It above all launched a crusade against the deformation of the workers' movement which the 'Economists' propounded; it mocked and flayed them cruelly for their desire at all costs to lay the workers' movement upon the Procrustean bed of peaceful economic demands. Its beacon was the idea of the hegemony of the proletariat and the confidence that the working class would be the liberator class and the main force in the revolution. In addition, the newspaper waged a campaign against the Socialist-Revolutionaries. As early as 1901 they were called in its columns for the first time not Socialist-Revolutionaries but Socialist-*Reactionaries*, and this at a time when they had only just emerged, when members of their party were carrying out effective terrorist acts and it was still difficult to detect their reactionary essence. But the sharp eye of Comrade Lenin and the *Iskra* editorial board had already taken a hard look at this party of future Socialist-Revolutionaries, the future representatives of the kulak petty-bourgeoisie. *Iskra*'s campaign against the S.R.s, however, produced deep disquiet among the circles of Narodnik intellectuals which still survived at that time and also among a certain section of workers who said: why fight amongst ourselves? Let's all march together in one column against autocracy. The psychology of workers living under the yoke of Tsarism was such that they said: let all revolutionaries irrespective of party and their differences unite closely together and teach us jointly how to fight against autocracy. And so *Iskra* had on the one hand to take under its wing workers of all opposition and revolutionary tendencies, students and liberals, zemstvo members and S.R.s — and on the other, in laying the foundations of its purely proletarian and irreconcilable workers' party, to fight simultaneously against the liberals and the S.R.s, exposing their petty-bourgeois essence and proving that they were not proletarian revolutionaries. Finally the third main idea of *Iskra* consisted in fighting for a centralized, single, all-Russian political organization of the proletariat.

'*Iskra*'s' literary and practical activity

These days such an idea seems a commonplace. But in 1900-1901 when revolutionaries were in the habit of huddling away each in his own small circle, when no one

Iskra

had all-Russian perspectives and understood that only in this way could anything be achieved, when no one had a clear vision and when no one could conceive what an enormous force would have to be put into battle to gain any results—in those days the concept of the centralized party, the all-Russian political organization striving to unite the whole proletariat, was a new and in the highest degree a difficult one. The newspaper not only propounded this idea in its articles: it formed a special *Iskra* organization which was formed of some 100-150 *Iskra* men — the foremost revolutionaries of the time. And this group put into practice those plans which in the paper Lenin and Plekhanov developed in a literary form.

'Osvobozhdenie' and *'Iskra'*

But at the same time there were people taking part in *Iskra* in the beginning who already stood with one foot outside the workers' camp. This resulted from the necessity of a united front with the liberals and the S.R.s against autocracy. In this respect the following episode which Martov recounts in detail in his personal memoirs, is worthy of note.

As I have said there had been for some time people like Struve and Tugan-Baranovsky, the future leading lights of *Osvobozhdenie*, clustered round *Iskra*. What is more, in the very beginning, Prince Obolensky, who was then even a party member, collaborated on it. A year after its foundation when the paper quite clearly showed its political physiognomy as the leader of the working class, and the propounder of the idea of the hegemony of the proletariat, Obolensky in the middle of 1902 wrote to *Iskra* from Orel the following: 'I think it is time for us to reject the hegemony of the liberation movement'. On this basis Obolensky soon broke from *Iskra* and was in fact expelled from the party. With his departure ended the last link that still existed between *Iskra* and those liberal revolutionaries who could in the beginning still count on a definite bloc and a coalition with the *Iskra* men.

This episode is in the highest measure a curious one. In my view it is extremely significant that people like Struve,

Tugan-Baranovsky and Prince Obolensky could move around and about the workers' party at all. Today this will appear incomprehensible to many but then it was inevitable. And Comrade Lenin was right when he would from time to time derive benefit from Struve, Tugan-Baranovsky and Obolensky and said that in a big house even a bit of string has some use: Obolensky too had his uses. Remember: the working class had been driven underground and was outside the law; its agitators and propagandists had neither refuge nor a single penny. But these representatives of the liberals, who in their own way hated Tsarism, were rich in contacts and money and had roomy flats. And for this reason alone it was entirely correct to make use of them for a certain period.

But if it was a noteworthy thing that people like Prince Obolensky could be around the party at that time then their break from it is even more interesting. On what account did it take place? Because of trifling differences? No, because of a basic idea. Obolensky said: 'I think that it is time to renounce our hegemony in the liberation movement'. In other words it was time to renounce the fact that the worker strives towards the leading role in the revolution: rather he must be merely an auxiliary force. This is how these people looked upon the worker. It's okay for him to pull the cart of the revolution, but on this cart there have to sit the liberal gentry like Struve, Tugan-Baranovsky or Prince Obolensky who must keep the reins in their hands and determine the programme, aim and tactics of the revolutionary movement. But when they became convinced that *Iskra* was not amenable to this they said: 'We are leaving'. Of course, having made use of these people, there was nothing else for Comrade Lenin and his sympathizers to do but to bid them a pleasant journey.

'Iskra's' success and influence

Iskra, which had the support of its own organization which we have mentioned above as well as its printed columns (as you saw from the letter I quoted it was read until it was in tatters; especially as it was printed on thin cheap paper), succeeded in winning control of the work-

LECTURE THREE

ers' committees, the provincial committees of that time, in a whole number of cities and above all in the two capitals.

Besides *Iskra* an exceptional role was played by Comrade Lenin's book *What is to be Done?* which was published in the spring of 1902. This was not merely a book: it was a book marking an era. It drew up a two-year account of the work of *Iskra*. At the same time it was a handbook and gospel for all revolutionary Marxist activists of the time. And it was only in 1903 that the Mensheviks, having seen the conclusions which had been drawn from this book, began, in retrospect and through a magnifying glass, to seek disagreements with it. The main ideas of *What is to be Done?* are the same as those of *Iskra*: that is, the self-same idea of the hegemony of the proletariat. But *What is to be Done?* above all posed with particular emphasis the question of so-called 'primitiveness'* and professional revolutionaries.

Lenin's Collected Works, Vol. 5, pp. 347-529.

* Primitiveness—the Russian word means more exactly 'cottage industry methods'.

Primitiveness

Comrade Lenin christened with the name of 'primitiveness' the wretched practice of that time of self-contained circles. He criticised and scoffed at the revolutionaries of those days who complacently boasted that in such-and-such a city they had a circle and in another one all of two. Comrade Lenin wrote: this is small fry, this is primitiveness, but we need a revolution on the scale of large-scale factory production; it is necessary to put an end to primitiveness; in the days when nothing else could be done it was essential, but now when the masses are on the boil, when working men and women write that they demand struggle and ask to be taught how to 'go into battle', when strikes like the actions by the textile workers can involve up to 80,000 people, when clashes take place in the Vyborg district and when even the students, the sons of the bourgeoisie, come out on to the streets in their thousands and tens of thousands and fight the Tsarist mounted police with their bare hands — to limit yourself now, in this day, to discussion-groups means to engage in primitive handicrafts and hair-splitting when we need revolutionary factory production. No, said Lenin in *What is to be Done?* we need to create an all-Russian party with a division of labour within it where everyone knows what he must do and what his obligations are. Comrade Lenin was pounced upon over this division of labour especially by the then right wing. He was reproached for aiming to turn individual revolutionaries into mindless screws and cogs in a big machine and for thereby debasing the vocation of the revolutionary. But Comrade Lenin replied: being a little screw or cog of a great revolutionary party pursuing world historical objectives does not at all mean debasing the vocation of the revolutionary. And in connection with this Comrade Lenin advanced the idea of the corporate association of professional revolutionaries, if it can be put that way, that is of people occupied with revolution by profession.

Professional Revolutionaries

This term — 'professional revolutionary' — played its part in the controversies between the Bolsheviks and the Mensheviks as well. The latter were for years after to fight against it and to assert that professional revolutionaries would become a self-centred caste of people divorced from the masses who would not breathe the same air as the workers' movement, but would degenerate into a conspiratorial group and so on and so forth. In reply to them Comrade Lenin demonstrated a very simple truth: against us, he said, there is Tsarist autocracy's enormous force, its whole apparatus which it has created over its 300 year term of office; against us are all the technical resources of the old Russia, its schools and its press; yet we have a completely juvenile workers' movement. If we want to forge the working masses together and to merge the separate little fires flaring up here and there into one single big flame, then we need an exceptional, almost miraculous apparatus which is capable of realising all this. And for this it is no less necessary in turn that people really dedicated to the working class are brought together by us into one organization of professional revolutionaries; that is, people who would serve only the revolution and not concern themselves with anything else, and who in conditions of illegality and inconceivably rigorous situations would be capable of forming a very complex revolutionary system of co-operation with a precise division of labour, and mastering the art of easy and free manoeuvrebility.

Their work and importance for the party

Comrade Lenin had to sustain a major battle in order to uphold the idea of the organization of professional revolutionaries. For, at that time, this idea was a completely new one and appeared to many to be an 'organizational delirium'. But Comrade Lenin was right and this idea of his proved to be one of his most fruitful. Indeed if, from the standpoint of the personal composition of the leadership, you take a close look at how our party and even our state live today then it will become clear that to a considerable extent even today, twenty years later, the party is nourished so to speak by a group of professional revolutionaries whose basis was laid at the beginning of the 1900s. The old active workers of our party form a minute section (party members with a membership dating from before 1917 throughout Russia number today ten thousand), but enjoy an enormous popularity and prestige and form the mortar which binds our party together. These ten thousand are a glorious cohort of professional revolutionaries who have waged a revolutionary struggle year in and year out and do not know any other occupation. They were put in prison but on leaving, either after escaping or serving their time, again took up revolutionary work in exactly the same way as a worker, after going home from the factory in the evening and going to bed, once again goes off to the factory in the morning.

A considerable part of *What is to be Done?* is devoted to the idea of an organization of professional revolutionaries. It proved in its time to have a huge influence and produced a powerful impact. A certain Bund member, a supporter of Menshevism, who did not approve either of the organization of professional revolutionaries or of the struggle against primitiveness, or even of the division of labour, recently wrote in recollection of the 1900s:

> 'I often found myself thinking: how good it would be, all the same, to resemble just a little the ideal of the revolutionary which Lenin depicts in his book *What is to be Done?*'

The breaking up of the Kiev 'Iskra' organization

When they had read *What is to be Done?* the best of the Mensheviks, the opponents of Comrade Lenin, if not admitted then at least felt what a great vital revolutionary truth was laid out on the pages of this book.

Meanwhile the *Iskra* organization continued to grow. The Tsarist government, convinced that it was becoming a highly influential revolutionary breeding-ground and that it would stir up the whole of the revolutionary camp, launched a number of repressive measures against it. In February 1901, in Kiev, which was an important point of support for *Iskra*, the authorities broke up the organization and arrested its leaders. Let me remind you of some of them. First N. Bauman, who was killed in Moscow in 1905, a definite Bolshevik. Then there was V. Krokhmal who later became a vehement Menshevik; he was the chairman, or one of the chairmen, of the Pre-Parliament which we dissolved in the October days and afterwards, it has to be admitted, he was more than once arrested in Petrograd by our G.P.U. for counter-revolutionary activity. Then also there was Basovsky who has left the revolutionary scene; Radchenko, who I have already spoken about, is now dead; Litvinov, our present comrade in the People's Commissariat for Foreign Affairs; Pyatnitsky, a Bolshevik who at the present time is working in the Comintern — and a few others. In short, in the *Iskra* organization which was in essence Bolshevik there were people working together for a short space of time from whose ranks emerged the best leaders of Bolshevism and the most graphic representatives of Menshevism.

N.E. Bauman

O.A. Pyatnitsky

In April 1902 an attempt was again made to call an all-Russian congress. Only half a conference managed to meet at Bialystok at which both future Bolsheviks as well as future Mensheviks including the notorious Dan were represented.

1902

On the 4th April 1902 Balmashev killed Sipyagin* who was succeeded by Plehve. This was the highest point reached by the student movement, which had led a section

* Sipyagin—then the Minister of Internal Affairs.

of students who at that time acted together with workers and social-democrats but who then began to move away from the workers and go over to the S.R. party. But parallel to this, the revolutionary movement amongst workers spread. At this point the celebrated Nizhni-Novgorod* workers' demonstration took place, and brought with it the arrest of many comrades. In connection with the workers' demonstrations the first major trial was held at which Zalomov, Denisov and others made public speeches. Denisov, today a member of our party and one of the oldest Bolsheviks, made a speech before the court which, under the conditions of Tsarist reaction, was truly heroic. It was snatched up from the streets of Nizhni-Novgorod and was afterwards read in a whole number of Russian cities.

* Now Gorky.

The Rostov events

Finally in November 1902 the Rostov events broke forth which bore a nakedly pre-revolutionary character. It must be said of course that all of 1902 abounded in strikes, especially in the south of Russia. But towards the end of 1902 — in November — a powerful political movement arose in the city of Rostov out of what was apparently, initially, an economic one. First of all a meeting was held which brought together some 40,000 people and which the police could not disperse. A continuous meeting ran for a period of several days with the demonstrators uttering inflammatory speeches in the spirit of *Iskra*. At the head of this movement stood principally the Bolshevik Stavsky, a Rostov worker, today a member of our party, and Comrade Gusev who now works with us on the military side. (He was then a member of the Rostov committee and a guiding spirit of this movement).

The Rostov events drew up the balance-sheet of a specific phase. At this point the Economists were finally smashed. Movements such as those at Nizhni-Novgorod, at the Obukhov works, in the Vyborg district and in Rostov were clearly political and had nothing in common with 'Economism', but brought forward workers who raised their voices as the future leaders of the revolution.

I.I. Stavsky

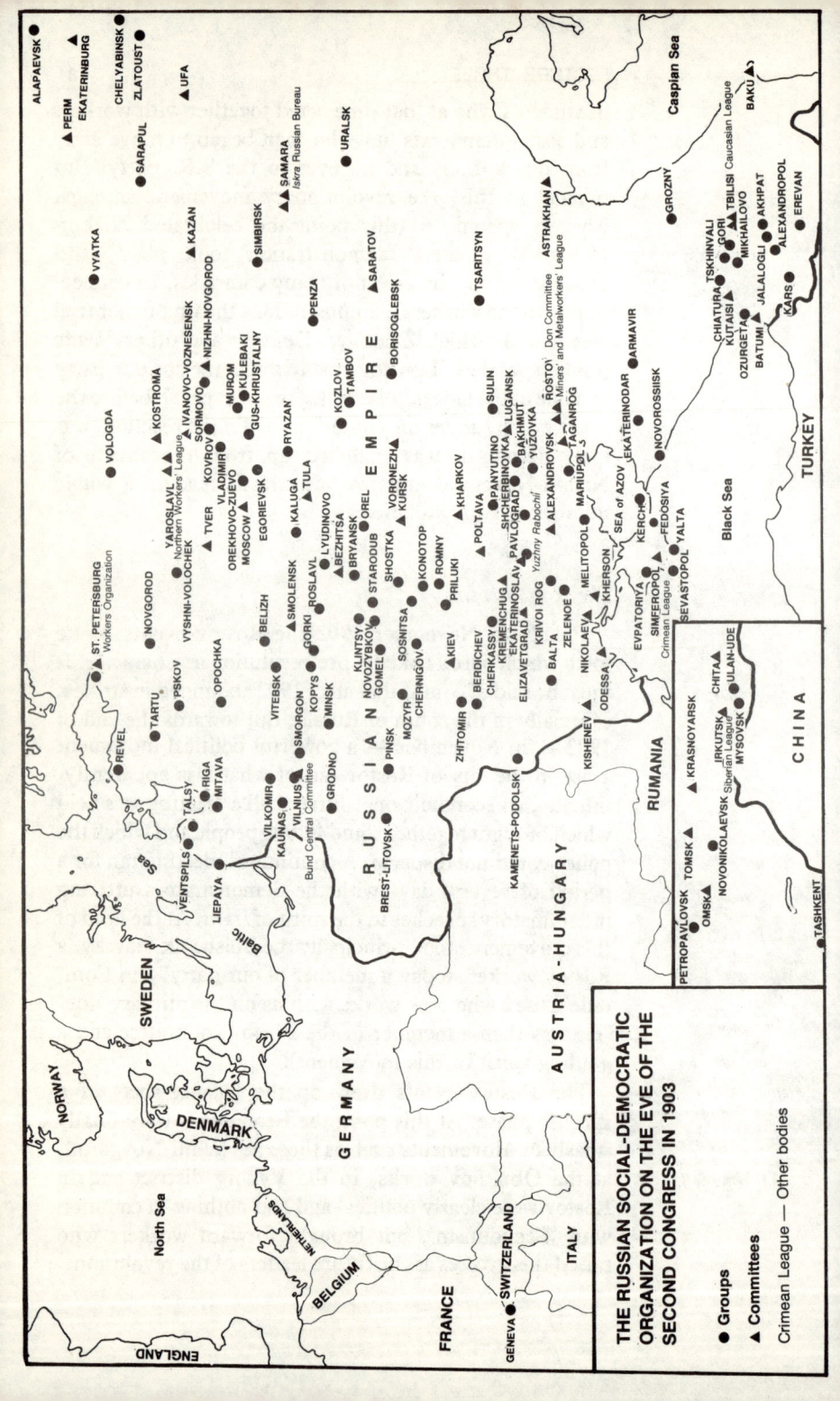

The first Central Committee

All these events preceded the Second Congress of our party and formed the background to its preparation. After the arrests in Kiev and the escape from the local prison in which Litvinov and Pyatnitsky took part, the *Iskra* organization formed its organizational committee, which was in essence the first Central Committee of that time. And here it is no less interesting to enumerate those who made up this committee. This listing shows clearly that the nearer we approach the revolution the more frequently we encounter the names of present-day Bolsheviks.

G.M. Krzhizhanovsky

On this organizational committee there sat: today's electrifier of Russia, Krzhizhanovsky, about whom I have already spoken; Alexandrova, the future Menshevik; Lengnik who is now working in the People's Commissariat for Education; Krasikov, one of our principal colleagues in the People's Commissariat of Justice; a representative of the St. Petersburg Committee, Krasnukh; a representative of *Yuzhny Rabochii*, Levin, and finally Rozanov about whom we shall have to speak again. (In 1920 he was arrested in connection with the so-called 'National Centre'). Portnoi came from the Bund. A good half of them are today Bolsheviks, and were then sympathizers of Lenin who was directing this work from abroad.

The draft Party programme

This organizational committee had the task of convening an all-Russian Party Congress, which would have to lay the foundation of the party on the basis of the programme which *Iskra* had worked out for this purpose. By this time the latter had printed the draft programme of our party prepared by the editorial boards of *Iskra* and *Zarya*. (*Zarya* was a theoretical organ which was published abroad by the same group of Plekhanov and Lenin).

This preliminary draft which was written in the main by Plekhanov and Lenin has, upon the insistence of Comrade Lenin, been carried in large part over to our programme of today. Included in its theoretical section were propositions relating to the development of capitalism, the concentration of capital, the formation of the proletariat and the transfer of power to the proletariat. By 1903 this draft programme was ready. And by this time the Organizational Committee had brought the party to the congress.

At the same time the lightning of revolutionary struggle flickered in different places. In 1902 a peasant movement began in Saratov with a number of peasant rebellions, which were suppressed by the governor, Stolypin. They showed that following the working class which had aroused the students and had provided an impetus to the bourgeois opposition, the peasantry was likewise beginning to rise up. Simultaneously the shots of individual terrorists rang out: Karpovich, Balmashev, and Hirsch Lekert who shot Von Wahl. In some cities demonstrators fought with the Tsarist police.

The Second Party Congress

It was against the background of these events that our party's Second Congress met in the summer of 1903. It started in Brussels, but as the Belgian authorities created obstacles it moved to London where it was concluded. Some sixty people having 48 votes were present at this congress. Among them were: Comrade Schottmann from the St. Petersburg Committee who works now in a Karelian commune; Lydia Makhnovets, a second representative from St. Petersburg, the sister of Akimov Makhnovets, one of the extreme 'Economists' who stood on the right wing; N. Bauman from the Moscow Committee; from the Northern League, which linked together a number of committees in the north of Russia, came Lydia Knipovich, whom old working men and women of Petrograd should remember as she worked many years there under the name of 'Dyadenka'* — she died the year before last; from the same Northern League came a second representative, Stopani, the founder of the Baku workers' movement and one of the most distinguished Bolsheviks; from the Ufa Committee were Makhlin and Leonov who was subsequently an anarchist; from the Kiev Committee, Krasikov; from Tula, the brother of Vladimir Ilyich

* 'Auntie'.

LECTURE FOUR

Ulyanov, Dmitri Ulyanov who is now in our ranks; from the Odessa Committee, Zemlyachka; from the Crimean League, the Menshevik, Panin; from the Don League, Mashinsky, also a Menshevik; from the Don Committee, Gusev, now a Bolshevik, and the Menshevik Akkerman; from the Saratov Committee, Galkin and Lyadov, both now Bolsheviks; from the Kharkov Committee, Levina and Nikolaev; from the Siberian League, Dr. Maldenberg, a Menshevik and a member of the Second Duma and also Comrade Trotsky who was at that time a Menshevik; from the Batumi Committee, Zurabov, subsequently a deputy in the Second Duma, a Menshevik and an internationalist; from the Baku Committee, Bogdan Knuniants who took part in the first Workers' Soviet in 1905 and who during the counter-revolution went over to the Mensheviks; from the Tbilisi Committee, Topuridze; from the Bund, Kremer, Eisenstadt, Portnoi, Lieber, and Kosovsky, all Mensheviks; finally Comrade Lenin represented the *Iskra* organization in exile and Martov, the editorial board; also present at the congress were Plekhanov, Axelrod, Deutsch and others.

The Party's social composition at the beginning of the 1900s

By the way, two words on the social composition of the party in those days. The *Iskra* organization, this congress, as well as our committees at that time, did not have a majority of workers. This fact is extremely important in clarifying our present-day controversy over the social composition of the party. Sometimes this is judged in a highly primitive fashion. Statistics are taken of how many workers, peasants and officials there are in the party and then it is said: as the workers are not in a clear majority then of course it is not a workers' party. However it is not so simple in practice. We know that there are purely workers' organizations in composition but whose policy is not revolutionary nor imbued with a proletarian spirit. The party's social composition does not decide everything. It is of course an important factor but not the only one.

The *Iskra* organization and our committees then con-

'Bolshevik' Delegates at the 2nd Party Congress (l. to r.)
V.F. Galkin, S.I. Gusev, R.S. Zemlyachka, A.G. Zurabov
P.A. Krasikov, M.N. Lyadov, L.D. Makhlin, G.M. Mishenev
I.K. Nikitin, D.A. Topuridze, D.I. Ulyanov, A.V. Schottmann

sisted more of students and partly too of professional revolutionaries; there were few workers and they were still isolated figures like Babushkin and Schottmann, who were beginning to come forward from the working masses. By dint of this, the Second Party Congress which laid the basis of the party also consisted of a majority of nonworkers. But despite this the *Iskra* organization, which formed essentially the first Bolshevik organization, played a large and active role in the revolution — the role of the communist vanguard. Made up of professional revolutionaries led by Comrade Lenin yet not composed purely of workers it nevertheless carried the working masses with it and its grass roots took shape there in the depths of the proletarian masses. And it was just this working mass which in turn carried upon its crest the group which was subsequently to create the party.

The controversy with the Bund

But let us return to the Second Congress, at which the split between the Bolsheviks and the Mensheviks became clearly revealed. The first point of divergence was the attitude of the different sides to the national question, in other words, towards the Bund. While paying a tribute to the heroism of the Jewish workers and artisans, who during the dark night of reaction first rose to the struggle, it must at the same time be said that this organization came into the history of the party as a Menshevik and an opportunist one. At the Second Congress these traits manifested themselves sharply over the national question. The Bund demanded that it be regarded as the 'only representative of all the Jewish proletariat living in Russia', evidently not wishing to take into account the fact that Jewish workers, like all the Jewish people, were scattered throughout the country and that therefore it would be more correct for Jewish workers, like the Finnish, Estonian and other workers to join the organization of the locality where they lived. We could not agree to fragment our organization into separate national sections for we are a single international party waging a struggle against international capital. The *Iskra* men stood for precisely this point of view, conceding only that Jewish workers could have their subsidiary organizations and special groups and publish their own newspapers in their native tongue and so on. But the Bund, expressing its future social-chauvinism for the first time, adamantly demanded the division of workers by nationality and their right to have their separate parties. This controversy, which might appear to be an organizational one, was in actual fact an extremely important political disagreement which contained in itself the future discussions on the attitude to the national question and towards internationalism. The *Iskra* men, marching in a common front with both Lenin and Martov, fought against the Bund, but at the congress the future Mensheviks and Bundists began to move together having sensed that they were close to one another and that they had identical views on certain other basic questions. However for the time being it ended with the Bund splitting away from the party and walking out of the congress.

The controversy over the first paragraph of the Party's statutes (party membership)

The second controversy, which was no less serious, arose in connection with the first paragraph of the party statutes which spoke of the obligations of a party member. Comrade Lenin formulated it in this way: a party member is one who *participates in any of the organizations* of the party, fulfils the *obligations of a party member*, pays members' dues, observes discipline etc. Martov proposed this formula: a party member is one who works *under the direction* of the party and provides any assistance to party *organizations*. At first sight it might appear that the controversy was really one of words only. And many attending the congress actually thought so too. But in actual fact the controversy was not over words but over what the party should be.

Comrade Lenin said: if a worker wants to be a member of the party he must enter this or that cell and work in this or that party organization — that does not put workers off; by observing this condition we shall know whom the party consists of, and we shall not have a loose party mass, not a mish-mash, but a firmly cast organization comprising genuine proletarians. Martov, Axelrod and the rest of the Mensheviks maintained otherwise. 'We have outlived the period of illegality', they said, 'when participating in the party was no safe affair. The worker will come to us perhaps but there is besides the worker, the student, the professor, and the petty-bourgeois, who will not come. Therefore if, in relation to the obligations of a party member, we adopt a broader formula and say that anyone may enter the party who gives it assistance and works under its direction, without the obligation to enter a cell or organization then the student, the professor and the petty-bourgeois will come to us.' Comrade Lenin energetically objected to such a formulation of the question: 'Your argument threatens the party with doom', he said. 'In the party we need not students, not professors nor petty-bourgeois: we need workers. We are prepared to make use of the student and academic movements; we do not reject the services of Prince Obolensky, or the very eminent Petr Struve or anyone whom we meet along our way, but we must remember that the leading class is the proletariat and that its party must be a proletarian one'. And thus the controversy revolved not around verbal formulas but around the vital question: should our party be a workers' proletarian revolutionary party or should it become what German Social-Democracy had become; by picking up tens and hundreds of fellow-travellers and numbering as many innkeepers in its ranks as workers it swelled incredibly yet during the war suffered the bankruptcy which is well-known to all. What Martov and Axelrod had proposed threatened us with the same end that was met by the S.R. party which, through taking in everyone it met, had swollen so much by 1917 that individual revolutionaries drowned in it like flies in milk amid the sludge of the bourgeois democrats.

This question was a completely new one for the congress and it did not grasp it very clearly; moreover things were further complicated by the fact that the party was still on an illegal footing. Even such acute minds as Plekhanov's did not take full account of how serious this controversy was. Plekhanov delivered a jocular speech in which he said: 'When you listen to Lenin he seems to be right; when you listen to Martov he seems to come close to the truth also'. He apparently wanted to reconcile the two sides. But Lenin firmly stuck to his position and the struggle raged bitterly. In the very end victory was won by Martov who, thanks to an insignificant majority, carried the Menshevik formula. The congress resolved that everyone who assisted the party and worked under its direction could enter it. In other words the decision was taken which opened the party's doors to the non-proletarian element which without doubt would have destroyed it had not life later introduced its own particular amendments. Martov, in describing this point at the congress much later on said: 'I sustained the victory but Lenin contrived within a short space of time to so crop short my formula with the aid of several other points and take such a revenge that, in the final analysis, hardly anything of my victory remained'.

This controversy over paragraph I of the Statutes was an extremely instructive one, as it showed that within the framework of a single party we then had two parties, rather as within the framework of Legal Marxism there had existed at the same time two world-outlooks.

The controversy over the attitude to the liberal bourgeoisie

The third divergence at the Second Congress was still more important and serious. This was on the question of the attitude towards the liberals.

By that time the liberal bourgeoisie, which now had the support of its own organ, began to show its claws to the working class. In the 1900s it was still the case that the main enemy of the liberals was autocracy. But in 1903 when political relationships began to crystallize more rapidly, especially after the strikes in the south and the Rostov events as a result of which workers spoke up with the voice of a hegemonic class concerned with its *own* interests, the liberals began to look askance at the left and opened a struggle on two fronts: not only against Tsarism but also against the workers. With their class instinct they sensed that sooner or later they would have to do battle with the working class and the workers' party.

In connexion with this situation the question arose at the congress of what attitude to take towards the liberals. Comrade Lenin, who had said at one time that we ought to make use of the liberals for even a bit of string has a use in a big house, when he could see that the liberals were getting organized and showing their claws said: Yes, we make use of the liberals against the Tsar, but at the same time we must tell the working class that the liberal bourgeoisie is getting organized, that it is creating its own party, and that as it becomes more and more counter-revolutionary it will move against the workers and against carrying the revolution through to the end. Therefore inasmuch as the bourgeoisie acts against the Tsar we shall support it, but we must not forget that this class is our enemy. In other words: for the first time, at this congress, the question of the attitude towards the bourgeoisie, the question which in the end led to the split between ourselves and the Mensheviks, was clearly and precisely formulated. The latter, in the persons of Martov, Potresov and some others, introduced the following motion: we must go along with the liberals but set them the condition that they come out in favour of universal suffrage; those of them who sincerely come out for this will prove that they are not counter-revolutionaries. The Mensheviks asserted that (in the words of Potresov) this condition would be a sort of test, a piece of litmus paper, for the liberals. But their presentation of the question clearly showed that they wanted not to use the bourgeoisie, but to go hand in hand with it — for which purpose they had thought up conditions acceptable to it.

Lenin and Plekhanov sharply criticised this motion and showed that 'litmus paper' was of no help; liberal after liberal would for the moment accept any conditions you like only to trick you the next day. It was necessary to teach workers distrust and not instil them with naive Manilovian† ideas that one could, with the help of some 'conditions', come to an agreement with the liberal bourgeoisie which wished merely to use the workers in their struggle against autocracy.

† Manilov—a character in Gogol's *Dead Souls* noted for his inane schemes and dreaming.

In 1903 the picture was as follows: there were three forces present — the Tsarist autocracy, the working class and the liberal bourgeoisie. The working class said: let us use the liberal bourgeoisie against the Tsar but let us tomorrow fight against it; the liberal bourgeoisie said: let us use the workers against the Tsar but tomorrow we will fight against them. In this state of affairs it is clear that the attitude towards the liberals and towards the bourgeoisie was a central and basic question which would define future tactics for a whole era.

But the congress did not see this disagreement with the same clarity as we see it nowadays. And as Martov who had fought for many years hand in hand with Lenin enjoyed the popularity and confidence of the party, the congress made a Solomon-like decision: by an almost equal number of votes, it carried both motions taking the view that they did not contradict each other. This shows how much the disagreements were in reality still undefined.

Besides the three we have mentioned there were yet other disagreements at the congress of a minor importance. For example there was the question of whether or not the party ought to be built upon the principle of a strict centralization or the contrary. Comrade Lenin stood for a centralized party. The Mensheviks began cautiously to defend decentralization and the federal principle of giving greater power to the areas.

The controversy over the composition of the 'Iskra' editorial board

There also arose a dispute over personnel — in connection with the composition of the editorial board of *Iskra*. It had latterly consisted of six: Plekhanov, Lenin, Martov, Potresov, Axelrod and Zasulich. After the disagreements had emerged at the congress, Comrade Lenin stated that an editorial board should be formed which would express the opinion of a majority of the congress and proposed the trio Plekhanov, Lenin and Martov. But in that case the majority would be against Martov and thus a heated argument blew up. Comrade Lenin's proposal was

A.N. Potresov

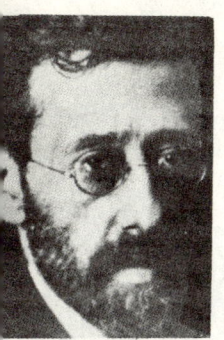

Y.O. Martov

declared a sacrilegious slight on the most senior and best people in the party and Martov in protest refused to take his seat on the editorial board and a whole number of his colleagues supported him. The congress could do nothing. Finally it was left with Plekhanov and Lenin and this decision was carried by a majority, apparently of 25 votes to 23. It was from this point that the 'Bolsheviks' and 'Mensheviks' came on to the world scene. As is well known, during the revolution these terms were frequently invested with quite a different content. In the countryside they started talking about the 'Bolshaks'. Many quite simply considered that the Bolsheviks were the ones who wanted a bit more and the Mensheviks were the ones who were prepared to make do with less. But in point of fact these pithy words were born at the congress when the majority (*bolshinstvo* — the 'bolsheviks') voted for the Plekhanov-Lenin editorial board and the minority (*menshinstvo* — the 'mensheviks') were against it.

The controversy over the party programme

There was finally at the congress another controversy over the party programme. It is worth dwelling on it in some detail because Plekhanov again emerged in it as an energetic defender of the idea of the idea of the hegemony of the proletariat.

Plekhanov was one of the chief authors of the party programme which the Economists, headed by Martov, strongly criticized and to which they proposed some dozen amendments. The controversy turned on certain points which had a deeply principled, and one might even say, topical importance, primarily over the question of universal suffrage. In one of his speeches on the programme in the programme commission delivered at the congress, Plekhanov formulated his view in this way: we of course today advance the slogan of universal suffrage but as revolutionaries we must say openly that we do not wish to turn it into a fetish. For you can quite easily conceive a situation where the victorious working class will for a time deprive its enemy, the bourgeoisie, of the franchise. These words deeply antagonized the future Mensheviks.

During the subsequent discussion the question of the Constituent Assembly and of the terms of parliament arose. In the minimum programme we had demanded the calling of a parliament every two years, i.e. as often as possible. One of the future Mensheviks stated that it would be better once a year for that would be more democratic. Then Plekhanov got up and delivered a remarkable speech. He said: 'You must bear in mind, friends, that the question of the terms of parliament is, for us revolutionaries, a subsidiary one. If a given parliament is advantageous to the working class then we will of course attempt to prolong it; but if it is against the working class we will attempt, if we are able, to dissolve it within a fortnight'. Hardly had Plekhanov uttered these words than the congress was gripped by the greatest excitement. One section of the delegates broke into applause while others began to whistle and boo. The chairman called the booing delegates to order but one of them stated with a haughty posture: 'If at a congress of a workers' party such unheard-of words are voiced then I am bound to boo them'. By an irony of history this individual was none other than Rozanov, the self-same person who under the alias of 'Martyn', worked in Petrograd, was a member of the P.C. and C.C. and an outstanding figure in the generation of revolutionaries of that time; this same Rozanov started off with a protest against Plekhanov's abovementioned words, and ended by becoming the organizer of Denikin's party, and was arrested for his part in the 'National Centre', sentenced to death, but thanks to our typical leniency is now roaming at liberty, having apparently abandoned politics.

Plekhanov on capital punishment

In this small incident there was reflected like sunshine in a droplet of water the controversy of the Montagne and the Gironde, the future Bolsheviks and Mensheviks. At the Second Congress those basic questions which were subsequently to play such a decisive role were posed point-blank and marked the final dividing line between ourselves and the Mensheviks. Plekhanov was at that time a Bolshevik in the best sense of the word: he was proud of his nickname 'The Jacobin'. When the question of the death penalty was examined and the Mensheviks demanded its abolition, Plekhanov tipped a tub of cold water over them by saying: the abolition of the death penalty is all very well; but I consider that some qualifications are necessary. What do you think? Should we leave Nikolai II alive? I think we must preserve the death penalty for him. The Mensheviks were now arguing like liberals: it is bad to spill blood, they said — and not like revolutionaries who say — it all depends on the circumstances: there can be nothing at all wrong with destroying the tyrant Nikolai II. When Kerensky attempted to introduce the death penalty for workers and soldiers we then aroused all the people against this measure and we were right. But the death penalty carried out against Nikolai and the landowners is quite a different matter.

On all the sharp questions like universal suffrage, parliamentarism, the Constituent Assembly and the death penalty, Plekhanov came forward as a real Bolshevik, as a true defender of the idea of the hegemony of the proletariat and as a revolutionary, he called himself a Jacobin with pride. Plekhanov remarked at the congress: Yes, our Social-Democracy is divided into a Montagne and a Gironde; you Mensheviks, you are the Girondists, the future traitors to the workers' revolution. Some people know Plekhanov only in the latter years when his star had waned and when he had gone over to the enemy's camp during the war. But he is in a certain measure one of the founders of Bolshevism. In 1903 he was on the same side as Lenin and entered the Party Council and the editorial board of its central organ as a representative of the same views that Lenin held.

After the Second Congress

The congress closed with a split. The Central Committee was elected by the Bolsheviks alone. Martov brought out a pamphlet, *The State of Siege in the Party,* in which he accused Lenin of every deadly sin and of diverse insults inflicted on many worthy people. The Menshevik delegates set off for Russia and formed their own special 'bureau' which at once declared a boycott of the Bolshevik Central Committee. No one worked for *Iskra* except Lenin and Plekhanov. There took place as Plekhanov expressed it with his characteristic wit: *une grève générale des generaux*.* These 'generals' who had collaborated on *Iskra* laid down their pens and refused to write for the paper on which there was neither Martov nor Axelrod. Six issues of *Iskra* came out under the editorship of Lenin and Plekhanov and in these issues the latter once again revived the spirit of the old days. He began to insert articles in which he taught the tactics of street fighting; he, the learned Marxist, wrote on how to construct barbed-wire entanglements for battles with the Tsarist gendarmes. He did what the Bolsheviks were then doing, sensing in advance the revolutionary thunderstorm. But very soon, only too soon, Plekhanov gave up his position. Before several months had passed he had deserted. He proposed to Lenin that they bring the 'striking generals' back to the editorial board and yield to their strike, hoping somehow to get a hold on them even though he might be in the minority. But Lenin as always with principled questions proved to be irreconcilable and left the editorial board. Plekhanov remained alone and, as the joke was then, 'unanimously' invited the four Menshevik almighties back on to *Iskra*. The new *Iskra* became the Menshevik organ. Plekhanov at first attempted to restrain the 'generals' from an excessive deviation to the right but then he gradually made his peace, resigned himself to fate and himself became a Menshevik.

In this way by the end of 1903 we already had two clear-cut groups, two organizations and two parties. It might be said that Bolshevism and Menshevism as ideological tendencies had already become formed at that time and that they had taken their final shape before the revolutionary thunderstorm broke out.

* 'a General Strike by generals'.

LECTURE FOUR

The Russo-Japanese War

The most important event of 1904 was of course the Russo-Japanese War. It had an enormous significance as a factor which revolutionized our country and brought closer the first, 1905 revolution without which 1917 was in turn inconceivable.

It will be useful to say a few words about the causes of this war over which a certain divergence of view within Russian Social-Democracy of that time was perceptible. The Mensheviks laid principal stress on its dynastic character explaining it as an attempt by the House of Romanov to establish itself more firmly on the throne by diverting the people's attention from domestic events to foreign ones. To a certain extent this was true of course. The country was discontented and deeply disturbed and it was entirely natural that the government of the day, which was lorded over by Pobedonostsev, Witte and company, should resort to such a diversion. More than one example can be found in history where kings and emperors at critical moments for them have tried to use a war to artificially foster a patriotic fever in the people and thereby to postpone the day of reckoning within the state itself. But from the same history it is well-known how most of these attempts usually brought about merely the hastening of the collapse of the monarchist governments. So it was also with the Russo-Japanese War.

The Mensheviks' standpoint

But the question was not exhausted by the dynastic factor. Alongside the dynastic motive a considerable role in this war was doubtless played by purely imperialist and aggressive ambitions and the desire to gain new markets and so on. Many party committees which were operating in Russia emphasized precisely this aspect of the war, but the Mensheviks fought against such a view, trying to prove that nothing of the sort applied in this instance. And if today one looks closely into the evolution of Menshevism, it has to be said that as early as in their analysis of the Russo-Japanese War a seed of their future political thinking was contained, for they did not wish to see the underlying economic motives of the conflict in 1917 either.

Defeatism

During the Russo-Japanese War the tendency first arose which in 1917 was to receive the name of 'defeatism'. It is necessary to examine this as it has the most direct bearing upon the subsequent evolution of Bolshevism and upon the controversies with our political adversaries.

Defeatism embraced not only both sections of the workers' party, i.e. the Bolsheviks and the Mensheviks, but also all liberal bourgeois society. This far from accidental phenomenon indicates that in the years when Tsarism was treading on the pet corns of the bourgeoisie, if you can put it that way, the latter knew how to carry on regardless and even to permit the defeat of 'its' government in a foreign war if only to win concessions in domestic policy. Let me recommend to those who wish to become more familiar with this question that they read the anthology *Against the Current*; for my part I will confine myself merely to several demonstrations of the fact that during the Russo-Japanese War, defeatism rolled right across Russia in a broad wave.

> The contributions written by Lenin are contained in his *Collected Works* Volumes 21-23.

In 1904 the well-known liberal writer — and at the same time convinced monarchist — Boris Chicherin (not our present People's Commissar for Foreign Affairs but a relative of his, a journalist) wrote:

> The consequences of this war will in the end assist the solution of the domestic crisis. *It is hard to say which outcome of the war would be most favourable to this end.*

LECTURE FOUR

These lines which quite unambiguously imply that the defeat of Tsarist Russia would be more desirable than its victory were written under the Tsarist censorship. Can one conceive, even for a minute, that in 1914 during the imperialist war there could be found a single bourgeois capable of saying anything of this sort? This would be impossible because, through the First, Second, Third and Fourth State Dumas the Tsarist autocracy had reached a certain more or less close agreement with the leaders of the Russian bourgeoisie; and because in 1914 the monarchy, at least in form, was not what it was in 1904. The sharing of power between the landowners and the bourgeoisie had in 1914 already been accomplished, and for this reason the bourgeoisie in 1914 did not treat the war as they had done in 1904. In 1916, in the very heat of the war, Milyukov delivered a speech in the State Duma where he stated that if the path to victory over the Germans lay through revolution then he would reject victory. This most enlightened representative of the bourgeoisie was thus saying that if the Germans could not be beaten without a revolution, then it would be better to renounce victory over the hated Germans as long as a revolution could be avoided. In other words he meant that he feared a revolution more than a victory by the Germans. These two statements, on the one hand by Boris Chicherin, an eminent representative of the revolutionary bourgeoisie in 1904 and on the other by Milyukov, the principal representative of the liberal bourgeoisie in 1916, show the path traced by Russia in the evolution of its bourgeoisie.

In 1904 a considerable part of the bourgeoisie stood for the defeat of Russia in the Russo-Japanese War, hoping in this way to win certain concessions and to share power with the landowners who would otherwise never yield. The bourgeoisie knew perfectly well that if Tsarism was victorious the position of the landowners would be even more strengthened and any hope of a constitution, i.e. the sharing of power between the landowners and the bourgeoisie, would disappear.

Gershuni's reminiscences

The defeatist mood was of course shared, but in sharper form, by the revolutionaries, including the S.R.s. This party, which in 1914-1917 did not break free from the bondage of 'patriotism' was also arch-defeatistly inclined during the Russo-Japanese War. For example, here is what one of the acknowledged leaders of the S.R. party, the late Gershuni, who was at the time sitting in the Fortress of St. Peter and St. Paul, wrote in this connexion. He first learnt about the defeat of the Russian forces and of the Russo-Japanese War as a whole from his defence counsel, the lawyer Karabchevsky, who went to see him in prison. This meeting of the well-known Russian terrorist and the highly renowned Russian lawyer, a typical representative of opposition society of that time, is extremely interesting.

> You wait with impatience (*writes Gershuni*) for all this comedy to end and to remain alone with your defence counsel at last — the only living being not from the enemy camp who has the right to do so.. After a long and tiresome ceremony the door of the cell slams shut, and the two of us are left together, just the two! (*A long and feverish questioning begins.*)
> 'Plehve's still in power, is he? Is he alive?'
> 'Yes. But there's some bigger news: do you know that war has been declared?'
> 'War?! Against whom?'
> 'Against Japan. Some of our cruisers have already been blown up and we are being defeated . . . '
> 'A second Crimean campaign? Port Arthur, another Sebastopol? *Ex oriente lux*? . . . '
> 'Something like that'.
> 'And how's the country; seized with 'patriotic ecstasy and thirsting to close ranks around the leader of the state'?'
> 'Well that's about it of course. But everything is inflated and artificial to a large degree. The war is unpopular. Nobody expected it and nobody wants it'.
> It's strange (*adds Gershuni*) that here in a half-dark cell of the Fortress of St. Peter and St. Paul everything somehow at once became clear. One felt that something infinitely menacing, infinitely grave and infinitely grievous was approaching and that it would for the state play the role of a thunder-clap which would arouse the sleeping, and explode and turn to ashes that veil which had concealed the true essence of the autocratic regime from the majority of the country . . . .

Further on in his reminiscences, the same Gershuni relates how from a screwed-up bit of newspaper picked up while walking in the courtyard of the Schlüsselburg Fortress he and his prison mates learnt about the fall of Port Arthur. The prison gendarme gave away this 'military stratagem' by confirming the news for them. It is hard to describe what the Schlüsselburg captives experienced. 'We trembled, Port Arthur had fallen ... autocracy will fall too!' wrote Gershuni. A nakedly defeatist mood.

Defeatism in Savinkov's novel

And not only for Gershuni. Likewise for a man like Savinkov who, in his famous novel *The Pale Horse*, which he published under the pseudonym of Ropshin, describes the condition of his hero who had travelled to Russia from abroad on terrorist work. On the journey he learns about Tsushima, that colossal defeat of the Tsarist fleet, and the most contradictory feelings grip him: on the one hand as a Russian, he laments the smashed fleet, and the men who have perished — the dead and drowned Russian sailors, and on the other, as a revolutionary, he understands that the defeat at Tsushima signifies the victory of the revolution and that the rout of the Tsarist fleet will benefit it.

We can see the same mood in *Notes on the Russo-Japanese War* by Veresaev, who excellently reflects in his works all the new trends arising in the Russian intelligentsia today. Every line of his *Notes* bears witness to the fact that nearly all the Russian intelligentsia were inclined towards defeatism and clearly understood that the defeat of Tsarist Russia in the Japanese war would signify a victory for the liberation movement.

Bolsheviks and the Russo-Japanese war

Now let us turn to the camp of social-democracy at that time. As regards the Bolsheviks they spoke out without the slightest hesitation for the desirability of the total defeat of Tsarist Russia. When *Iskra*, which had by now become Menshevik (after Comrade Lenin had left it and Plekhanov had invited the four Mensheviks to come to his aid), put forward the slogan of 'peace at all costs', the Bolsheviks objected that this slogan was incorrect. 'We do

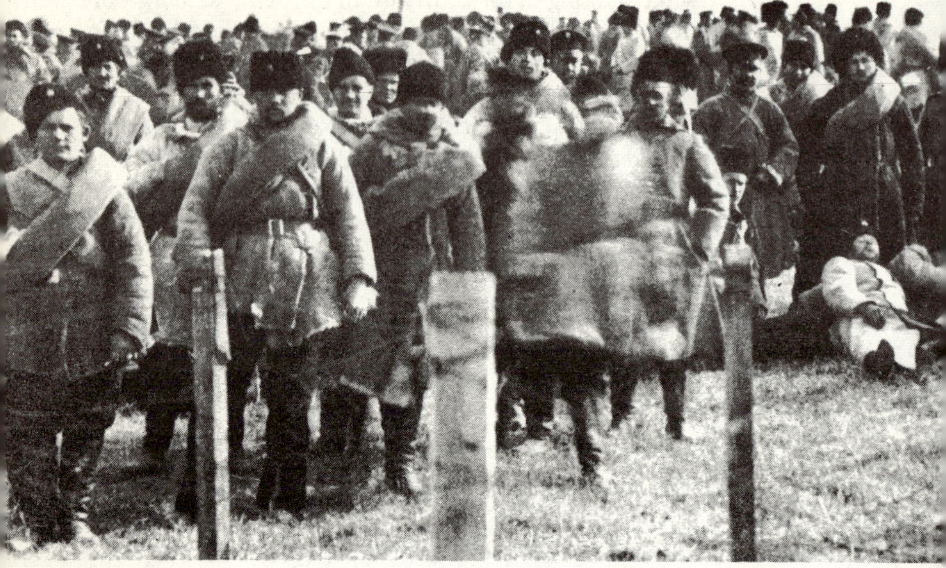

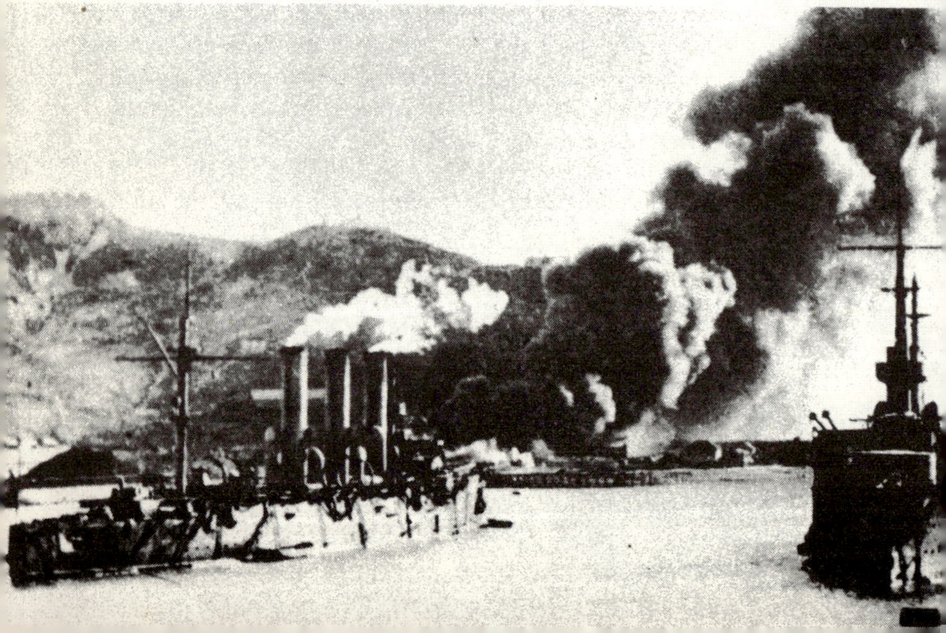

not stand for peace at all costs', they said, 'we are not pacifists. There are wars which in the final count benefit the people'. This means that as early as then the rudiments of the future ideology of Bolshevism were revealing themselves in their world-outlook: namely the idea of turning the imperialist war into a civil war.

The Mensheviks' position

The Mensheviks also, though not without hesitation, adopted a defeatist position. At the International Socialist Congress at Amsterdam in 1904 our party was represented by two delegations: one was the official one led by Mensheviks (because they then controlled the central party organ) and the other was our Bolshevik one, recognized but numerically weak and permitted only the right of a deliberative voice — at this congress Plekhanov met our present-day comrade, Katayama, whom many of you have probably seen and represented there the Japanese movement. Between them a scene of fraternization broke out: they kissed each other to the rapturous cries of the whole congress which had applauded Plekhanov's defeatist speech with enthusiasm. This is how he described the event:

S. Katayama

> I said that in the event of a victory of the Tsarist government over Japan, the vanquished would turn out to be none other than the Russian people itself. The triumphant Tsarist government would take advantage of the aura of victory to draw the chains with which it had fettered the Russian people even more tightly. I reminded the congress of that unfortunately indisputable historical truth that the foreign policy of the Tsarist government had for long been a policy of plunder and conquest; that this government had invariably striven to dominate all those nations surrounding it which had not been strong enough to give it a firm rebuff and that it had enclosed strictly Russian land with a solid ring of defeated nationalities which repaid it in hatred what they received from it in oppression. And I added that from such a policy the Russian population itself suffered not less but most of all, because not a single nation can be free if it serves as the instrument for the oppression of its neighbours ... And in saying all this I acknowledged that I was expressing the thoughts and feelings of the vast mass of the Russian people. Never before had the voice of Russian Social-Democracy been in such strong measure the voice of the Russian people.

The Russo-Japanese
War:
Russian prisoners
of war
Port Arthur
under Japanese attack

The whole Second International in the form of the Amsterdam Congress, subscribed to the words of the Menshevik leader, that a victory of the Tsarist government would be considered a defeat for the Russian people. In this way under the pressure of the whole revolutionary situation and the circumstance that even the bourgeoisie tended towards defeatism the Mensheviks themselves occupied a defeatist position.

The Mensheviks' treachery

It is necessary to bear all this in mind in order to explain the treachery of the Mensheviks during the 1914-1917 war when they presented matters as if our defeatist position was nothing but an unprecedented betrayal of the Russian people. As is well-known, later on, in the July Days of 1917, they even asserted that we were being well paid for our 'defeatism'. Anyway this page of Russian history is extremely noteworthy, displaying as it does the curious fact that in the days when the Russian bourgeoisie was not yet in power and the landowner sat over it the former was greatly in favour of defeatism. Today, in his *History of Russian Social-Democracy*, Martov attempts in retrospect to disown the Mensheviks' defeatist position during this war. He writes:

> As soon as typically 'defeatist' moods developed in liberal society and revolutionary circles following on the setbacks of the Russian army, and the hope grew that Tsarism would meet a subsequent military disaster almost without fresh efforts on the part of the people; as soon as a certain 'Japanophilia' appeared in connection with this together with an idealization of the role that Japanese imperialism would play in this war, *Iskra* [i.e. the Mensheviks who controlled the paper at this time] came out against 'defeatism' and upheld the interest of the people and the revolution to see that the war would not end with the infliction of heavy sacrifices upon Russia and that freedom would not be brought to the Russian people on Japanese bayonets.

Japanophilia and Bolshevism

Martov blatantly slurs the question and today attempts in retrospect to atone for his revolutionary sins before the

LECTURE FOUR

bourgeoisie. He deliberately confuses two questions when he speaks about Japanophilia and *Iskra*'s fight against it. Such a sympathy for the Japanese had nothing in common with 'defeatism'. During the war when the Japanese battled against the forces of the Russian Tsar, certain layers of liberal society (especially the students) went so far that individual groups of students reputedly sent greetings telegrams to the Japanese Mikado. This fact has not been fully confirmed, but the Tsarist press circulated it and spread it around vigorously. At all events, if symptoms of Japanophilia did exist then we revolutionaries naturally came out against it. We said: the Japanese monarch is in no way better than our Russian one, and we do not expect him to bring us freedom on the bayonets of his own soldiers. And it was from this standpoint that we condemned any extreme view on the part of the liberals and shallow minded revolutionary students who, if not actually sending one, were possibly on the point of sending a telegram to the Japanese emperor. In this sense Martov was right: yes, we were against Japanophilia but we did stand for the defeat of the Tsarist army in this war and Martov deliberately shuffles the cards when he recounts the following fact:

> The leader of the Finnish bourgeois 'activists' and subsequent head of the Finnish government in 1905, Konni Zilliacus, openly proposed that Plekhanov and also foreign representatives of the Bund enter into talks with agents of the Japanese government on assisting the Russian revolution with money and arms.

Martov goes on to say that this proposal was rejected. This is true. When the Russian revolutionaries and even a section of the Russian bourgeoisie came out as committed defeatists the Japanese and certain hired agents of theirs made an attempt to toss us a bait: as you stand for the defeat of the Tsarist monarchy then we, if you like, will readily support you with money and arms. It is quite self-evident that all these offers were indignantly rejected by our organization, all honest revolutionaries and also Plekhanov and the Mensheviks. The Bolsheviks said: we are against the Russian Tsar but this does not mean that we are for the Japanese monarch. But this still did not prevent all of us, including the Mensheviks, from being defeatists.

The growth of the liberal movement

Parallel with the development of the events caused by the Russo-Japanese War the liberal movement grew and broadened. Not only did a powerful strike movement among workers and a student movement arise, but an enormous shift took place among liberal zemstvo members who saw that autocracy was getting into a mess it would never get out of. The liberal bourgeoisie sensed that the war would inevitably bring about a constitution, in the way that the Crimean War had brought about the emancipation of the serfs in 1861. The more the Japanese struck at the Tsar's forces and the more clearly the autocracy demonstrated that it was a colossus with feet of clay, the bolder and more arrogant the Russian bourgeoisie became. What is more, plucking up courage, they began to organize themselves with amazing speed: quite understandably their organization was cast in forms peculiar to itself. Where an upsurge had begun in the depths of the working class, the movement generally took the form of strikes, mass demonstrations and then armed uprising; but quite different tools of struggle were typical of the liberal bourgeoisie: meetings, banquets and petitions. The most exalted zemstvo members, among whom there were many of princely descent, waged a systematic campaign at provincial zemstvo meetings and there drew up their resolutions, which they called addresses, covered them with their signatures and sent them in to the Tsar. In these addresses they said to him that he must listen to public reason and the 'voice of the country' i.e. *their* voice, and grant the people a constitution and summon them, the zemstvo members, to power. This zemstvo movement was soon to reach its highest point, which expressed itself by sending a deputation to the Tsar. This, though, was all that the liberals could decide upon doing.

LECTURE FOUR

The relationship between the working class and the bourgeoisie in 1904

Linked to this awakening of the bourgeoisie to political life such as had not been hitherto observable in Russia, the question of the attitude of the working class to the bourgeoisie again arose with particular acuteness — the same basic question with which we collided at every stage of the history of the party and to which in the end all our disagreements with the Mensheviks could be reduced. This question, as we have seen, had already come up in Legal Marxism and in the struggle against the populists, with Struve, with the Economists and at the Second Congress of the party where on the one hand Lenin and Plekhanov's motion and on the other that of Martov and his supporters were carried. But this time, in 1904, the question arose for the first time not as a theoretical one, but as a political and extremely burning one: the liberal bourgeois had begun to move, and the working class had to decide: how, in this instance, should they treat the bourgeoisie? It was here, as previously, that major disagreements between ourselves and the Mensheviks emerged.

The Mensheviks advocated the so-called zemstvo campaign, which amounted to the following. The working class, in the Mensheviks' opinion, had to take into account that provincial meetings of repesentatives of the liberal zemstvos were being held everywhere which discussed the situation in Russia and addressed petitions to the Tsar, and it had to send its own representatives to these meetings charging them to tell the noblemen and liberal bourgeoisie that the workers would support them and go along with them if they eagerly continued their campaign of petitions. In addition, the Mensheviks insisted that the workers must not intimidate the liberal bourgeoisie with their excessively proletarian demands. The Menshevik *Iskra* said so directly and openly:

> If we take a look at the arena of struggle in Russia then what do we see? Only two forces: the Tsarist autocracy and the liberal bourgeoisie, which is now organized and possesses a huge specific weight. The working mass, however, is atomized and can do nothing;

as an independent force we do not exist; and thus our task consists in supporting the second force, the liberal bourgeoisie, and encouraging it and in no case intimidating it by presenting our own independent proletarian demands.

From this exposition of the question the Mensheviks' plan emerges with exceptional clarity: the working class as an independent force must be erased from the account, and only two forces must be kept in mind: the Tsar and the liberal bourgeoisie. Which of them is the better one? The liberal bourgeoisie of course. If this is so, then let us support it. In this formulation of the question the Mensheviks' opportunism spoke, and their course was revealed: towards a bloc and an alliance with the bourgeoisie and not towards an independent role for the working class.

Comrade Lenin's position

Against this Menshevik plan, which produced the first major practical disagreement following the Second Congress where the Bolshevik party had begun to take shape, Bolshevism, in the figure of Comrade Lenin, came out strongly, writing a number of articles and pamphlets on this question which can be regarded as the first important political documents of Bolshevism. *These articles are contained in volume 7 of Lenin's Collected Works.*

Comrade Lenin said in reply to the Mensheviks: you demand of us that we do not intimidate the liberals and the liberal-minded noblemen but really you yourselves are intimidated by the shadow of an intimidated liberal. You maintain that one must take into account only two forces: Tsarist autocracy and the liberal nobility — but you have forgotten something, you have not noticed one small thing; there is, you know, besides these two forces, yet another one, enormous, decisive and sovereign: the working class, which has organized itself and which, in spite of its party being underground and being lashed at every step with three whips, nevertheless forms the chief motive power of the revolution. You have forgotten that the proletariat has its own independent task and not just the choice of either the Tsar or Rodichev, either the Tsarist monarchy or the liberal constitution; you have forgotten that it has its own path which leads to unity with the peasantry and a really popular revolution which will uproot the monarchy and burn out the vestiges of feudalism with a red-hot iron, so forming the first step to a genuine proletarian revolution.

Basing ourselves upon these lines of Comrade Lenin we Bolsheviks advocated another plan: when the bourgeoisie tangles itself up around the feet of the monarchy when supposedly fighting it, then we for our part must come out as an independent force, go on to the streets, raid the police stations and so on. The last project was not at all to the Mensheviks' liking and they turned to laughing at us; what do you think we are, burglars? Surely this isn't the job of revolutionaries — raiding police stations? In their opinion it was far more important to go along to meetings of liberal noblemen and support them without intimidation. Should the working class play an independent role in the revolution or remain a stooge of the liberal bourgeoisie? Is it to be a mere appendage of the bourgeoisie, its left wing, or is it on the contrary to be the independent and chief driving force of the revolution which will produce by its intervention a definite reshuffling in the inter-relation of class forces? That was how the question was posed.

Parvus

L.D. Trotsky

Defections from the Mensheviks

And it was at that point, amid this zemstvo campaign when the Mensheviks' position and their tactic of support for the bourgeoisie in an alliance had been delineated, that Parvus and Comrade Trotsky, who had until then supported them, started to move away from them.

At the same time Bolshevism began to grow stronger, as all those revolutionaries and workers began to move over towards it who had until then regarded all the disagreements as merely arguments over trifles and details but now became convinced that it was not a secondary question but one of the historical role of the working class in the revolution: in other words of the character of the Russian revolution itself; whether it was to be an ordinary bourgeois revolution, of which there had been more than one back in

1848 and before, or whether it was to become a revolution of a new type in which the chief motive force and leading factor would be the working class. From that moment, let me repeat, a process of consolidation began within Bolshevism and like a sponge soaking up water it began to draw in the most revolutionary elements of social-democracy of that time who had finally become convinced of its correctness.

Here it is necessary to say a few words in passing about the inner party and organizational issues which put ourselves and the Mensheviks on opposing sides.

The controversy over democracy within the party

In 1904 and 1905 the issue of democracy played a great part within the party. This is an extremely interesting episode which throws a sharp light on certain disputes of our own time. The Mensheviks stood firmly for 'consistent democratism' within the party and for a strictly elective principle, while the Bolsheviks headed by Comrade Lenin were then strongly against it. At the present moment it might appear strange to young comrades that the Bolsheviks were against democracy and against the elective principle in the party, while the Mensheviks stood for both of them. But it is easy to clear up the confusion.

The fact was that the Mensheviks did not believe in the independent role of the proletarian party in the revolution and did not believe that we could succeed in creating a serious proletarian party under the autocracy. As I have said earlier, they wanted to have a party which could be easily and freely entered by both the student and the professor; they thought that our party would always be one of intellectuals and therefore strove towards such a fully finished structure under which every 'His Majesty the Intellectual' could receive his share of rights, where nobody would 'oppress' him, and where he would vote and listen to reports—in short where there would be 'real democratism just like in Europe'.

The Bolsheviks in the words of Comrade Lenin, objected to this as follows: We too stand for democracy but only when it is actually possible: for at present democracy would be an idle game, and this we do not want because we need a serious party which can strike at the Tsar and the bourgeoisie. At the present moment when we are underground we shall not be able to realise genuine democracy in the party; we need an organization of tested revolutionaries who have proved by long years of work that they are prepared to give up their life for the revolution and the party; and it is these people that we take in, placing our fate in their hands. If we were to chase after the elective principle under autocracy and its barbaric repressions, we would only assist the Tsar's gang to smash our organization and facilitate the hunting down of our people by Tsarist provocateurs and detectives.

The Mensheviks sought, like cunning demagogues, all the little experienced workers, published their letters and cried: 'There you see! Here are workers demanding the elective principle and you are offending them by not agreeing to it'. In St. Petersburg there is a worker Glebov-Putilovsky (he was a Menshevik at that time) who wrote a very muddle-headed pamphlet supporting democracy in precisely this vein. The Mensheviks immediately published it with a foreword by Axelrod himself who stated: here you can see the whole proletariat speaking out through his lines, all the workers are demanding the elective principle but you are not granting it.

Comrade Lenin replied with the article *Fine words butter no parsnips*. Its point was as follows: We too know the workers: they do stand for democracy, as we do, for the sort that we really need; when it is possible we shall be the first to carry it out. But you are only hoodwinking them with your stories. The serious worker of today understands that democracy and the elective principle are not ends in themselves, but a means to the liberation of the working class. We are building in the way that will be the most advantageous to us for the struggle at the present time. And at this very moment we require a strict hierarchy and centralism.

Lenin's *Collected Works*, Vol. 8, pp. 56-62.

Today it is clear to us that the Mensheviks were at that time attempting to play around with the workers by means of 'democratism' and reckoned on hooking them on this bait. At every street corner they shouted: 'We propose elections but the Bolsheviks are against; this means they are against you so come to us'. But workers soon bit through the bait.

In this respect events developed organizationally in the following fashion.

The predominance of the Mensheviks

At the Second Congress the Bolsheviks, as is well known, won control of the party's Central Committee, its central organ which was led by Lenin and Plekhanov and the Party Council. Forming the last-mentioned were two representatives of the Central Committee, two from the central party organ which was based abroad, while the fifth, the chairman, was elected at the Congress itself. Plekhanov was elected as this fifth man. In the Party Council we thus also had a majority. However a few months later Plekhanov turned tail, part of the Bolshevik delegation on the Central Committee was arrested in Russia, and this situation came about: first *Iskra*, the central party organ, passed over to the Mensheviks; then after the arrest of our comrades Mensheviks were elected to the Central Committee, which slid out of our hands; finally Plekhanov, who had crossed over to the Mensheviks' side, made them a dowry of the Party Council. In a comparatively short time we lost all the central positions. Mensheviks were sitting on the Central Committee, on the central party organ and on the Party Council and Martov could walk round handing out skull-caps to everyone, for he had become 'three in one and one in three': the Party Council, the Central Committee and the central party organ.

Such a situation was extremely difficult for us. It must be said that at that time the whole of the party's prestige lay on the side of the Mensheviks. Comrade Lenin, notwithstanding all the weight he carried in the party, was nevertheless still a young figure in comparison with Plekhanov. And this had great importance of course. For example, let me recall my first conversation with Plekhanov (at that time I was rather more of a Young Communist than now), when he frightened us by saying: Who are you going along with? You should consider who is on our side: Martov, Zasulich, Axelrod and the rest; but over on your side there is only Lenin. And you know, things will eventually turn out that in a few months all the sparrows will be laughing at your Lenin. And you go along with him! A section of the party was in actual fact under the hypnosis of these old doyens whose contribution — if only of such a man as Plekhanov — had indeed been enormous.

The Bolsheviks' position was, let me repeat, an extremely hard one and complicated further by the impossibility of referring to the party membership, as the party had been driven underground and was being subjected to savage persecution by Tsarism.

The Bureau of Committees of the Party Majority

As a result of this situation it became increasingly apparent to the Bolsheviks that it was necessary to organize themselves separately and to strengthen such an organization formally. Comrade Lenin who for many, and especially the Mensheviks, had become renowned as a frantic and indefatiguable 'splitter' — although in fact he decided upon such steps only with the greatest difficulty and after much reflection when there proved to be no other way out — Comrade Lenin after lengthy reflection and an all-round examination of the question decided upon such a split. The pressure of the Russian committees and in part the impatient young Bolshevik youth of the time also influenced him to a certain degree; the latter said: time does not wait, the revolution is close, major events are at hand (this was not long before January 9th) so we must organize our party. And so a whole number of regional party conferences — from the north, the south, Moscow and other areas — put forward a plan for creating in Russia a 'Bureau of Committees of the Party Majority' as a counterweight to the Menshevik Central Committee. Once an all-Russian central organization of Bolsheviks had been founded in this way and came into direct conflict with the Menshevik Central Committee Comrade Lenin gave his final agreement to an organizationally separate party, whereupon we embarked upon publishing abroad the first Bolshevik newspaper which was called *Vpered* and appeared at the beginning of 1905 in Geneva, subsisting on miserable resources gathered penny by penny amongst the Bolsheviks sympathizing with this movement. *Vpered* continued the work of the old Leninist *Iskra* but now in a new situation laying the basis of the Bolsheviks' tactics. Thus by the beginning of 1905 the Bolsheviks had in Russia the 'Bureau of Committees of the Party Majority' and abroad the Bolshevik organ *Vpered*. The Mensheviks for their part had at their disposal the Central Committee, the central organ and the Party Council.

January 9th

It was in this situation, with the party still atomized and still remaining underground and within it a struggle of two fully formed tendencies in progress — that the events of January 9th were played out. I shall not speak about them in any sort of detail; they are well known to you.* Their fundamental content lay in the fact that non-party working masses came out on to the streets over the head of the constituted party organization, filling the square of the Winter Palace and showing that the Mensheviks were mistaken when they said that only two forces were in action on the field of struggle: the Tsarist monarchy and the noblemen's opposition. January 9th proved that there was yet another force which the Mensheviks completely overlooked and this was precisely the *working class*. It is true that the working masses did not yet know clearly what they wanted, that they were unorganized and had no leaders of their own but put forward in this capacity accidentally chosen people; it is true that they marched with icons, unconscious politically, and that they were shot down like a flight of ducks; all this was true but this mass existed and formed a powerful political factor. Its action on January 9th shook all Russia, and this was far more priceless than any liberal resolutions and petitions. On January 9th the working class proved that it was alive, and that the task of genuine revolutionaries was not to run round provincial meetings and prominent distinguished zemstvo members nor to make calm and 'unintimidating'

* **January 9, 1905**—Refers to the infamous 'Bloody Sunday' when a large and peaceful procession of workers led by a priest Father Gapon, marched on the Winter Palace to demand political freedom, the eight-hour day, a fair wage and the gradual transfer to the people and the convening of a Constituent Assembly based on universal and equal suffrage. Hundreds of the demonstrators were shot by the Tsarist soldiers and thousands more were seriously wounded. (See Trotsky's *1905* for the significance of this event in the development of the revolutionary movement.)

speeches, but to head the workers' movement, which had burst forth tumultuously and broken through like a torrent over a weir despite lacking in the beginning both leaders and a clear political programme. In other words, there was a trunk to which a head had to be put: the party had to intervene in this mass, take its great movement in tow and lead it along the historical path of the working class.

January 9th and subsequent events, as you know, thrust forward several chance non-party figures. This fact is wholly understandable and can be explained by the fact that the party was then underground and could not form the necessary links with the rising working masses. Among these accidental figures were Gapon, Khrustalev and Lieutenant Schmidt—men sharply contrasted, but all completely new to the revolution. Gapon, who played a major role on January 9th, afterwards turned out to be a provocateur and was punished by revolutionaries; Khrustalev, who subsequently left the party, showed himself to be a semi-adventurist. As for Lieutenant Schmidt, though a fairly attractive figure, he was still not a conscious revolutionary. The other day his letters to a close friend were published and I advise every one of you to read them as they present great interest as human documents which take up in passing certain questions of personal ethics. From the pages of this book, Schmidt appears to us as a man profoundly dedicated to the revolution, marching for it calmly to his death; but we can see at the same time that, politically speaking, he was a man without rudder or sails. This can be said while maintaining every respect for his memory. In a letter to his close friend, Schmidt wrote: 'We must have a meeting with Milyukov and discuss important matters with him'. Thus, in the beginning he was a semi-Cadet. But this does not prevent us from bowing before his grave: he was a man who died heroically for the cause of the revolution.

P.P. Schmidt

The significance of January 9th

I have quoted these names in order to show what unexpected figures the movement pushed forward at that time,

January 9, 1905: March to the Winter Palace; Bloody Sunday.
Inset: Father Gapon and the Chief of the St. Petersburg Police.

thrusting up to its surface men who had no clear programme, and who did not know how to lead the awakened masses. The same Schmidt, who led the uprising in the Black Sea fleet, at the same time dreamt of parleying with the Cadets, i.e. the landowner and monarchist party which the 'Constitutional Democrats' were. It is therefore in no way surprising that the three brought forward by 1905, though each in his own way a major figure, remained episodic figures having no roots in the working class.

January 9th placed on the agenda the general question of how the party should lead a mighty movement of workers who were charging into battle yet at the same time had no programme and did not know what they wanted, but marched to the Winter Palace with icons and ecclesiastical banners. And yet January 9th, whose rumble resounded throughout Russia, destroyed faith in the monarchy. This is not an exaggeration. Workers who had, only the day before, believed in the monarchy, and who had thought that it was only his ministers who were bad, saw that their most terrible enemy was nothing other than the monarchy and the Tsar himself.

The controversies over the slogan of the 'Provisional Revolutionary Government'

As for our party, January 9th posed before it in full measure the question of power or, as we then said, of participation in a provisional revolutionary government. The Bolsheviks advanced this slogan with every effort: the organization of an armed uprising and the formation of a provisional revolutionary government. But the Mensheviks firmly opposed this. And again it was extremely typical that they adduced supposedly 'Marxist' arguments against our participation in a provisional revolutionary government. They said: how can we socialists enter a government which will not be a socialist one? They alluded to recent western European experience.

Only just before, in France, the period of so-called 'Millerandism' had come to an end. This word originated from the name of the present president of the French bourgeois republic, Millerand. In those years he was a socialist and even at one point a Left. But then the bourgeoisie bought him off and drew him into participation in the government. He joined the French bourgeois cabinet saying 'I am going there to defend the workers' interests'. But he did not nor could not do any such thing there of course, but gradually became an agent of the bourgeoisie. All orthodox Marxists fought against Millerand and Millerandism and at the Amsterdam Congress even the Second International spoke out against him. A duel took place over this at the Congress between the late Jaurès who defended (to be sure, only in half) Millerand's tactics, and Bebel who was opposed to participation in a bourgeois government. Bebel triumphed, and it was resolved that participation by socialists in a bourgeois government was in no case permissible, for every such socialist becomes in effect the hostage and the steward of the bourgeoisie who will use him. In France this was what happened. After only a year Millerand shot down striking workers, and now he is president of the French bourgeois republic.

A. Bebel

The Mensheviks did not fail to drag this French experience into our controversy. They said: 'But what about Millerandism? Just look what came of that. Could we, after that, participate in a provisional revolutionary government in Russia?' But we replied to them: 'But you, with respect, do not notice one small detail: in France Millerand entered a stable bourgeois government when there was no revolution or, put simply, he sold himself to the bourgeoisie. But with us in 1905 it is a question of overthrowing the Tsar whose throne is already creaking, and to this end we must, in the course of the struggle, create some sort of central revolutionary workers' and peasants' organization, in other words a provisional revolutionary government'.

The Mensheviks' standpoint on the question of the Provisional Revolutionary Government

But the Mensheviks stuck to their guns, indulging in sophistry and shuffling the facts by referring to Millerandism; rehearsing, as it were, an entirely different opera. What would have happened if their view that we ought not to enter a provisional revolutionary government had won out? What would have happened would be that after the fall of Tsarism the bourgeoisie would pass into the government (for you know, the government has to be organized by someone). And this was just what the Mensheviks wanted. Their viewpoint was as follows: workers must not poke their noses into politics: their job is a small one — the economic struggle and giving support to the liberal zemstvo members; but as for a provisional revolutionary government, or rather a provisional non-revolutionary government, Milyukov will know how to organize that. And in actual fact in 1917 they leapt with joy because Milyukov was there and delighted them by agreeing to accept out of the hands of the S.R.s and Mensheviks the power conquered by the workers.

From the above it is clear why the Mensheviks came out against the slogan of the 'Provisional Revolutionary Government'. Their at first glance purist arguments were nothing other than opportunism. True to their invariable tactics, they made use of everything — including even Marxist terminology — to push the workers away from power and to deprive them of the leading role. Menshevik purism was, in fact, opportunism throughout. They shrieked in protest against workers drawing closer to the peasants on the grounds of 'class purity'. But they themselves stayed all the time in a bloc with the Chernovs, Savinkovs and Kerenskys, that is, with the most rotten and counter-revolutionary section of the 'peasant' party.

The Third (Bolshevik)·Congress in London and the First Conference of Mensheviks in Geneva

In the middle of 1905 the Third Congress of the party was held which, as we have already said, could be regarded in a certain sense as the first congress of the Bolsheviks since only they participated in it. The Mensheviks, carrying in their right pocket the seal of the Central Committee and in the left that of the Party Council, said that they did not need any congress because all power was in their hands. Consequently in order to get out of this situation, we Bolsheviks were compelled to call a new congress. But the Mensheviks opposed this very firmly and we had to convene it in spite of the then Central Committee. The Congress was called by the Bureau of Committees of the Party Majority, and was held abroad in London in the middle of 1905. The Mensheviks simultaneously convened their first All-Russian Conference (as they called it) in Geneva. And so in the summer of 1905, before the revolution itself, a review of forces was held, on the one side those of the Bolsheviks at the Third Congress in London, and on the other, those of the Mensheviks at the 'First All-Russian Conference' in Geneva. At these two congresses both sides worked out their respective detailed tactics in relation to the 1905 revolution: for everyone sensed that the decisive days would come any day now.

The Third Congress had an enormous importance. Its main contribution lay in that it for the first time advocated, in a fully worked out programmatic form, the idea of unifying a general strike with an armed uprising. Nowadays this, like much else, appears to be a relative commonplace but at that time it was something quite new. Let us dwell for a few moments on the question of the general strike.

The question of the general strike

International Social-Democracy, in the shape of the Second International, had at that time rejected this idea. In the Second International the little catch-phrase of the late Auer, the famous opportunist ringleader in the German party, was current: *Generalstreick ist Generalunsinn.** Why? Because, he said, if we could really carry out a general strike so that all workers stopped work as one, then this would mean that we could make a revolution as well; but if, on the other hand, we are such a force then we do not need a general strike; if we cannot do that it means that we will not get a general strike either. Hence Auer drew the conclusion: a general strike is an absurdity. The Mensheviks chimed in with the Second International on

* 'A General Strike general lunacy.'

LECTURE FOUR 121

this question. At that time there was really no question of a general strike: it was a period of such deep lull, that when small strike took place in Belgium over the question of universal suffrage, lasting two days in all, this was a huge event on which whole studies were written by, amongst others, the late Rosa Luxemburg.

Given this attitude towards the question of the general strike by the Second International and, even more, by the Mensheviks, the Third Congress did a great service to the revolutionary movement by advocating this idea, and by stating that the general strike was *not* an absurdity, that it stood on the order of the day in Russia, and that we would carry it out.

The question of the armed uprising

Even more sharply posed was the question of the armed uprising. The Second International would hear nothing of this, arguing that this was anarchism and making reference to Engels' foreword which he wrote in the 1890s.† In this foreword Engels pointed to the frenzied growth of the military technology of bourgeois armies, and the reconstruction of the streets in the major cities which had become too wide and did not facilitate the waging of barricade battles, and drew the conclusion that under such conditions an armed uprising would be a very difficult thing as the bourgeoisie would smash any movement of this kind in a matter of hours. All the opportunists hung tightly on to this foreword and asserted with one accord that an armed uprising was impossible and that this had been 'proved by Engels', completely losing sight of the fact that conditions in Russia were different and that moreover imperialist wars could create a different situation within the armies of western Europe.

In this regard too, the Third Congress of our party again made a major contribution to the revolutionary movement by declaring that it placed the armed uprising on the order of the day as a real possibility and that the opportunists were incorrectly interpreting Engels. Moreover, it not only advanced each of these ideas individually but proceeded to propose their synthesis, that is the conjunction

†Engels' foreword: See Glossary.

of the armed uprising with the general strike, as if foreseeing with a prophetic eye the course of events of 1905 and afterwards of 1917.

The achievements of the Third Congress

Thus at the Third Congress an indestructible foundation of Bolshevik tactics was laid, and a precise programme for the coming revolution mapped out. It should not be forgotten that this congress was in session two or three months before the decisive events of 1905, and so its resolutions represent for revolutionary parties throughout the world, a model of how revolutionary Marxist thinking when connected with a mass movement of workers, can predict the path of a revolution. Reading over the resolutions of the Third Congress, it can be said that by putting an ear to the ground and listening closely to events in Russia, it foretold their future course on the basis of a Marxist analysis.

Lenin's Collected Works Vol. 8, pp. 359-424.

The question of arming the workers

Meanwhile the Mensheviks were completing and perfecting their opportunist programme. At their All-Russian Conference they put forward an entirely different idea — that of so-called 'revolutionary self-government'. They were preparing to participate in the Bulygin Duma and worked out all the questions facing them in an opportunist direction. The question of arming the workers provides a perfect example of this. The Third Congress of our party had put it forward very forcefully and energetically. In our time it seems, like much else, elementary, but in those days of the peaceful development of the Second International, when Kautsky and his crowd feared rifles like fire, the arming of the workers seemed to many a wild rebellious lunacy. So when the Third Congress of our party posed this question point-blank, the Mensheviks at their All-Russian Conference set up a hue and cry that this was unprecedented anarchism and rebellion! 'We have to arm the workers not with weapons but first with the burning consciousness of the necessity of arming themselves' they said. Bolshevism gave an excellent answer to this. 'You regard Russian workers as little children, you want to 'arm them with consciousness'; but that time has already passed; they have the consciousness, now they need to be armed with rifles to strike at the Tsar and the bourgeoisie.'

That is just how sharply we differed from the Mensheviks at that time. On the one hand there was a fighting workers' phalanx preparing itself for the revolution and on the other, bittersweet talks about burning consciousness and revolutionary self-government, that is the improvement of the zemstvos and the city Dumas and participation in the Bulygin Duma.

The Shidlovsky Commission

After the events of January 9th the Tsarist autocracy found itself forced to make certain concessions to the workers, and to this end it set up the so-called Shidlovsky Commission, which many workers probably still remember. The Tsar appointed the senator Shidlovsky as chairman of this commission, and proposed that workers send their representatives there for joint discussions on questions of certain improvements to their living conditions in the spirit of Gapon's demands. It can be easily understood that the fundamental political questions were not touched by this commission, which confined itself to utter trivialities. This commission had to be made use of, like any legal opening, and we did. But the Mensheviks built a whole philosophy out of it and rushed into the commission like flies into the sugar.

The Bulygin Duma

Later on when the workers' movement had acquired a further development, the Union of Unions had been organized, the movement amongst the peasantry began to grow stronger, and when a mood began to mature in the army and the navy, especially in the warships, which led later to the uprising on the battleship *Knyaz Potemkin-Tavricheskii*, the Tsarist autocracy gave thought to more substantial 'reforms', and decided to call a Duma which was to receive the name of 'Bulygin'. The preparation of this outfit, in the sense of drafting an appropriate

franchise, the Tsar entrusted to Bulygin. The idea of the Tsar's gang was to call a State Duma that would have no serious rights and would form merely a consultative organ which put forward its views for the monarch's 'kind consideration', who would decide all questions. The franchise drafted by Bulygin was such that the workers received hardly anything, while the nobility and the bourgeoisie had all the rights.

When the outline of the Bulygin Duma had become clear enough the question arose: what attitude should be taken towards it? The Bolsheviks proposed to reject any sort of participation in this Duma, boycotting it, and mobilising the masses to thwart it. We felt that the incipient movement was exceptionally powerful and that the Tsarist autocracy's underdone gingerbreads could no longer feed anyone; they had to be snatched out of its hands and flung on the ground and the movement had to proceed against Tsarism. The Mensheviks, as might be expected, saw in the Tsar's project the beginning of parliamentarianism in Russia, and at first proposed to participate in the Duma. But when they began to be ridiculed, they rejected participation declaring that, in that case, they would convene an election meeting and elect their people not to the Duma, but to organs of revolutionary self-government. But this plan was later likewise thrown out and the revolution moved on to the immediate matters, passing over Bulygin and his Duma, and also over the Menshevik project of 'revolutionary self-government'. The workers said: we do not intend to play games; grave times are upon us; powder is in the air and a real revolution is approaching; there is no reason to elect people to a Duma that the Tsarist autocracy is foisting upon us.

The October events of 1905

It was in this situation that the October events of 1905 took their course: the all-Russian strike, the energetic activity of the Union of Unions, October 17th, certain concessions on the part of autocracy and finally the constitution. The details and the behind-the-scenes events of the granting of the constitution can be learnt from Witte's notes where he gives an all-round depiction of the game of recriminations, parties and court intrigues. At the same time the first St. Petersburg Council of Workers' Deputies (the 'Soviet') was born. Let me stress: Council of *Workers'* Deputies and not Council of *Workers' and Soldiers'* Deputies. This is very important because herein lay its chief weakness. The Bolsheviks said: for them to become a force we must have not only Soviets of workers, but of soldiers and peasants deputies. This however could not then be achieved, as the movement was too weak.

The idea of Soviets itself, like all major ideas, was born in the masses. The Mensheviks later attempted to make out that their bob-tailed idea of revolutionary self-government had been embodied in the idea of the Soviets. But the Soviets were as far from their idea as the stars from the earth. It was not the Mensheviks who put forward the idea of Soviets: it was born in the masses, in the grass roots in the factories and plants of St. Petersburg. The St. Petersburg Soviet became an embryonic government. This was the reality of the matter: either this Soviet took power in its hands and dissolved the Tsarist government or the latter would dissolve the Soviet. As you know the latter occurred. A section of the Bolsheviks had made the mistake of demanding that the Soviet officially adopt the Social-Democrat party programme. But Lenin and the Bolsheviks' Central Committee soon corrected this major mistake.*

*Trotsky's role as leader of the St. Petersburg Soviet is 'missed o by Zinoviev as part of attack on Trotsky. In fa the Soviet was to play crucial role both in 19 as well as 1917, as Ler came to realize. S Trotsky's *1905* for account of this unsucce ful revolution as well an outline of the theo of Permanent Revolutic For an account Trotsky's role in the 19 Revolution see Isa Deutscher, *The Prop Armed*, Ch. 5.

The December armed rising in Moscow

The culminating point of this movement was the December rising at Presnya in Moscow. The leading organizational role in it belonged to Bolsheviks and their committee at whose head stood the late Schanzer (Marat) who died abroad in 1911, today's Deputy Minister of Internal Affairs, Vladimirsky, another member of our party, Sedoi, who is still alive, and several other comrades. It was this committee that organized workers' combat units for the first time.

The Moscow armed rising, which had an enormous historical significance, was smashed and drowned in the workers' blood. And almost immediately after it even the best of the Mensheviks, like for example Plekhanov, hastened to disown it. Plekhanov wrote in this respect a cold, soulless, almost treacherous, phrase: 'They should not have taken up arms'. We replied to him: whether this movement was mistaken or not, such words could only issue forth from the pen of someone hostile to the working class. When in 1871 the Paris Communards suffered a defeat, Marx, who had warned Paris workers against an uprising, did not tell them that they should not have taken up arms, but wrote his brilliant book *The Civil War in France* and perpetuated the great cause of the Paris Communards in a truly immortal creative work which forms a masterpiece of Marxist journalism. Plekhanov, like many others, did not follow Marx's path; like some lord of revolution, he remained aloof and like some astrologer discussed the movement only from an abstract standpoint —'they should not have taken up arms'. The Bolsheviks did not act like that. Comrade Lenin treated this movement with the greatest affection. His first watchword was: study everything, even the most minor episodes of this struggle, the technique of fighting and the biographies of the individual participants. Lenin was not one of those 'revolutionaries' who only show solidarity with a victorious uprising (you can find many enthusiasts for that) — equally dear to him was a smashed uprising of our class. There are defeats which are more valuable than any victory. And the December rising of 1905 was just such. This was the first rising of the politically advanced workers under the slogans of our party, when they now knew clearly what they wanted and did not march with the banners of the Gapons. This very fact showed that the movement had risen to a new level, that the working class had grown up into a gigantic independent force, had a clear programme and was imbued with a readiness to crack down upon a Tsarist army armed to the teeth. So the movement suffered defeat: but we had not promised immediate victory. Workers usually reach it across a series of defeats. And so the Bolsheviks showed complete solidarity with this uprising and declared a decisive struggle against Plekhanov with his renegade's phrase — 'they should not have taken up arms'.

**Rail strike
Barricades in Moscow**

Cossacks forcing peasants to work on the estates

The Ivanovo-Voznesensk Soviet of Workers' Deputies

Workers on strike in Moscow

Aftermath:
Destruction of workers' quarters in Moscow
The results of a pogrom in Odessa

LECTURE FIVE

The experience of the 1905 Revolution

Let us now examine the period from approximately 1906 to 1909. The first revolution of 1905 was, to a certain extent, a rehearsal for the revolution of 1917. Without 1905 such a comparatively easy victory in 1917 would have been impossible. Despite the fact that the idea of Soviets had flashed past like a meteor in 1905, it had nevertheless settled deeply in the sub-conscious of the working class, and in 1917 when the first thunder claps of the February revolution sounded every worker regarded it as self-evident that the country needed to be covered by a network of Soviets. Let me repeat, many events in 1917 would have taken a different course had we not had the great experience of the 1905 revolution. But taken by itself the 1905 revolution suffered a defeat. Thus the question arises: how? Wherein lay the cause of its failure?

The Mensheviks gave an answer to this, which was set out in profuse detail in their five-volume work written under the editorship of Martov, Potresov, Dan and other Menshevik leaders during the period of the counter-revolution, that is from 1909 to 1910. Their explanation was the following. The 1905 revolution suffered defeat because the working class had proceeded too far with its purely class, proletarian demands. Thus it had advanced, and on its own initiative had even realized, the eight-hour working day at the end of 1905. From the standpoint of the Menshevik philosophy of history this was the first crime of the working class in the 1905 revolution. The working class, said the Mensheviks, had driven a considerable part of the bourgeoisie away from itself and encouraged them into an alliance with the landowners, i.e. Tsarism, by their excessive demands. The Mensheviks regarded all the activity of the first Soviet of Workers' Deputies in St. Petersburg as misguided and even blatantly demagogic in spite of the fact that, at one point, its leadership belonged in considerable measure to themselves, the Mensheviks. In their opinion the Soviet had spontaneously taken the path of Bolshevism. This was true to a certain extent. As regards parties, the St. Petersburg Soviet of Workers' Deputies was by no means composed exclusively of Bolsheviks yet, under the influence of the whole contemporary situation, it did in fact take the path of Bolshevism. More than that, history played ever such a cruel trick on the Mensheviks. Their daily newspaper *Nachalo*, which was published from the end of 1905, also swung markedly towards the Bolshevik path, and we reached a point where subsequently the entire Menshevik general staff disowned their press organ. Let us say a few words in passing about *Nachalo*, and also about *Novaya Zhizn*.

F.I. Dan

'Novaya Zhizn' and 'Nachalo'

At the end of 1905 legal daily newspapers of the Bolsheviks and the Mensheviks appeared for the first time: *Novaya Zhizn* for the former and *Nachalo* for the latter.

Until the arrival of Comrade Lenin and several other of our leaders from abroad, *Novaya Zhizn* was led by more or less incidental people. At the head of the editorial board stood Rumyantsev, who subsequently departed from the revolution and whose whereabouts today are unknown. An active part in the paper was taken by intellectual writers, not only Gorky but also Minsky, Teffi and other literary figures who have long since taken their stand on the other side of the barricades. Today it is really hard for us to conceive that these people could have been at any time in the Bolshevik camp. The situation only changed when the basic leading group of Bolsheviks arrived from abroad and *Novaya Zhizn* became a definitely Bolshevik newspaper.

Novaya Zhizn

Things took a somewhat different course with the Menshevik *Nachalo*. This newspaper fell into the hands of Parvus and Comrade Trotsky. Starting from the middle of 1905, when the disagreement on the question of the attitude towards the bourgeoisie took shape, these two outstanding Mensheviks began to move away from Menshevism. When for a number of reasons *Nachalo* came under their leadership they imparted to it a considerably Bolshevik tenor. This trend, headed at that time by Parvus and Comrade Trotsky, has gone down in the history of the party as the tendency which defended the so-called 'permanent', i.e. uninterrupted, revolution. This idea consisted of the following.*

* See Appendix V for a note added here by Zinoviev in the 1924 edition.

The 'Permanent Revolution'

Nachalo asserted that the 1905 revolution had opened up an era of revolutions which would only end with the complete victory of the world proletariat. The paper stressed that the Russian revolution was a part of the international one and that as a consequence its complete victory could be only under the conditions of the victory of the international revolution. There were many attractive things about this tendency, but it had a number of erroneous aspects too. Its main delusion lay in the fact that it either ignored or seriously underestimated the role of the peasantry, and completely lost sight of the fact that the Russian revolution could not be victorious if the working class did not establish firm collaboration with the countryside. In other words, the leaders of this tendency underrated the Bolsheviks' slogan which had been formulated by Lenin as early as the middle of 1905, proclaiming the dictatorship of the proletariat and the revolutionary peasantry.*

* Here Zinoviev seriously distorts Trotsky's theory of Permanent Revolution, and obviously quite knowingly. The so-called 'under-estimation' of the peasantry was to be one of the most persistent of the many false charges laid against Trotsky by the Stalinists in the years following these lectures. Trotsky in no way belittled the peasantry's role; what he did insist upon was the fact that the working class must take the lead in the revolutionary struggle. Hence, said Trotsky, the old slogan of the 'democratic dictatorship of the working class and the peasantry' lacked precision. The revolution would have to result in the dictatorship of the working class, with the peasant masses behind it. Trotsky's *The Permanent Revolution* (New Park Publications, 1971) should be studied, particularly Trotsky's summary of his theory (pp. 152-161).

Be that as it may, the Menshevik newspaper *Nachalo* of its own accord followed by no means a Menshevik path. And the Mensheviks, in drawing up a balance sheet of the defeat of the 1905 revolution, had to lament not only the tactics of the Bolsheviks, not only the line of conduct of the St. Petersburg Soviet, but also the trend of their own newspaper *Nachalo*, which at that time exerted of course a strong influence upon the whole movement. Entirely understandable in this connection was their explanation of the failure of 1905: the working class, they said, had bent too much towards maximalism, as they then put it, and, carried away by unrealizable demands had taken the Bolshevik path and come unstuck; the chief mistake of the working class, in the Mensheviks' opinion, was that they had not trimmed down their programme and accommodated their tactics to the demands of bourgeois 'society' but had transcended them and put forward the eight-hour working day and other purely class claims.

Causes of the failure of the 1905 movement

The Bolsheviks thought otherwise. Even if it was true, they said, that to advance the eight-hour working day at that point was a mistake, a movement in support of it was inevitable. Only functionaries can conceive of a revolution where the awakening millions of the oppressed class renounce their demands and do not advance what is for them the most important question. If, we said, there had not been a single Bolshevik either in St. Petersburg or the world in general, the working masses, awakening from decades of oppression, would still have put forward the demand for the eight-hour working day and would not have confined themselves to support for the bourgeois constitutionalists. In point of fact this demand was not a mistake: it could not, nor should not have been otherwise. The working class of Russia, which at that time numbered at least eight million people (possibly ten), felt that the outcome depended upon it. And having once got to its feet, of course it could not help putting its *own* fundamental class demands on the agenda. If it was smashed in 1905 then there would nevertheless come a time when the demands of 1905 would eventually triumph. Such were our firm objections to the abovementioned Menshevik philosophy.

But what diagnosis did Bolshevism make of the defeat of 1905? It held and still holds the opinion that the failure of 1905 had three basic causes. The first and principal one was the international situation. The Russian revolution

LECTURE FIVE

was, and indeed had to be, an episode of the international struggle. The fact that our revolution of 1917-20 was closely linked with international events is now clear to everyone.* But the 1905 revolution was also no less closely linked with the whole international situation. The loan which the minister Witte managed to negotiate with foreign bankers without doubt played a decisive role. Moreover the international bourgeoisie which gave Tsarism financial assistance also provided it with great moral support. At that time the western European bourgeois world was not as split as it is these days. In those days it conceived itself as a single, fairly stable whole. Tsarist Russia enjoyed the most cordial relations with bourgeois France, this notorious Franco-Russian alliance being in reality an alliance between millions of Tsarist bayonets and millions of French francs. It must be admitted that it was a powerful alliance. But Russian Tsarism received a powerful support not only from France: almost all the major western European powers likewise assisted it quite liberally. And although the defeat of Tsarist Russia in the Russo-Japanese War played into the hands of individual capitalist groups who were in rivalry with similar such Russian groups, the western European bourgeois world as a whole supported Tsarism unconditionally and did not let it collapse. Beisdes, western European bourgeois politicians reconciled Russian Tsarism with the Cadets and the Russian liberals whose leaders were in favour of the link with European capital. Today it is beyond doubt that the French and other foreign bourgeoisies played the role of brokers and intermediaries between a section of the Russian opposition bourgeoisie and the Tsarist autocracy. Russian Tsarism felt on its back the hand of the most civilized European states. This was the first cause of the defeat of the 1905 revolution.

The second cause was the lack of political consciousness in the peasantry. Plekhanov had said that the Russian revolution could triumph only as a workers' revolution. This was true and indisputable in the sense that the working class had to be the hegemonic, basic force in the revolution. But Plekhanov's formula suffered from incompleteness. It should have been set out like this: the

*'Closely linked'. Here again Zinoviev fails to pose the central theoretical question. The Russian revolution was not closely linked' with international events, but was actually made possible only because of the international capitalist, political and economic breakdown which World War One created. Again this was at the centre of Trotsky's theory of 'Permanent Revolution'. See, apart from reference in last note, Trotsky's *History of the Russian Revolution*, Vol. I. Ch. I.

Russian revolution must triumph as a workers' revolution but the working class must at all costs achieve a firm alliance with the peasantry. In 1905 this was impossible to realize. The Soviet of Workers' Deputies was a council of only workers' deputies while the peasantry was as yet uneducated. If it is borne in mind that on January 9th 1905 the workers of the Putilov works still believed in the Tsar and marched to him with icons, then it is all the more understandable how such a mood reigned among the enormous mass of the peasantry who had still less political experience. This explains the mood in the army at the time which in the final count helped Tsarism to triumph over the workers' uprising. Its mood at that time was such that the Tsarist monarchy could still handle it comparatively easily and despatch it against the workers. If the working class of St. Petersburg and other central cities of Russia underwent for some eight to ten months from January 9th until October 17th 1905 an intensive course in political science and learnt what the monarchy was, then for the peasantry and the peasant army far more time was required. Mutinies in the forces, which had become a very widespread phenomenon from 1902, still bore for a long time a purely local character and did not carry a definitely revolutionary programme. The first glimmers of a movement in the army were of course very significant, and even more symptomatic was the uprising in the Black Sea fleet. This was quite a large-scale and serious occurrence, but Tsarism in 1905 still had nonetheless a sufficient degree of control over both its army and its peasantry. In the 1905 revolution the latter proved to be still insufficiently prepared to be an ally to the proletariat: it remained more or less neutral while in the form of the army it lay more in the hands of Tsarism than in the hands of the revolution.

And finally the third cause was the betrayal by the bourgeoisie. Those Mensheviks were profoundly mistaken who presented matters as though the workers were to blame for everything by putting forward too great class demands. Truth was on the side of the Bolsheviks when they emphasised that at the decisive moment the bourgeoisie had shrunk back from the movement and betrayed it by doing a deal with Tsarism. They snapped up the gnawed-off bone which had been tossed to them on October 17th. From that moment on, all the liberal bourgeois camp turned firmly against the proletariat. The same Struve who was always very happy with his catch-phrases, put into circulation this phrase about the 'elemental lunacy' of the strike movement, which was by then moving forward with class, proletarian slogans. The liberal bourgeoisie depicted matters as though a wild elemental force had broken loose and waves were running high which it was essential at all costs to still as otherwise a universal deluge would burst forth across the country, a complete breakdown would ensue, and any order would disappear. In actual fact the bourgeoisie had a correct class instinct and reckoning. When they saw that Tsarism had been cracked and was coming to meet them with its hands outstretched for an agreement, they at once turned to the right, betrayed the liberation movement, and became the effective ally of the Tsar.

Those were the underlying causes which are sufficient to explain the defeat of the 1905 revolution.

The results of 1905

What results did 1905 give us? What were its consequences, inevitable after every revolution including those which suffer a defeat? Foremost was the regrouping of class forces. This lay in the main in the fact that the bourgeoisie finally became a counter-revolutionary class. As you know this was far from always the case. In France in 1789 the bourgeoisie in its struggle against feudalism, the landowners' regime, and the monarchy was a revolutionary class. In Russia prior to 1905 it had played likewise a more or less oppositional role. There had been a time when a section of the Russian bourgeoisie had sought an alliance with the working class and hovered around our workers' party. The attempts of Struve, Tugan-Baranovsky and its best representatives to reach such an agreement with us are well known. Milyukov arrived in London where Comrade Lenin was then living, bowed low before him as the leader of the workers, and offered to make a pact on collaboration. There had been a time when

LECTURE FIVE

all the opposition bourgeoisie had, out of its hatred for Tsarism, been inclined towards a certain measure of collaboration with the working class, secretly hoping that the latter would become an obedient tool in its hands and would drag its chestnuts out of the fire as had been the case in 1848 in Germany and other countries. But the sharper the class nature of the workers' movement became, and the more distinctly the bourgeoisie could pick out the tune of class demands within it, the more they turned aside from the liberation movement, and the clearer it became to them that however bad the Tsar might be for the bourgeoisie, he was nevertheless preferable to the victory of the working class. And when it was finally convinced that the working class was already strong enough, that it was not marching behind Gapon but its own party, that it had its own class programme, put forward the demand for the eight-hour working day and formed its own Soviet of Workers' Deputies, the bourgeoisie quickly began to shed its coat and rapidly became a definitely counter-revolutionary class. The decisive factor in this instance was the rise of the St. Petersburg Soviet of Workers' Deputies. This assembly, which met at the Free Economic Association, became a bogeyman to all of the bourgeoisie, which had a very keen sense of smell. It sniffed it out as a future workers' government, i.e. a class organ of the proletariat that the bourgeoisie could never control. And from that moment on it began to repaint its pink tint with black. From that minute even such theoreticians of the Second International as Kautsky understood that the Russian bourgeoisie could no longer play the role that the French had in 1789, for the proletariat of our country had grown stronger. The Russian bourgeoisie had to become a counter-revolutionary class, while during the French revolution the working class was still in diapers, which alone made it possible for the bourgeoisie to play an objectively revolutionary role.

Thus the first result of 1905 was that one of the most important classes, the young Russian bourgeoisie, became at once a counter-revolutionary class. Its second consequence found expression in the incontestable awakening of the peasantry from its age-old lethargy. If the movement

St. Petersburg Soviet before their exile: Trotsky second from left front row
Bolsheviks in exile: 3rd, 4th and 7th from left, back row: Stalin, Kamenev and Sverdlov
A group of exiles in Siberia

of 1905 had not ended in victory, then the land question had nevertheless been posed extremely acutely, a fact which the appearance of the first land committees had augured. The peasantry had, despite everything, been aroused and shaken by the events of 1905. Its representatives in the First and Second State Dumas showed this quite graphically. In these two Dumas not only the Trudovik peasants, that is, the semi-S.R.s who formed the Trudovik party, but also the right wing, which had been regarded as Black Hundred* in political matters, delivered speeches full of revolutionary ardour on the land question. For when it came to a matter of their patch of land, these right-wing peasants whom the landlords and the Tsarist monarchy had banked upon, spoke up in a language that the Bolsheviks could do nothing but applaud.

* **Black Hundreds** — Counter-revolutionary terrorist gangs which waged attacks on the workers' and democratic movements in Russia.

The formula: 1847 or 1849?'

Thus the second great result of the 1905 revolution was the rapidly growing consciousness of the peasant masses. A fundamental shift had occurred in this respect: the bourgeoisie had moved over to the right while the gradually awakening peasantry began to push leftwards.

The question that stood before the party in 1906 was: what now then? Has the revolution ended? The following formula emerged from the controversies that arose at this point: are we going through our 1847 or our 1849? This meant, in other words, what had we then: an 1847, the eve of the 1848 revolution, or an 1849, the period following the half-victory, half-defeat of the 1848 revolution? As you know the 1848 revolution ended in exactly this way in a number of countries, that is, as an abortion or a compromise where the bourgeoisie clearly snatched the fruits of victory. In party circles the question was posed: what are we experiencing in 1906: what Germany and a considerable part of Europe experienced in 1847, or what they experienced in 1849? Put another way, was 1906 merely the herald of new battles or were the major battles already behind us and the movement on the wane? Were we having our 1849 when the revolution could be regarded as finished? An exceptionally acrimonious discussion flared up between the Bolsheviks and the Mensheviks around this formula.

The Bolsheviks defended the view that we were going through an 1847, that the revolution was not finished, the objective tasks brought to the fore by the revolution had not been formally satisfied and that sooner or later the revolutionary wave would rise up again. The peasantry, we said, have not got their land, nor have the workers received fulfilment of their demands; these two classes comprise the overwhelming majority of the country. In this respect the tasks put forward by the revolution remain unsolved; it may be that the Tsar and Stolypin will drive the revolutionary movement down for a while, but only temporarily, for new battles are inevitable. What has taken place in 1905 was only a preliminary skirmish, a mere rehearsal, a mere 1847, while the really big battles still lie ahead.

The Mensheviks of course maintained a different view. They said: we have taken the path of Prussia after her unsuccessful 1848 which ended half in favour of the revolution and half in favour of the monarchy. The Tsar remains, but we have a constitutional monarchy, so we must now adjust ourselves to this reality. Hence the Mensheviks' slogan: legalize the party at all costs or, as we then mocked them, 'crawl into legality'. Yet this Menshevik standpoint was understandable. For, once they had considered the revolution to be over and that there would be no further battles and that Russia was entering a peaceful phase after the Prussian fashion, then it was clear that the party had to leave the underground, become legalized, trim down its programme, adapt to legality and find a means of co-existing with the monarchy and the bourgeois parties.

The re-unification of the Bolsheviks and the Mensheviks

Such were the two platforms, Bolshevik and Menshevik, in the spring of 1906. By that time, as a consequence of the revolutionary battles of late 1905 and under the influence of the masses, the staffs of the Bolsheviks and the Mensheviks were compelled to re-unite. In effect the masses forced the Bolsheviks to reconcile themselves to the Mensheviks on several questions.

It was not surprising. Even as late as 1917 voices could be heard to say: 'Why should we be split? The more the merrier; if we add to each Bolshevik a Menshevik and then an S.R. we can certainly conquer the bourgeoisie and Tsarism.' That was how broad masses of workers uninitiated in political struggle, and even party members, argued. At any event a strong movement favouring reunification had started as early as 1905. In many areas federated committees of Bolsheviks and Mensheviks were formed, and these created evenly constituted joint organizations which led the struggle as a single unit. This ended with the Central Committee of the Bolsheviks having to enter into such a federated relationship with the Menshevik Organizational Committee, and afterwards under the pressure of the masses a unifying congress was convened, and held in Stockholm in 1906. At this congress the chief difference between the Bolsheviks and the Mensheviks was that the former said, '1847', and the latter, '1849'. In other words the Bolsheviks stated: 'We have been smashed in the first revolutionary engagement, but another revolution faces us ahead whose tasks 1905 has not solved'. The Mensheviks declared on the other hand: 'You are Utopians and fantasists, for you do not want to admit the hard fact that this is not 1847, but 1849. We have been utterly smashed and the Russian revolution has been irretrievably lost. Russia has embarked upon the road of a constitutional monarchy and the party must march under the sign of such a struggle along the path trodden by European Social-Democracy'.

The victory of the Menshevik tendency

At the Stockholm Congress the Mensheviks won a victory. This demonstrated that throughout the country the revolutionary mood of the working masses was declining under the effect of the defeat inflicted upon them, and that party circles were similarly depressed by the inevitable disappointment following the failure of the December rising and the arrest of the members of the St. Petersburg

LECTURE FIVE 143

Soviet. Only thanks to this circumstance were the Mensheviks able to muster a majority (and then only a narrow one), and so dictate their tactics to the party. When the question of the armed insurrection came up at the Congress, they introduced a motion opposing it, though of course doing so in a disguised, diplomatic fashion. They then carried Maslov's and Plekhanov's agrarian programme which was also directed against revolution, and meant that the land would necessarily be transferred through the intermediary of the municipal organs, the zemstvos, to the better-off peasants. Finally they adopted a resolution to participate in the elections to the First State Duma and to form a social-democratic faction there.*

* This decision was made too late for the party to participate officially in the elections to the First Duma, but it did so the following year for the Second Duma.

The Bolsheviks' tactics

The Bolsheviks could do nothing except formally abide by these decisions as they were in the minority and the workers were demanding unity. But the Unification Congress did not in practice re-unite the Bolsheviks and the Mensheviks in any way and we left Stockholm in fact as two separate factions. Several of our comrades were elected to the Central Committee, 'taken as hostages', as we then said. But at the same time the Bolsheviks had set up during the Congress their own internal and, for the party, illegal, Central Committee. This period of our party's history when we were in the minority on both the Central Committee and the St. Petersburg Committee and had to conceal our separate revolutionary activity, was very arduous and unpleasant for us. It would often happen that two secretaries, one a Menshevik and the other a Bolshevik, would stalk each other because of their mutual distrust. It was a situation where two parties were seemingly operating within the structure of one.

From the literary documents of the period which record this struggle between the Bolsheviks and the Mensheviks, we can single out above all the pamphlet *Report on the Stockholm Congress to St. Petersburg Workers* which was written by Comrade Lenin who attended this congress as a delegate of St. Petersburg workers, and also his book *The Cadet Victory and the Tasks of the Workers' Party*.

Lenin's *Collected Works*, Vol. 10, pp. 317-382.

Lenin's *Collected Works*, Vol. 10, pp. 199-276.

Subsequent controversy over '1847 or 1849'

The controversy over '1847 or 1849', over who was right, the Bolsheviks or the Mensheviks, still continued after the Stockholm Congress when a phase of decline in the revolution and the predominance of Menshevism ensued. The Mensheviks repeatedly pointed out to us exultantly: 'See how wrong you were, you thought that the revolution was not over and that new battles lay just ahead but in the meantime see how much time has passed since then'. And in actual fact the next revolution only came about in 1917, that is, ten years later. But does it follow from this that the Bolsheviks were wrong? No. The Bolsheviks did not set a precise date: though, to be frank, they did assume that things would move faster than they did and did not foresee that another entire decade would pass before a new victory of the working class. But, as you know, everybody makes mistakes over dates, not least Marx himself who several times warned of the proximity of the world revolution. It is quite natural that any sincere revolutionary will tend to set shorter rather than longer time-scales. Our prognosis was in any case correct in general terms: the revolution had not yet finished, its fundamental demands had not been fulfilled in practice, the proletariat and the peasantry had not been satisfied and new battles were unavoidable, thus we would not follow the Prussian road but a *Russian* one fraught with great social upheavals. These predictions of ours *came true*. All this was to become clear and rapidly so.

The Stockholm Congress coincided chronologically with the overwhelming victory of the Cadets, the party of the liberal bourgeoisie, in the elections to the First State Duma. They gained the greatest number of seats in the Duma and thereby political leadership of the first Russian parliament and installed the notorious Muromtsev as its president. The Cadets were the leading party in the State Duma and its leaders, Nabokov and others, became the leading parliamentary orators. In the final count the First Duma represented a major triumph for the Russian bourgeois-liberal party which called itself

'Constitutional-Democrat' (C-D, hence 'Cadets'). This presented us with a very serious new political factor and the workers' party was confronted with the problem of how to respond to it.

Responsible (Cadet) government

The Menshevik-controlled Central Committee which then led the party was ecstatic over the Cadet victory. It considered that a new era had opened in Russia and that the Constitutional-Democratic Party could now, by asserting its views, assist the country peacefully to solve the land question and many others too. Consequently the Mensheviks put forward the slogan of a Cadet, or as they then put it, 'responsible government'; that is, one that would be responsible not to the Tsar but to the State Duma. That is by and large the classic formula of all bourgeois parliaments. With them you always have a government which is seemingly responsible to parliament but in point of fact only responsible to a clique of bankers. As soon as Menshevik social-democracy put forward this slogan they embarked on feverish agitation in working-class districts to win support for this idea of 'responsible government'. As you can see, the Mensheviks were logical and true to themselves: here too they were seeking a suitable form of support to the bourgeoisie, so dear to their heart. But here things came unstuck, as they say. This slogan was to be the Mensheviks' undoing, for it helped us to win the majority in St. Petersburg. I remember that the Vyborg district, where many factories were situated, was then, unlike nowadays, solidly Menshevik. The workers would hardly listen to us wicked Bolsheviks there. But as soon as it came to the slogan of a 'responsible government' and it became as clear as daylight to them that the Menshevik tactic amounted to giving support to a bourgeois government, the picture changed. From that moment on, the Mensheviks began to lose the Vyborg district factory by factory. Following this the St. Petersburg City Conference likewise declared itself against the Menshevik slogan. This conference was held in Finland where life was relatively free. I recall how on the Saturday we boarded a train at the Finland Station under the furtive glances of a whole posse of police spies and went to Terijoki.* The conference ran for the whole Sunday and at certain moments it almost came to blows between the Mensheviks and the Bolsheviks. Finally, in spite of pressure from the Menshevik Central Committee, we managed for the first time to obtain the majority in St. Petersburg and subsequently in a whole number of other towns. This was already half the victory on an all-Russian scale because St. Petersburg was the political focus of the country. The Menshevik Central Committee was powerless when faced with the Bolshevik St. Petersburg Committee, and bourgeois newspapers at the time liked to joke that the little Bolshevik St. Petersburg Committee had beaten the big Menshevik Central Committee.

* Now Zelenogorsk.

The State Duma

The First State Duma, notwithstanding the fact that Cadets held its political leadership, had to pay heed to the revolutionary movement and especially the revolutionary peasant movement which was still growing and spreading, and it was forced to raise the land question, albeit somewhat indecisively. It came into conflict with the Tsarist government over this. The First Duma was dissolved. The Cadet Party in a fit of temper also went off to Finland for its own illegal conference and there issued the notorious Vyborg Appeal, which was later called the 'Vyborg pretzel'. This document called upon the population not to pay taxes, and was in essence a repetition of the revolutionary gesture which the moderate liberals in the 1848 revolution had permitted themselves when they cocked a snook at the monarchy, having already decided not to support the revolutionary struggle and knowing beforehand that nobody would listen to their appeal not to pay taxes. The Tsarist monarchy did not take the 'Vyborg pretzel' seriously of course and sentenced its bakers to three months' imprisonment, quite a trivial penalty.

The dissolution of the First State Duma was a little tiff between Tsarism and the liberal bourgeoisie. But it was soon to be forgotten, and in the Second Duma generally

First Duma in session
Illegal conference of
Cadet Party in
the Vyborg wood

fairly good-neighbourly relations were established between both sides, whereby a section of the liberal bourgeoisie began openly to praise Stolypin.

The London Congress of 1907

The London, or Fifth, Congress of our party was held in the spring of 1907 against the background of these events. For a long time we argued over what it should be called. We, Bolsheviks, counted from the Third, Bolshevik, Congress, regarding Stockholm as the Fourth and London as the Fifth. But the Mensheviks did not recognize our Third Congress, and not wanting to call this Congress the Fifth called it simply the London Congress. Three new sections merged with the party at this congress: Polish Social-Democracy, Latvian Social-Democracy and the Bund, which, as I have said earlier, had left our party in 1903. These three organizations (the first two overwhelmingly and the Bund to a considerable degree) then stood on our side. In London, therefore, despite the fact that the revolution was on the ebb, thanks to the adherence of three new sections to our point of view, we did obtain a majority which, though a relatively weak one, often depending upon a couple of votes, was nonetheless a majority. The Mensheviks dug their heels in over the control of the party and we had to tear this control from them by force, using very indelicate methods, so as to liberate the party from their hands.

At the London Congress a debate revolved around parliamentary tactics, which was waged by Tsereteli for the Mensheviks (he was a member of the Second State Duma) and Alexinsky, who was then a Bolshevik and had been elected from our party to the Duma by St. Petersburg workers. (He doesn't want to forget this to this day when he has long since been a monarchist: today in Wrangel's company he still signs himself 'State Duma deputy elected by the St. Petersburg workers'.) Then a heated theoretical struggle arose at the Congress over the questions of the attitude of the liberal bourgeoisie towards the revolution and the character of the revolution generally. This discussion, which assumed a wide-ranging scope, was

I.G. Tsereteli

conducted by the best theoreticians and most outstanding speakers on each side. Plekhanov for the most part spoke for the Mensheviks, and Comrade Lenin and the late Rosa Luxemburg (who had joined our party and participated in the Congress as a representative of Polish workers) for the Bolsheviks. The speeches on the question of the nature of the Russian revolution and our attitude towards the liberal bourgeoisie delivered to this congress by Rosa Luxemburg and Comrade Lenin rank to this day as models and masterpieces of political analysis. And in this sense the debate which took place at the London Congress has in no way dated: for there of course a basic question was being decided—should the working class serve merely as an auxiliary to the bourgeoisie or should it play an independent role in the forthcoming revolution?

The Central Committee elected at the London Congress

Our majority on the Central Committee elected by the congress in London was, however, very unstable and extremely insignificant. Martov in his book has reminded me of some things I had forgotten. The Central Committee elected at the London Congress comprised the following: from the Mensheviks: Martynov (who has now come over to us); N. Zhordania (who was since president of the Menshevik Georgian Republic and is now in Paris); Goldman-Gorev and Noi Ramishvili (a member of the First State Duma, a Menshevik). From the Poles: Tyszka (who was shot during the Spartacist Rising after Karl Liebknecht) and the communist, Warski (today in our party). From the Bund: Abramovich and Lieber. From the Bolsheviks: Comrade Lenin, Zinoviev (I was then elected to the Central Committee for the first time), Goldenberg (he was to become a Menshevik for a while but then came back to us and died a Bolshevik), Rozhkov (whom many of you probably know; at that time he was one of our best friends and representatives of Bolshevism), and finally the late Dubrovinsky. From the Latvians: Rozin (now deceased, a Bolshevik) and German. This latter was none other than our present-day military specialist, Comrade Danishevsky. I remind you of that

N.N. Zhordania
J. Tyszka
I.F. Dubrovinsky

LECTURE FIVE 151

because he was then a conciliationist; on certain important occasions we had a 'Germanization' of the Central Committee, as we then joked, for German voted alternately with the Bolsheviks and the Mensheviks. You can imagine what an unstable policy resulted from such a co-existence. The Bolsheviks appreciated this and made an attempt at the same London Congress to elect their own illegal Bolshevik Centre. We said: we will work and suffer dutifully for the Central Committee but we will do the real work in our Bolshevik Centre, for it is clear that this forced marriage with the Mensheviks cannot last. Thus in summarizing the results of the London Congress we can say this: it yielded a theoretical victory to the Bolsheviks and deprived the Mensheviks of overall party control; but the Central Committee was beyond our control and the position was highly unstable; moreover the system of separate factions continued, and the Bolsheviks had to be independently organized.

Before we managed to arrive back from the London Congress the Second State Duma had been dissolved. The social-democratic faction had been arrested on charges of conspiracy, and a famous criminal case was opened against it which ended with hard labour sentences for a whole number of deputies. We entered a period of illegality. Our newspapers were closed down. Although they made protests against the disbandment of the Second Duma the bourgeoisie no longer thought of bothering with such stunts as trips to Vyborg. It sat quietly in St. Petersburg and just now and again uttered speeches of opposition to Stolypin to clear its conscience, or sharp phrases about Stolypin's 'neck-ties', i.e. gallows, as, for instance, did Rodichev. But this was merely appearances, for in practice the whole of the bourgeoisie stood entirely upon the basis of Stolypin's constitution.

The Third Duma

Having dissolved the Second State Duma, the Tsarist monarchy raised the question of a third, slightly 'adjusted', franchise, and this they did in a very odd fashion. The principal adjustment consisted in depriving the peasants of the franchise. By the way, there was nothing to deprive the workers of since they had almost no electoral rights as it was. This measure was quite to be expected. Up till the Second Duma the autocracy had still pinned its hopes upon the old peasant. Even the cleverest representative of the Tsarist monarchy, that old reptile, Pobedonostsev, had believed in him. The monarchists considered that they had to stake their money on the old peasant: he'll not betray us, we understand each other, they said, the peasant believes in his old father Tsar and won't go against him. But the Second Duma showed Tsarism that the peasant also was losing his faith in the Tsar. And thus the principal operation enacted upon the franchise amounted to removing it from the peasantry. This was done quite skilfully. The peasant electors were to be vetted by landlords who had a majority and could choose any peasant whom they liked. In this way we can see that the essence of the evolution of the monarchy in the period from the Second Duma to the Third lay in the fact that it had lost faith in the peasantry, for the reason of course that the peasant had lost all faith in it.

For the party the question arose: should we take part in the Third State Duma which would be blatantly Black Hundred? Over this, serious differences appeared among the Bolsheviks. The vast majority of them declared themselves against participation and for a boycott of the State Duma, hoping to be able to achieve what had been done in 1905 with the Bulygin Duma. A sharp conflict developed within the Bolshevik faction. Comrade Lenin together with a very small number of supporters defended taking part in the Third Duma but the main body of the Bolsheviks was against it. Pamphlets appeared which argued that Lenin had moved to the right just because he wanted the workers to go into the Black Hundred Duma that the Third was. He replied to this: the Third Duma is a cowshed; but if in the workers' interests it is necessary to spend a little while in a cowshed then we shall. Comrade Lenin's argument was as follows: in 1905 the correlation of forces was such that any day revolution would flare up and we would triumph over both the Tsarist monarchy and the Bulygin Duma; in 1907 such a balance of forces did not obtain, and it was clear that the Tsarist monarchy had been assured another few years of life and for the moment we would not be able to drive it out; if we were to boycott the Duma, then it would assemble just the same and we would have to prepare ourselves for several years of the darkest reaction; the Black Hundred Duma was indeed a cowshed, but in there we would be able to bring some benefit to the working class by using the Duma platform for agitation.

The controversy over legal opportunities

Hence arose the controversy over the utilization of legal opportunities. The party as a whole was illegal: its original parliamentary deputies had been transported to labour camps and it only had isolated legal bases: certain trade unions and workers' clubs, and in addition the Third State Duma where workers could send a few people to tell the people the truth over the heads of the Black Hundred deputies. At one stage this controversy put the Bolsheviks in quite a critical situation. If the anti-Lenin tendency had prevailed for long at that time our party would have probably turned into a sect. As a matter of fact our party's work in the trade unions had been insufficiently successful precisely because we had missed our opportunity there. At one point the upper hand was gained by people who said: Why go into trade unions? Our concern is the party. We will go underground and work there and as far as the trade unions are concerned the Mensheviks can sit tight. This was a major error for which we paid a high price. We did not win the trade unions from the Mensheviks until after October 1917 and they held the majority in them until that time. Comrade Lenin's main idea was that we had to remain with the working class and be a mass party and not to coop ourselves up exclusively in the underground and turn into a narrow circle. If the workers are in the trade unions then we must be there too; if we can send just one man into the Tsar's Duma then we shall: let him tell the workers the truth and we can publish his speeches as leaflets; if something can be done for the workers in the workers' clubs then we will be there. We have to use every legal opportunity, so as not to divorce ourselves from the working masses; we must live their lives and not become merely pure propagandists who just have the idea in their head that there will be a revolution some time. Workers, said Comrade Lenin, will have no respect for people of this sort. They demand that the party keeps in touch with them, that it is with them at every turn of the road and that it provides answers to all the everyday questions.

It was only on account of Comrade Lenin's enormous prestige that although he was in the minority, the Bolshevik faction resolved to take part in the Third State Duma and managed to get a few of its own deputies there, including as a representative of St. Petersburg, Poletaev who was later to play significant part in the work of organizing *Pravda* and *Zvezda*.

It is necessary to recall this controversy within the Bolshevik faction, because we will have to return to it when I speak about the tendency in Bolshevism which subsequently acquired the name of recallism.*

* Recallism is sometime referred to by the Russian word Otzovism.

'*Liquidationism*'

At the same time as this division had begun to appear within the Bolsheviks over the question of boycottism and anti-boycottism, for or against utilizing opportunities for legal activity, a division developed within the Mensheviks along another line. A tendency began to emerge among them which acquired the name of 'liquidationism'. The origin of this term is as follows.

A number of Menshevik leaders had come to the conclusion that it was necessary to liquidate the underground, as they put it, put an end to the illegal organization, adapt to the regime of Tsarist legality, prune down the party's programme to make it acceptable to the Tsarist, or as it was then called, the June 3rd Monarchy†, admit once and for all that the revolution was finished and take the path of a simple struggle for workers' economic demands. The clearest representative of this liquidationist tendency was none other than our present-day colleague and dear comrade, Larin. Then he was an extreme liquidator Menshevik, a fact which does not prevent him now from

† June 3, 1907, was the date of the government *coup d'etat* which dissolved the Second Duma and introduced the new franchise.

sometimes adopting the posture of the 'left' wing of Bolshevism. Transformations can be of all sorts. At that time Comrade Larin founded in St. Petersburg the little legal journal called *Vozrozhdenie* which was consciously tolerated by Stolypin. Ezhov, Potresov, Lewicki and other Mensheviks were also members of this group. Comrade Lenin proclaimed this group of Liquidator Mensheviks to be the 'Stolypin Workers' Party'. And they were to carry this nickname like the mark of Cain. Then they started up a second journal, a learned one called *Nasha Zarya* in which Martov, Dan and Co. also participated. They made fun of our illegal organization. Larin himself wrote 'In any city it is not hard to knock together a score of discussion groups of raw youth, but what importance have they? The real people will not go into the underground'. They wrecked our common Central Committee and their leaders, Mikhail, Roman and Yuri, three Menshevik members of the Central Committee, issued this statement: although we are Central Committee members we are not so stupid as to play around: we will not go to the meetings of your Central Committee: we have to disband all our illegal organisations which have outlived their day; the time has come to build a social-democratic party as in Europe. Martov and Dan, who were abroad, attempted to occupy a moderate position as they did not wish to lose the positions that they had inside our party. Thus they established a definite division of labour, as Lenin put it: Potresov, Ezhov, Lewicki, Larin and their colleagues were based in St. Petersburg to disrupt the party from there while Martov and Dan stayed within the illegal apparatus so as to sabotage it from the inside.

Liquidationism and the bourgeoisie

The liquidationist movement encountered throughout Russia strong support from the liberal bourgeoisie. The newspaper *Rech* readily set aside columns for these Mensheviks: their trade unions enjoyed support from the liberals (at a time when ours were being subjected to arrests); the Mensheviks began to work legally in the clubs and started to penetrate the trade union press. The monarchists and liberals openly took the side of the liquidators, thereby hoping to dissolve the party and demoralize the revolutionary vanguard of the working class.

From 1908 this movement became fully evident and the term 'liquidationism' acquired its right of citizenship. A whole number of old working-class Mensheviks went over to the extreme group of *Nasha Zarya* headed by Potresov and became liquidators. Open renegacy occurred at every turn. The party's old past was besmirched with filth, the illegal period was declared to have been nonsense, immaturity and a lack of political consciousness, and adaptation to Stolypin's regime began to be preached. This was how you had alongside Stolypin's liberal party also the 'Stolypin Workers' Party'. The liquidators advanced freedom of association as their main slogan, implying that the Bolsheviks were opposed to such a liberty. This was rubbish of course. The Bolsheviks stood for freedom of association but they also said that under the Tsarist monarchy the working class would gain no freedoms. In the final analysis the divergence between the Bolsheviks and the Mensheviks was here a complete one: the former set the revolution down as the cornerstone of their programme while the latter proposed reforms within the monarchist system. The Mensheviks became definite reformists, but the Bolsheviks remained revolutionaries. We said to them and to the workers: if you want freedom of association then you must overthrow the Tsar, who will never grant you it, to which the Mensheviks replied: if you want freedom of association you must overthrow the illegal party, adapt to the existing regime and become a 'European' social-democrat.

Party Mensheviks

In addition to these two basic tendencies, the one inspired by Martov who sat inside the party and undermined it from within and the second led by Potresov which openly described itself as liquidationist, the Mensheviks had another third group, which was headed by Plekhanov. This tendency harked back once again to the old days, and returning to the side of our revolutionary tactic formed a separate group known as the 'Party Mensheviks'. They participated in *Sotsial-Demokrat*, which was edited by Lenin and myself for the Bolsheviks and Martov and Dan for the Mensheviks. Plekhanov as a Party Menshevik published a number of brilliant articles in defence of the illegal party. The Mensheviks began to jeer at him, saying that he had become in his old age the 'bard of the underground'. But Plekhanov was unruffled, for, as opposed to many of the Mensheviks, he had nonetheless pretty often been a revolutionary. For example it was news to me to read Martov's account in his *History of Russian Social-Democracy* of how at the beginning of 1905, when the struggle against Tsarism had become particularly sharp, Plekhanov spoke out in favour of terrorism. This I didn't know. Martov wrote:

> There was a point when even Plekhanov, the long-standing opponent of terrorist methods, raised in the Party Council the question of an agreement with the Socialist-Revolutionaries on the subject of acts of terrorism which might be entirely expedient in certain political circumstances. An agreement was wrecked only as a consequence of an ultimatum by Axelrod and Martov who declared that if one were reached they would resign from the Council and make an appeal to the membership. Amongst the Bolshevik elements in the party sympathy for terror had likewise grown but the party by and large stood firm on its previous position of rejecting terror.

This is an extremely interesting point in Plekhanov's biography for it proves that he was at any rate no average mediocrity. He came out against terror when he could see that it would undermine the mass party and mass struggle, but when he understood that the decisive blow was approaching he posed the question of terror.

Plekhanov as the 'Bard of the Underground'

In these difficult years for the party (1907, 1908 and 1909) Plekhanov then once again rendered it an inestimable service by coming over to our side to become the 'bard of the underground'. He supported us in our illegal literary organ and subsequently in our legal one, and reinforced the position of the Bolshevik section of the Duma faction giving us energetic assistance in the struggle against those who wanted to bury the party. This was extremely important in the atmosphere of that period, one which is hard to conceive of today. At that time following the defeats we had undergone, when a considerable part of our forces were forced to go abroad and when demoralization could be felt everywhere, there was not a single organization in the areas into which a provocateur had not wormed himself, and everyone trailed each other around, one member fearing and not trusting the next. Pornography blossomed in literature—*Sanin* appeared.*. All this affected revolutionary groups too. The State Duma had become utterly counter-revolutionary. The party was dispersed into tiny groups. At the same time the liquidationist section of the Mensheviks openly sang a requiem for the party and its funeral note sounded in St. Petersburg and Moscow. And just at this moment Plekhanov, who commanded prestige among the Mensheviks, spoke up and, while remaining a Menshevik himself, flailed them for their liquidationism. Yes, his voice proved a great support to the Bolsheviks standing as they did for the idea of the underground.

It must be said generally that the party was to know its true leaders in precisely its hardest hours. Comrade Lenin's enormous stature as a leader most clearly emerged in just this difficult time: not so much in 1905 when everything was on the upturn, and the revolutionary wave was rising up and it was easy to lead the party, as in 1907-1909 in the days of the hopeless breakdown, demoralization and decline, when nobody believed either in the revolution or the party and when Comrade Lenin had alone, or almost alone, to defend the idea of the party with his pen, his spoken word and his organizational work. Such was the period when the division appeared within the Bolsheviks over boycott or non-boycott, utilization of legal openings or their non-utilization. Likewise the division within the Mensheviks took place which put them into two main camps, the liquidators and the Party Mensheviks: on the one side Potresov and Larin, on the other Plekhanov, and in the middle, but standing closer to the liquidators, Martov.

By 1909 the struggle within the Bolsheviks had

* *Sanin* was a best-selling pornographic novel of that time by M. Artsybashev.

A game of chess Bogdanov and Lenin in exile in Capri, 190

acquired quite a sharp character. At the opening of the Third Duma in 1908 we had debated whether to take part in it. But by now, the boycottist tendency had formed itself into a whole faction and the so-called 'recallism' appeared.

The Bolshevik faction had divided over the following three questions: 'recallism', 'ultimatism', and 'godbuilding'. At first glance all this might appear fatuous but when you hear the explanation you will see that it is far from being so. So first, 'recallism'.

'Recallism'

A section of the Bolsheviks, including some veterans and some of the local organizations like the Regional Committee of Central Russia, declared themselves in favour of the recall of deputies from the State Duma. (Hence the word 'recallism'.) They advanced the following thesis: the Tsarist Duma is a Black Hundred institution and the true revolutionary has no place there; anyone who enters it has become a liquidator and has thereby renounced the revolution. In taking this argument further they drew the conclusion that to derive benefit from legal opportunities is largely impossible, and a proper Bolshevik has no place in a trade union or a worker's club either. This was a very dangerous tendency which aided the liquidators. In our newspaper *Proletarii*, which was published by Comrades Lenin, Kamenev and myself, we called them 'liquidators from the left' and pointed out that their concept, while outwardly attractive and revolutionary, tended in practice to cut us off from living reality. All the Mensheviks needed was for us to leave the trade unions, the State Duma and working-class milieus. They would very much have liked us to shut ourselves up in little circles and turn away from harsh political reality. Let me repeat: this tendency was very dangerous to Bolshevism, and had we not dealt it a sufficiently strong rebuff we would not have become a mass party. The strength of Bolshevism lay in the fact that over decades and at every stage of its difficult path, it knew how to wedge itself into the masses and to answer not only the key

L.B. Kamenev

LECTURE FIVE

questions of the revolution but also any mundane problem of the worker's life. When we today observe how the young communist parties in other countries are taking shape we can see that it is frequently this very elasticity that they lack: instead, they become sectarian, turn in on themselves and move away from the masses, as was the case for a while with the Italian communists. In this respect they were repeating the errors of 'recallism'.

'Ultimatism'

'Ultimatism' originates from the word 'ultimatum'. A whole group of Bolsheviks who at that time carried great authority, having as their leaders A.A. Bogdanov, the author of the textbook *Political Economy* (he has now left the party and preaches counter-revolutionary Menshevik ideas through the 'Workers' Truth' group, the Proletkult and the workers' faculties into which he tries to creep: then however he was an influential Bolshevik leader), A.V. Lunacharsky, M.N. Pokrovsky and several other distinguished comrades (they were also supported by M. Gorky who was then extremely 'left'), accused Comrade Lenin of opportunism and formed their own 'ultimatist' faction. In essence the difference between ultimatism and recallism was only one of nuance. The ultimatists said: 'We propose not to recall our deputies, but to give them an ultimatum; those who do not accept it must go'. We objected to this and said:'This is to pass out of the frying pan into the fire'. This is the same old recallism. Under the guise of an ultimatum you nevertheless want to recall our representatives from the Black Hundred Duma where our comrades can still manage to deliver their revolutionary message to all Russia. The ultimatists had a substantial influence within the Bolshevik faction and among a section of members of the Bolshevik Centre, that is, in the Bolshevik Central Committee.

A.A. Bogdanov
A.V. Lunacharsky
M.N. Pokrovsky

'God-Building'

Finally the third tendency, that of so-called 'god-building', was headed by A. Lunacharsky and M. Gorky.

The chief literary documents of this tendency were several articles by our friend A.V. Lunacharsky and Gorky's novel *The Confession*, a fine book which many of you have probably read but which is 'god-builder' in its world-outlook. The god-builders in one way or another paid tribute to religious attitudes. They said that they did not of course believe in a god pure and simple, but that there was some sort of special Marxist god-figure. At that time degeneration could be observed—as is always the case after defeats—in all spheres of culture, both in science and literature, which brought forth a flowering of pornography, mysticism, and every kind of religious outlook. Such moods affected on one side the most sensitive people who were inclined that way in our party, including Gorky and Lunacharsky. They made an attempt, however strange that may seem, to wed god-building with recallism. Collecting together a party school of some twenty workers (more than could be brought into the party organizations at that time) they took them to the island of Capri where Gorky was then living, with the idea of teaching them Marxism. However they in reality did not teach Marxism so much as recallism plus god-building. The workers who were taken there were for the most part good people and many of them now occupy prominent posts in our republic. But the god-builders' scheme on the island of Capri came to grief. The workers listened readily to Marxism and the history of literature on which Gorky lectured, letting recallism go in one ear and out of the other, but when it came to god-building the proletarians said 'No, that's enough'. It ended by more than half of these pupils, under the leadership of the late worker Vilonov, the school organizer, stealing away from the island one fine night and going to see Comrade Lenin and others who lived in exile with him and published *Proletarii*. They moved from the 'god-building' school to ours and then went back to Russia as representatives of our tendency.

This party school in exile of ours played a major role. In those days when there was no party this group of some twenty leading workers was a force and virtually our party's Central Committee.

LECTURE FIVE

The struggle against Recallism and other tendencies

We had to pursue a desperate struggle against recallism, ultimatism and god-building, which was to be crowned by the splitting of the Bolshevik faction. We attracted a number of delegates from the areas and from St. Petersburg and Moscow, and called a Bolshevik conference where we expelled God's slaves like Bogdanov and others, from our faction. This chapter in the history of Bolshevism is one of the most important. It is set out in detail in the newspaper *Proletarii* in which Comrade Lenin published many brilliant articles in this connection. The struggle was an incredibly hard one because our adversaries had more contacts and because everyone knew them and many supported them. Bolshevism took its final shape only through waging this struggle 'on the left'. Our antagonists stigmatized us for our alliance with Plekhanov. But we were right, and to this day we have maintained a pact with the Plekhanovites for the defence of materialist philosophy. But Lunacharsky and Bogdanov were opponents of Marx over philosophy, the latter being and remaining not a supporter of Marx but of Ernst Mach, whose philosophy has nothing in common with Marxism, as Comrade Lenin established in his philosophical study of empirio-criticism.[The reference is to Lenin's *Materialism and Empirio-criticism* (Collected Works, Vol. 14, p. 17).] At that time, however, many of our comrades who were in exile or prison engrossed themselves in Mach. Bogdanov upon the basis of literary degeneration and corrupt atmosphere drew conclusions opposed to Marxism. Let me repeat, this was a very serious factor in the history of Bolshevism. We concluded an alliance with Plekhanov for the struggle for philosophical materialism. Bolshevism only finally arose when it had passed through the struggle not only against liquidationism and Menshevism, but also against liquidationism 'from the left' and recallism which had also entered the party under the name of 'Vperedism'. This group of 'left' Bolsheviks used the title of our paper *Vpered* which had been published in 1905, and began to publish an anthology under the same name. The 'Vperedists' declared that they were the real Bolsheviks and that we were 'right-wing' Bolsheviks.

The history of the struggle against all these trends is particularly valuable for those who wish to become familiar with the theoretical basis of Bolshevism. The latter had never imagined that it had to be the most 'left' in the vulgar sense of the word. We had always rejected and firmly fought the leftism which was to sink into god-building, futurism and so on. In this struggle the Bolsheviks became finally steeled not only against rotten reformism and liquidationism but also against rotten idealism and adventurism in politics, for indeed recallism was nothing else but adventurism.

The whole of 1909 was spent in this struggle for the ideological rebirth of the party. The situation was, I repeat, incredibly tough. Many comrades lost any revolutionary physiognomy and turned into god knows what. The whole of our party was fragmented into groups, sub-groups and factions. In those hard days our central task consisted in assembling the party piece by piece, preparing its rebirth and, above all, defending the principles of Marxism against all possible distortions.

This phase in the history of Bolshevism was indeed an arduous one but a glorious one too. Had Bolshevism at that time made any theoretical or political concessions whatever to its opponents it would not have been able to play that great role which it accomplished later on. That is why this page of our history merits exceptional and painstaking study by our youth, especially today when 'fashionable' theoretical currents, recalling in many ways the period of degeneration that we have described, are again emerging.

LECTURE SIX

The years of Stolypin's counter-revolution were the most critical and most dangerous in the party's existence. In retrospect we can say quite unhesitatingly that in those hard times the party as such did not exist: it had disintegrated into tiny individual circles which differed from the circles of the 1880s and early 1890s in that, following the cruel defeat that had been inflicted upon the revolution, their general atmosphere was extremely depressed. Given this state of affairs, the co-existence with the Mensheviks, which had put a heavy pressure upon the party, concealed within itself a dangerous threat. The liquidator Mensheviks maliciously laid stress on the fact that the party did not exist as such. While every revolutionary who was dedicated to the party would conclude from this that it was necessary to devote every effort towards its construction, they drew the opposite conclusion: rejoicing that the party was smashed, they strove to create a new organization ideologically unconnected with the old party. Over the course of several years an intense struggle between the Bolsheviks and the liquidators was waged within the framework of a single party, where there was moreover no shortage of conciliationist groups which attempted to find a middle way and reconcile the two sides. We must then dwell upon the two most important of these attempts.

The 1908 Paris Conference

The first one took place in December 1908 at the All-Russian Conference of the party which was held in Paris. All the representatives of the party in exile as well as a number of the committees operating in Russia were present there. The wing of Menshevism represented by Martov and occupying the middle-ground between Plekhanov and Potresov, the party Mensheviks and the liquidators, also arrived at the conference in order to continue there their work of undermining and breaking up the party from inside. The Third State Duma faction had also been invited to the conference in the person of its principal leader, Chkheidze. But he did not come. This was a wholly deliberate step on his part, which had an important political significance. This refusal to attend the All-Russian Conference, although it was hedged round with various diplomatic pretexts, meant that the Menshevik majority of the Duma faction which was headed by Chkheidze did not wish to recognize the party, and considered that the faction was not subordinate to the party but stood above it. In other words, the faction once again underlined by this act its sympathy for the liquidationist wing of the Mensheviks in the party.

At the Paris Conference, more or less politically correct motions were carried which condemned liquidationism—though to be sure in a very moderate form. This was however understandable, since by wishing to preserve unity with Martov's group the conference and the then Central Committee, which had been elected back at the London Congress, was tied hand and foot and unable to declare open war on liquidationism, being restricted of necessity to making general theoretical formulae. Thus through its indeterminate nature the 1908 conference did not have a great significance for the party, especially since it met at the moment of the full bloom of counter-revolution and Stolypin's greatest triumph, and yet at a time when nothing but a crusade against the 'Stolypin Workers' Party' could make any practical sense.

P.A. Stolypin

The last united plenum of the Central Committee

Another attempt to preserve unity and to give shape to the conciliationist mood which then also pervaded a section of the Bolsheviks, took place at the beginning of 1910 at the plenum of the party's Central Committee, which

A.I. Rykov

was in fact the last plenum in which both Bolsheviks and Mensheviks participated, as subsequent events put an end to joint work together. Two groups of Bolsheviks emerged here: the conciliator Bolsheviks who called themselves party Bolsheviks, and ourselves, the irreconcilable Bolsheviks. Leading the first group were a group of comrades who today occupy prominent places in our party (Rykov, Sokolnikov, today's financial expert, Vladimirov, Lozovsky and some others), but their leader was Dubrovinsky ('Innokenti' was his pseudonym), one of the best, most dedicated and remarkable figures in our party on account of his personal appeal, who had done it great services. (He was to perish in Tsarist exile). Dubrovinsky committed the major political error in 1909-1910, when the necessity of a break from the Mensheviks was already clear, of blinding himself with the idea of unity and continuing to insist that we ought nevertheless to work together with them. His group formed an alliance with the party Mensheviks who had gathered around Plekhanov, and came out against us Leninists. At the 1910 plenum Dubrovinsky and his supporters once again carried a resolution on the need to work jointly with the Mensheviks, although at the same time a resolution against liquidationism was carried on the one hand and one against recallism on the other. Such a contradiction can be explained by the fact that at that time the liquidator Mensheviks were looked upon as erring brethren, and it was considered that a large part of them would still work on the basis of the decisions taken at this plenum.

At this plenum the Leninist Bolsheviks were in a minority and so could do nothing but submit to the decision adopted on the votes of the conciliator Bolsheviks, Plekhanov's supporters, and Comrade Trotsky, who was then publishing in Vienna the widely-read newspaper *Pravda* wherein he sustained the idea of the necessity of unity with the Mensheviks at all costs.

This plenum marked the end of a number of attempts to preserve the old unity: attempts which had been made against the background of a smashed workers' movement, a party driven underground and an all-round disillusionment which enveloped likewise a section of workers.

The Lena events and the revival of the workers' movement

But things were soon to change for the better. In only a short time after the above-mentioned plenum a revival commenced in the workers' movement. The first modest strikes occurred. The Bolsheviks managed to issue their limited legal literature which, notwithstanding government persecution, took the opportunity to counterpose Marxist views to liquidationist ones. The strike on the Lena and the events which followed formed a turning point in this respect indicating that a new page in the history of the Russian revolutionary movement was starting.* The 3rd June reaction had had its day. Interminable hanging and shooting of revolutionaries had temporarily driven the revolutionary movement underground but after the Lena events it became clear that, upon the basis of the start of economic expansion, the working class was again rising to the struggle with renewed energy.

* Lena events—In the course of a bitter strike in the Lena goldfields in E Siberia, Tsarist gendarmes massacred unarmed demonstrating workers.

The newspaper 'Zvezda'

We succeeded in organizing our first legal newspaper since the defeat of the 1905 revolution, *Zvezda*. This was initially an organ of Bolsheviks and Plekhanovite Mensheviks. Its effective leadership was located abroad, from where Plekhanov, Lenin and others sent in their leading articles; but there was an official editorial board in St. Petersburg consisting of Poletaev, a Bolshevik worker and State Duma member, and Pokrovsky, a Plekhanovite Menshevik deputy. In the beginning *Zvezda* expressed itself very cautiously and its political line could not be very explicit as the paper was the organ of a coalition bloc of Bolsheviks and Plekhanovites. But having made its appearance as the newspaper of two party groups, *Zvezda* very soon began to turn into the weapon of the resurgent workers' political movement, and as it became more closely linked with this it began gradually to lose its coalition character. In the end Plekhanov's group retired almost entirely into the background and *Zvezda* finally became our fighting Bolshevik organ which came out first twice and then three times a week.

Zvezda

Lena Strikes: The bodies of miners who were shot

Its role and significance

In my view, *Zvezda* played the same role for the new generation of workers which was rising up after digesting the experience of the 1905 defeat as *Iskra* had played at the beginning of the 1900s for that generation of conscious workers. *Zvezda* gathered under our banner the best workers that there were in St. Petersburg and all Russia. Cautiously at first, and then more boldly and firmly, it waged the same ruthless struggle against the liquidators as *Iskra* had done in its time against the Economists. In *Zvezda* we no longer spoke the semi-diplomatic language that we used at the end of 1908 or at the 1910 plenum. The newspaper was the organ of a militant tendency which hit out to the right and to the left, and which knew how to defend its line with vigour and open new frontiers in the workers' movement. It is only those party newspapers which really knew how to defend their tendency and clear their path through their innumerable enemies that have gone down in history as major landmarks. *Zvezda* was without doubt such a newspaper. It prepared for the appearance of *Pravda* which was to arise after the conference at Prague about which we must now say a few words.

The Bolshevik conference at Prague

By the time that *Zvezda* had emerged as the fighting organ of the Leninist Bolsheviks the split with the Mensheviks had become an accomplished fact. After the 1908 conference, and more especially after the 1910 plenum, we Leninist Bolsheviks said to ourselves that we would not work together with the liquidator Mensheviks and that we were only awaiting a convenient moment to break finally from them and form our own independent organization based upon the resurgent workers' movement.

Our group decided that such a moment had arrived at the beginning of 1912, and called a party conference in Prague which was to re-establish our party which had been routed since 1905. This conference has a major historical significance. Present at the conference, incidentally, were two or three delegates who were supporters of Plekhanov

LECTURE SIX

P.A. Zalutsky

and had arrived straight from party activity in Russia. Plekhanov himself however declined to take part, contending (and quite correctly) that the aim of the Prague Conference was to split from the Mensheviks. Plekhanov characteristically recoiled at the last minute from a split from the Mensheviks.

Its composition and results

At the Prague Conference the Bolsheviks predominated overwhelmingly. A new layer of Bolshevik workers was represented there which had grown up and politically matured in the phase of the counter-revolution which lasted approximately from 1907 to 1911. Here there first appeared Zalutsky, Serebryakov (now working in the People's Commissariat for Communications), Voronsky (the editor of *Krasnaya Nov**), Orjonikidze (currently a leading official in the Caucasus) and a number of other comrades who had either not taken part in the 1905 revolution at all or had been active in it only as rank-and-file party workers. At Prague they together formed a new generation of Bolsheviks which had grown up during the counter-revolution, and it was extremely important to establish organizational contact with them so as to benefit from the experience they had acquired.

Krasnaya Nov—a literary journal founded in Petrograd in April 1921 and subsequently a publishing house.

The conference at Prague consisted in effect of a handful of delegates (some 20 to 25 in number) led by Comrade Lenin, and took upon itself the presumption to proclaim itself to be the party and to break once and for ever from all other groups and sub-groups. This conference deposed the old Central Committee which had half rotted away and said to itself: it is we who are the party; whoever is not with us is against us; we will conduct a sharp struggle against everyone who refuses for his part to fight liquidationism.

L.P. Serebryakov

Among exile circles abroad, where the preponderant majority (roughly nine tenths) was then on the side of the Mensheviks, the Prague Conference was greeted with a great gnashing of teeth. For this venture the Mensheviks showed abuse upon us, declared us to be usurpers, and jibed that all the Bolsheviks could be accommodated on one bed, and that this conference would be of only a fleeting significance since no one would recognize it and it would play no role in the party. However, things did not turn out that way. While all the Menshevik exiles were against us, the rising generation of revolutionary workers in Russia was *for* us, and the Prague Conference succeeded in throwing a bridge across to the emergent Bolshevik workers' groups and in re-creating the party upon a new foundation.

The founding of the St. Petersburg 'Pravda'

At the Prague Conference the idea was put forward for the first time of creating the daily newspaper *Pravda*. One of the most passionate defenders of this idea was Comrade Voronsky. We at first treated this project somewhat sceptically, finding it hard to imagine that a daily political paper was possible for the Bolsheviks in Russia. Be that as it may, it was decided to have a go and so we carried out the necessary agitational work. *Pravda* of course was created quite differently from all other papers—by the half-kopecks collected by working men and women. The continually swelling influx of financial resources provided us with an accurate barometer for gauging workers' sympathies towards the Bolsheviks. We maintained a detailed record of workers' groups which had contributed this or that sum to *Pravda*, and the moment any group donated twenty kopecks it was noted in the register. Comrade Lenin especially took an interest in these statistics.

Pravda

In the beginning *Pravda* too was a coalition organ as both Bolsheviks and Plekhanovite Mensheviks took part in it. But it was to share the fate of *Zvezda*. In a very short space of time the Plekhanovites, who had been trying to keep a foot in both camps, were pushed out of *Pravda* by the course of events and the newspaper became the organ of the Bolsheviks of the Leninist tendency.

The Fourth Duma

At this point the elections for the Fourth State Duma were approaching. This time too a debate started among the Bolsheviks on whether to participate in the election campaign. But now this conflict was no longer marked by the animosity that it had during the first clash with the boycottists. The huge majority of Bolsheviks, mindful of the fact that it was necessary for us to utilize legal opportunities, recognized that we had to participate in the Duma. The electoral law was devised in such a way that the workers could have one representative in each of the six most industrial provinces, although the election procedure went like this: the workers had to vote for electors, and the latter in turn voted for the candidates, from whom the landlords and bourgeoisie, with their preponderant majority at the provincial meeting, had then to appoint one as the deputy. Thus for a Bolshevik to be a deputy it had to be arranged for all the candidates at the provincial meeting to be Bolsheviks so that the landlords could not avoid choosing a Bolshevik. This far from easy task confronted Bolshevism, and it succeeded brilliantly. Despite the Mensheviks' far greater legal opportunities, the Bolsheviks won the workers' curias in all the six provinces. The landlords and capitalists had willy-nilly to choose a Bolshevik, and if sometimes they attempted to choose a candidate other than the one we had proposed, so as to get their own back as it were, we had such firm discipline that all the remaining Bolsheviks would stand down and the particular one that the organization wished to send to the Duma got through. That was how Badaev in particular, who was elected from the Alexandrov works where he worked as a fitter, got through to the Stage Duma, in spite of the fact that the Octobrists and Cadets were in the majority at the provincial meeting. In the same way Petrovsky from Ekaterinoslav, Muranov from Kharkov, Samoilov from Ivanovo-Voznesensk, Shagov from Kostroma and Malinovsky from Moscow province reached the Duma.

The provocateur Malinovsky

The last-mentioned was an old activist in the workers' movement and the chairman of the metalworkers' union. For many years he had enjoyed such a wide popularity among the St. Petersburg workers (and elsewhere) that when he arrived in Prague as a delegate of a group of figures in the trade union movement we received him with

open arms. We placed him in a job in one of the factories in the Moscow area, and from the Central Committee elected at Prague issued him the directive to lie low for a whole year until the elections to avoid arrest and be able to enter the State Duma. And that was what happened. As you know Malinovsky subsequently turned out to be a provocateur and our party paid dearly for his exploits. Malinovsky succeeded in infiltrating the Duma faction, our party's Central Committee, and also the editorial board of *Pravda* and the Moscow newspaper *Rabochii Put*, on whose production he put in more work than anyone else. Nevertheless in retrospect we can see clearly that by force of the situation that had been created, this dirty game by the Security Department hardly turned out to their great advantage. Malinovsky of course caused us a great deal of harm, as with his assistance the Okhrana was able to arrest over a hundred of our best people; but despite this we can still say that the calculations of the Okhrana proved to be built upon sand. For in point of fact Malinovsky was forced by the circumstances to deliver revolutionary speeches, as like the other deputies he frequently read prepared texts which had been written abroad. Malinovsky was the chairman of our Duma six, and was compelled to assist us in our work so as not to lose credibility.

Malinovsky himself, when looked at as an individual, emerges as a man of a somewhat unusual, unstable, but talented character. He came from a Polish noble family, landed in proletarian circles and, having committed a criminal offence in his youth for which he was outlawed, soon fell into the web of the Okhrana. After he had handed in his deputy's credentials, sensing that he would soon be unmasked, he went in 1914 to the war and found himself in captivity where, as can be proven by dozens of letters received from prisoners of war, he conducted Bolshevik agitation. He could hardly have any reason for playing his double game in captivity. After October when we at last held power, he himself returned to Russia, gave himself up to us and was arrested and transported to Moscow where a tribunal sentenced him to be shot; and shot he was.

The Fourth Duma in session
Peasant Deputies to the Duma

The split of the Duma faction

In the same Duma alongside our six there sat the Menshevik seven, who were deputies coming chiefly from the petty-bourgeois population of the Caucasus and led by the notorious Chkheidze. The latter was in the Third and Fourth Dumas where he was to win popularity and acquire a certain importance, playing a fairly major role at the start of the February Revolution. When we split the Duma faction with the support of *Pravda*, the Mensheviks frantically agitated among workers in St. Petersburg and throughout Russia around the slogan of unity, which they had set against us on various occasions, thereby consciously capitalizing on the working masses' quite natural inclination towards unity. The latter sometimes presented the simple argument: the more of us the better. It was only with difficulty, and by learning the lessons that history taught, that the working masses digested the fact that there are situations when to split is the sacred obligation of a revolutionary, and when it is necessary to split an old organization which has become counter-revolutionary and hangs like a ball and chain on the feet of the working class. So it was with the single party in 1908-1910. So it was in 1912 when the Prague conference placed a split upon the agenda. In 1912 and the beginning of 1913 this split was carried through in the legal sphere between *Pravda* and *Luch* and between our Duma six and the Menshevik seven headed by Chkheidze.

N.S. Chkheidze

The 'August Bloc'

As a counterweight to the conference in Prague, the Mensheviks, meeting at Vienna in August 1912 at an all-Russian conference, formed the so-called 'August Bloc'. In this conference there took part liquidator Mensheviks, Mensheviks who supported Martov, and Comrade Trotsky's group, which was greatly to assist the creation of this bloc. At that time Comrade Trotsky led an energetic campaign against our St. Petersburg *Pravda* and the split in the Duma faction, considering it essential to preserve unity at any price. The August Bloc, which had united several groups, closed ranks against us, declared the conference at Prague a usurper, condemned the split which had started in St. Petersburg in the Duma faction, and once and for all formulated its own liquidationist political platform.

The controversy over partial demands

During the year a particularly sharp controversy took place over the question of partial demands. The Bolsheviks, at their conference at Prague and in their newspapers *Zvezda* and *Pravda* and their Duma faction, defended the 'three planks' as we then said, that is, three demands: the democratic republic, the eight-hour working day and the confiscation of landed estates. For their part the Mensheviks and their August Bloc formulated their own programme which departed radically from ours. They demanded the freedoms of speech, withdrawal of labour, assembly and association. In other words, instead of the Bolsheviks' revolutionary programme they proposed a programme for reforms, and instead of solutions to the basic questions, partial demands. The Bolsheviks said that they did not object to partial demands and that they were prepared to fight for any little improvement in the condition of the working class, but they maintained that any partial demands had to be put before the masses only in the context of the 'three planks'. Put briefly, our main demand was the overthrow of autocracy while the Mensheviks wanted to knit themselves into a constitutional monarchy and adapt the party to Stolypin's regime. Thus two sharply divergent platforms came into existence: one from Prague and the other from Vienna, i.e. from the August Bloc.

The question of the democratic republic

Let us say a few words in passing about the 'democratic republic'. The Bolsheviks had put forward this demand more than once. But looking back we have to admit that we did have some lack of agreement and confusion over this question in 1915-1917. Beginning with 1905 we considered that Russia was moving towards a dictatorship of the proletariat and peasantry and we therefore posed the question in this way: if our revolution was to be victorious and finally clean out the Augean stables of the Tsarist autocracy, and if it was to take place in an era of incipient revolution in the west it would not only be a democratic one but would become the start of the socialist revolution. In the theses published by the editorial board of *Sotsial-Demokrat* in 1916 (written by Comrade Lenin) when a wave of revolution was already forming, we were still however talking about a democratic revolution. And it was only when we had noted the profound changes that the imperialist war had brought about both here in Russia and throughout the world, that we finally formulated our platform of the *socialist* proletarian revolution.

Lenin's *Collected Works*, Vol. 21, pp. 401-404.

The evolution of Bolshevism

This evolution in our views over the years from 1905 to 1917 cannot be denied, any more than the fact that it proceeded with definite inconsistencies which were to produce amongst us very dangerous differences on the eve of October 1917.* Some of us (including myself) for too long upheld the idea that in our peasant country we could not pass straight on to the socialist revolution, but merely hope that if our revolution coincided with the start of the international proletarian one it could become its overture. But the terrible war of 1914 at one stroke advanced mankind many decades towards the victory of socialism. To be sure this war claimed countless victims, but it cut capitalism to the quick, upset the capitalist equilibrium, brought forward the world proletarian revolution and in Russia provided our party with the opportunity of posing it as a concrete question. Given such a train of events the evolution that we have noted in Bolshevism was unavoidable for us.

What then separated us from the August Bloc? Something very simple: we stood for a revolutionary programme while our opponents stood for a programme of reforms and a compromise with the constitutional monarchy, for they did not believe in revolution which they

* 'Dangerous differences'— Zinoviev hides the real depth of the differences which occurred within the Bolshevik Party throughout 1917, particularly on the very eve of the insurrection. Of course Zinoviev was right at the centre of these controversies, actually leaking the plans for the insurrection to the non-Party Press (see introduction). For the significance of these events see Trotsky's *Lessons of October* (New Park Publications, 1971) and *History of the Russian Revolution* Vol. 3, Ch. 5.

considered an impossibility. We differed from them not because we disputed with them the character of the future revolution, but because they simply did not want any revolution and did not anticipate one, but adapted to the constitutional monarchy of the time. Bolshevism thought otherwise. By carefully examining the path traversed by the working class during the period of the imperialist war, we gradually moved away from the formula of the 'democratic dictatorship of the proletariat and peasantry'* and drew closer to another: 'dictatorship of the proletariat leading the peasantry behind it'; we abandoned the formula of a 'systematic democratic revolution' in favour of the formula 'Soviet power and the proletarian revolution'; not the formula of the 'Constituent Assembly' which we were defending as late as the summer of 1917, but the formula of 'Soviet power'.

Thus by the end of 1912 following the appearance of the August Bloc, two distinct forces stood face to face, both of which had overcome the hard times they had undergone. The now recovered Bolsheviks created a new party, while the liquidator Mensheviks, conciliators and the supporters of unity gathered under the banner of partial demands striving to create a legal party under the constitutional monarchy.

What was happening at this time in the depths of the working class? With each month everything seethed more intensely within it. The movement was characterized by strikes. Many of you took part in them and will probably recall that in 1912 and 1913, St. Petersburg, Moscow and all working-class centres literally shook with incessant strikes. These later flared up anywhere and everywhere and it could be sensed that a new life was flowing through the workers' veins and they were beginning to flex their muscles again. Workers now took advantage of every pretext to turn any economic strike into a political one. The Mensheviks were at once up in arms against this strike movement, having sensed in it an enemy. Both their newspaper *Luch*, Chkheidze's faction, and their whole bloc recoiled in horror from it.

Still in everyone's memory are their newspaper articles that declared that St. Petersburg workers were seized by 'a

---

* **'Gradually** moved from the formula of the "democratic dictatorship of the proletariat and peasantry".' There was of course nothing 'gradual' about the transition at all. Lenin had to wage a sharp and ruthless struggle against almost all the Bolshevik 'Old Guard' who wanted to lend critical support to the Provisional government after 1917.

strike mania'. But these articles did not realize the expectations of the Mensheviks: when workers read them they could clearly understand who were their friends and who their enemies.

'*Pravda's*' victory

Pravda gradually wrested one factory after another from the Mensheviks. Workers would send tens and hundreds of dispatches into the newspaper, which had become a sort of general staff of the movement and an organizing centre. Every trade union meeting, the metalworkers' union election which had a great political importance and those of the workers' insurance societies took place under the shadow of *Pravda*, which came forward with its lists of *Pravda* candidates or other consistent Marxists who defended workers' democracy and 'immoderate' demands (as we then called them because of the censorship). The Mensheviks, who were suffering defeats everywhere, in their newspaper explained them by the '*Pravda* epidemic' which was raging through the working class of St. Petersburg and the main cities: the newly beginning revolutionary movement was a book with seven seals for them; they looked upon it as an accidental occurrence, and deliberately plugged their ears with cotton wool so as not to hear the rumble filling working-class districts.

Harsh repressions were launched against *Pravda*. Time and again its publication was suspended, it was fined for every article, its editors, collaborators and staff were arrested so that at one point it was impossible even to find a proof-reader for it. But the heroic workers of St. Petersburg courageously supported *Pravda* which, despite all persecution, grew stronger daily. The more blows that were loosed upon it, the dearer it became to the working masses, who collected money literally kopeck by kopeck to keep it running and to pay off the fines, and tirelessly supplied it with new editors to replace those arrested. All the contrivances of the police, who would stand guard over the printing press to confiscate the first copies, did not achieve their object thanks to the vigilance and energy of the St. Petersburg workers who had created an amazing organization to distribute the newspaper: hardly had the ink dried on the pages than hundreds of working men and women and their children would take the paper around to the factories and plants under their coats. Little by little *Pravda* became the best friend of any working-class family and today we can say quite frankly that an unquestioned place of honour belongs to it in the history of our revolution and Bolshevism.

War and Revolution

In 1913, and even more so at the beginning of 1914, the workers' movement entered a new phase in which it once again passed from strikes to demonstrations and open clashes. It is beyond doubt that the war initially was to retard this movement. As early as the beginning of 1914 the first barricades went up in St. Petersburg, while the strikes surged in such a broad and turbulent wave that from the start no force could halt this freshly maturing movement. Let me repeat, had there been no war we would probably have seen events in 1915 very similar to those of 1905, with the difference however that this time the peasantry was coming forward rather more consciously. But, on the other hand, if the imperialist war had somewhat postponed the revolution, the effects of this war revolutionized Russia and made it possible for us to replace the formula of the 'democratic revolution' with the formula of the 'proletarian revolution'.

The opening of 1914 found our party in the leadership of the working class in the broad sense of the word. The party was at that time illegal. A considerable portion of its Central Committee was abroad. Comrade Lenin and several other comrades moved over to Cracow. From there they could direct *Pravda* and *Zvezda* and dozens of comrades could come there from St. Petersburg to discuss pressing matters. In addition we had our headquarters in St. Petersburg and Moscow which operated both on a legal and an illegal footing. What the numerical strength of the party was by this time it is hard to say. The previous time that we managed to make an enumeration was when the party had been semi-legal—at the London Congress of

1907 when, in all the factions together, Bolsheviks, Mensheviks and the national sections, there were some 150,000 people. In 1914 we could not say exactly how many members we had, but we knew definitely that we had the huge majority of organized workers behind us. In the same year, as I have just said, the workers' movement began to come out on to the streets. The first barricades appeared only just before the declaration of war. The situation had sharpened to such a point that our Duma faction would have been arrested regardless, since our Duma faction led by Petrovsky, Muranov and Badaev was becoming a veritable hot-bed of revolution. Time and again they were seized: Badaev at illegal assemblies at the Putilov works and Petrovsky at illegal miners' meetings in the Donets Basin. All this clearly demonstrated that the workers' movement had made an enormous stride forward. The August Bloc had proven powerless and began to fall apart and fragment, with the result that, as this process developed, its best part gradually came over to us. The liquidator Mensheviks, notwithstanding their popular figures and orators (like Chkheidze in the Duma), remained in an insignificant minority in the working mass.

M.K. Muranov

A.E. Badaev

The War and the Party

This was the position we were in at the beginning of the war. It brought with it the almost complete destruction of the party. Above all, our Duma faction of five deputies was arrested. (The Mensheviks were not touched.) They were seized in one of the villages outside Petrograd at an illegal meeting, along with other comrades. The Manifesto of our Central Committee on the imperialist war, which had been written by Comrade Lenin abroad, was found on the arrested deputies.* It was in this manifesto that we first advanced the slogan of turning the imperialist war into a civil war. Today this slogan is the property of the broadest working masses and appears self-explanatory; but at that time this was far from the case, and in the camp of the Second International we were regarded literally as lepers. When we stated that this war

* See Appendix II.

LECTURE SIX

had to be turned into a civil war, a war against the bourgeoisie, they seriously began to suggest that we were 'not quite right in the head'. We approached Robert Grimm, one of the leftest of lefts in the Second International, with a request that he print short excerpts from our manifesto, but he looked at us with bitter compassion as if we were mentally defective, saying that he could not print documents which resembled political deliria. And when we had the temerity to suggest that the Second International had gone bankrupt and was finished, they openly began to deride us. But this was no joke: the Second International, as you know, then enjoyed enormous prestige and embraced, it was said, approaching 25 million organized workers. 'True, it couldn't manage to stop the war,' lamented the augurs of the day, Second International leaders like Kautsky for example, 'but what can we do? After all the International is a peacetime instrument and not an implement of a war during which class struggle should be suspended'. All these gentlemen then came to an arrangement among themselves for a mutual amnesty: let German Social-Democracy support its own government, they said, French Social-Democracy its own government, and the British their own government, and when the war is over all social-democrats can get together, forgive each other's sins and say: 'nothing can be done: it was a little misunderstanding—a few million workers have been slaughtered but it won't happen again'. So when, after all this, we Bolsheviks, the representatives of one illegal party among the dozens of parties which were in the Second International, threw it in their face that they were traitors, the Second International had suffered a shameful bankruptcy and they were betrayers of the working class, they declared a moral boycott of us and took pains to hush up everything that we wrote. Strange as it may seem, the first people to pay serious attention to our policy statements were bourgeois politicians. One German professor himself published a learned discourse in response to the manifesto we have referred to and our subsequent pamphlet *Socialism and the War*,* in which he said: 'This phenomenon should not be underestimated. You might find consolation in the fact that these people are lunatics

---

* *Socialism and War* was written by Lenin in July-August 1915 and published by the editorial board of *Sotsial-Demokrat* in Geneva in the latter month. (See Vol. 21 *Collected Works*, p. 295).

but it must be born in mind that a new trend has sprung up in socialism and the international workers' movement and we bourgeois must make a mental note of it'. Be that as it may, the Second International subjected us to moral ostracism, censored our statements regarding us as dreamers who had no followers but were obsessed with manifest ravings.

The arrest and trial of Central Committee members in Petrograd

It is sufficient to add that at that time even such people as Liebknecht, who spoke out against the war from the very start, did not however make up their mind to vote against the credits—so great was the pressure of the old social-democratic party discipline and bourgeois public opinion in the form of its hydra-headed press. It is clear, therefore, what sort of reception the manifesto of our Central Committee could expect. Not all of the latter was abroad. Part of it remained in Petrograd,* where it was arrested in connection with this document and put on trial. It should be said that at this trial not all our comrades behaved with sufficient restraint, but a number of our party workers, especially Muranov, Petrovsky and Badaev, did provide a model of what revolutionary parliamentarism consisted. In the court the diary of Petrovsky, who was thoughtless enough to make a record of his day-to-day activity, was read out. This of course should not be done in illegal work, but Petrovsky had counted on his deputy's immunity and thought that he could be permitted this luxury. This incriminating material fell into the hands of the gendarmerie and was read out to the court. But every cloud has a silver lining. Petrovsky's diary showed to workers of all countries, who were very deeply interested in this case, how a workers' deputy ought to work in parliament: it became known that Petrovsky had day in and day out devoted himself to oratorical work in the Duma as well as to illegal work, liaisons, meetings and illegal conferences; that is, as a parliamentary deputy he combined illegal with legal work. In this

* St. Petersburg was renamed Petrograd in 1914.

G.I Petrovsky

LECTURE SIX 185

sense the trial of the Duma faction had without doubt a great importance in exhibiting this model of Bolshevik work.

Bolshevism as a whole, and with a few purely individual exceptions, occupied an internationalist and anti-chauvinist position, i.e. against the war. The Mensheviks, likewise with several exceptions (like Martov who could not decide definitely to say yes or no), stood for the war.* It was their standpoint that the S.R.s shared.

The war was of course the most serious test for the whole party. It was a veritable crucible through which it had to pass. But it withstood the test and carried its internationalist tendency through to the end, proving in deeds its dedication to the working class. It was no accident that the Mensheviks and S.R.s ended up in favour of the war. This was the outcome of a logical chain of development. The Mensheviks had travelled a road from the right wing of Legal Marxism to Economism, liquidationism, defencism and social-chauvinism. Approximately the same was the case with the S.R.s. The Bolsheviks, though, had passed from *Iskra* to Bolshevism, anti-liquidationism, internationalism and communism.

*The Menshevik Duma deputies opposed the first war credit vote in 1914 along with the Bolsheviks but sooner or later went over to varying degrees of support for Russia's part in the war.

A united bourgeois-Menshevik front

Here it is of interest to note how rapidly a united front between the Russian bourgeoisie and the Mensheviks was formed. Two or three extracts will show this graphically. This is for example what Izgoev, a member of the Central Committee of the Cadet party and its former specialist on Marxism, wrote:

> Genuine historical forces have started to take effect and it has turned out that an international social-democracy which counterposes itself to the 'bourgeois world' does not exist. Only *national* workers' parties exist whose leaders style themselves social-democrats. (*Russkaya Mysl*, August-September 1914)

In other words, a prominent Cadet party leader said with the greatest exultation that international social-democracy did not exist, but only national workers' parties each of which marched behind the bourgeoisie of its own country. Petr Ryss, a no less major Cadet figure, expressed himself even more candidly. At that point Rosa Luxemburg and Karl Leibknecht were active in Germany against the war as internationalists. You would think that the Russian bourgeoisie, which was then at war with the German bourgeoisie, would, out of its narrow class interests, to some extent welcome this activity in that it weakened Kaiser Wilhelm. But the contrary proved to be the case. The bourgeoisie was no greenhorn either. It knew that it had fundamental class interests beyond its passing short-term interests. So although it was beneficial that Liebknecht and Luxemburg were weakening Wilhelm, the appearance of Bolshevism and a definite internationalist tendency in a belligerent country like Germany was unfavourable to it from the standpoint of the wider perspectives of the bourgeoisie. Petr Ryss wrote thus:

R. Luxemburg

> From the standpoint of the economic and political interests of Germany, Rosa Luxemburg and the small number of her supporters represent people who have no sense of duty towards their country. And if you look facts in the face and do not take cover behind the hypocritical phrases *you must say that the conduct of German Social-Democracy is as legitimate and reasonable as the conduct of social-democracy in France, Belgium and Great Britain. On the other hand Rosa Luxemburg and Karl Liebknecht are objectively committing a serious error, and display a lack of any conception of time or place.*

These words should be remembered well. The Russian bourgeoisie, while at war with the German bourgeoisie, at the same time stated that Rosa Luxemburg and Karl Liebknecht were bad people for they had betrayed their duty to their 'fatherland'; the Russian bourgeoisie hated the German and could not tolerate Wilhelm, but nonetheless it did not forget that Rosa Luxemburg and Karl Liebknecht, in weakening their adversaries by their political actions, were simultaneously blazing a trail towards internationalism, and were therefore its enemies. Consequently the Russian bourgeoisie at once took the path of supporting social-democracy, or rather, the Mensheviks.

K. Liebknecht

In Kerensky's own words, the S.R.s likewise declared from the very outset that they were for the war. Kerensky delivered a speech in the State Duma where he said literally the following: 'We are unalterably convinced that the great Russian democracy will, in alliance with all other forces in the country, put up stubborn resistance to the enemy which has fallen upon us'. This was a highly significant statement. At that moment Kerensky had, as it were, announced his candidature for the post of a future bourgeois minister.

Industrial War Committees

The Mensheviks dragged Petrograd workers into the so-called Industrial War Committees. These were organized under the aegis of the greatest representative of the Octobrist and merchant-landowner bourgeoisie, Guchkov, who had devised this method of raising production in the factories and thus waging war more effectively. A heated controversy flared up among Petrograd workers: should they participate in this bourgeois scheme or not? Bolshevik workers refused as consistent internationalists to take part in these committees, which represented but local branches of the Tsarist government, and existed to help it conduct the war. The Mensheviks, led by the notorious Kuzma Gvozdev, who subsequently became a minister in the coalition government, entered the Industrial War Committees. With the exception of some individuals like Chernov and Natanson who attempted to a certain degree to fight against Kerensky's view, no one among the S.R.s openly objected to this chauvinism.

Plekhanov came to the fore as the principal instigator of Russian chauvinism. This was especially unfortunate as he enjoyed tremendous prestige in the Second International, and in spite of all his waverings, no less an influence in our party either. Plekhanov showed himself to be a fanatical Germanophobe and steadfast social-chauvinist to the end. He argued to the point of saying that the war was a just one on the part of the Tsar. He declared: I am an old revolutionary: as you know, I have been at war with Tsarism for twenty years and I have suffered more than a little for this. So now let me say this to you, that the war which Russia is waging today is a just war and we must always stop any war against the Russian government. The Mensheviks' chauvinism reached a point where, for example, Yordansky, who was the editor of *Sovremenny Mir* (he was then an intractable chauvinist though now he has crossed over to our side) printed a gleeful article by Kleinbort who wrote:

> With a mere wave of the hand the conflagration in Petrograd has abated and the strikes in Moscow and the Baku area have ended: the workers, fully conscious of the historic gravity of the moment, have emphasized that this is no time to exacerbate internal conflict.

In these words was a direct betrayal of the working class, for it was being called upon to cease any struggle whatsoever, even an economic one, against the capitalists.

At the International Bureau of the Second International in Brussels on the eve of the war, a conference convened by its chairman Vandervelde was held with the object of reconciling all the tendencies in the Russian party, which then amounted to seven. At this conference the overwhelming majority carried a motion opposing us, and asserted that the Bolsheviks were to blame for everything and so on. At that time we had still not officially left the Second International and were forced to take account of its resolutions to some extent. But we did so only formally, in practice taking our own line. When the war broke out nearly all the seven tendencies assembled by Vandervelde in Brussels proved, with the exception of the Bolsheviks, to be social-chauvinists. There was then no party in the sense of a complete organization. Only the Bolsheviks upheld the party's banner and took on themselves all the blows of Tsarism. Tsarism punished the slightest manifestation of internationalism with hard labour and the last centres of the legal Bolshevik movement were stamped out.

The Zimmerwald conference

In the first years of the war it seemed that we were condemned to isolation. The section of Central Committee members which was abroad began to work on uniting internationalists on an international scale. We took part in the Zimmerwald conference where we constituted a weak minority and organized the Zimmerwald Left, which in fact served as the first nucleus of the future Third International. Then only a small number of German comrades, and a few Swedes and Latvians joined us. All the rest who were at Zimmerwald still came out against such a union. At Zimmerwald the majority declared themselves against the imperialist war, but also against a civil war. They were pacifists and well-meaning social-democrats, who did not want to betray the working class openly but at the same time did not believe either in proletarian revolution or in civil war, but wished to confine themselves to voting against war credits and similar such gestures. At their head stood Ledebour. A heated encounter occurred at Zimmerwald between him and Comrade Lenin. Ledebour said: it is easy for him (Lenin) sitting in exile abroad to preach civil war, but just let him go to Russia and show us who will support him. In the Second International it was said that we were just cranks who represented nobody in Russia, and that all Russian workers were for the war, which Kuzma Gvozdev, Chkheidze and Kerensky could confirm. In actual fact, though, a considerable part of the Second International reasoned to themselves in private as follows: the Bolsheviks may in fact be right but they are merely lone figures — there are no masses of workers behind them and nobody supports them.

Comrade Lenin in Switzerland

We proved to be in the minority at Zimmerwald. Yet out of the tiny crumbs collected among German workers and our organizations abroad, literally penny by penny, the first cell of the Zimmerwald Left was established which began to publish the journal *Vorbote* in German, which was to contain a series of excellent articles by Lenin, Roland-Holst, Radek and others.

We began in this journal to gather forces on an international scale. At that time we had to work in Switzerland, which had not been drawn into the orbit of the war. This little country, with its numerically small working class, could not have had any serious specific weight in the international proletarian revolution. The Swiss Social-Democratic Party was predominantly middle-class, so that when Comrade Lenin had perforce to collect small groups of young workers around him in Zurich in order to educate them in opposition to the war, the question arose in that party of expelling Comrade Lenin for engaging in criminal anti-war propaganda among the youth. During 1915 and 1916 we were an insignificant minority, which was attempting to establish these first international links and yet not lag behind events in Russia.

Commencing with the first half of 1916 our contacts with Russia grew firmer. We started to receive correspondence from workers and we gradually appreciated that workers were definitely swinging against the war. Our newspaper *Sotsial-Demokrat*, which we were then publishing and whose articles were reprinted in the anthology *Against the Current,* was, despite all obstacles, reaching Russia in small numbers of copies where it was absorbed with such interest that it was copied out by hand. This paper played an enormous part, notwithstanding the fact that it bore the now outdated name of *Sotsial-Demokrat*. This name seems these days a shameful term of contempt but, of course, our party was only renamed in 1918.

Lenin's articles for Sotsial Demokrat are contained in his Collected Works Vols. 21-23.

The paths of Bolshevism and Menshevism

Bolshevism was to prove during the imperialist war that it had not been at work for twenty-five years for nothing. Having laid a firm foundation of internationalist tactics, it convinced the workers that, right from Legal Marxism up until the ultra-illegal period of the imperialist war, it had remained true to its ideas. This, of course, was not accomplished without some errors, but nevertheless the line which it followed was the straight line of revolutionary communist tactics. The Mensheviks likewise followed their own straight line; but this passed from Legal Marxism to Economism, and then to liquidationism and social-chauvinism; this was the line of succession of petty-bourgeois reformism. The imperialist war, which proved a great crisis for all mankind as a whole and for the workers' movement in particular, sharply and conclusively brought out the true physiognomy of each of its tendencies. Three tendencies took shape in the camp of international socialism: on the one hand, social-chauvinism, on the other, internationalism, or communism, while the third tendency headed by Kautsky was called the 'Centre' tendency, a middle course which Martov supported for a long time and which the Independent German Social-Democratic Party was to maintain.

The 'Centre' tendency

We considered this middle tendency to be the most dangerous and so we concentrated all our efforts on the struggle against it. This was understandable. The blatant chauvinists, like Plekhanov for example, declared that the Tsar was waging a 'just' war and openly exposed themselves. Such a tactic did not greatly harm us because workers in the end saw through it and sooner or later turned away from its instigators. Much more dangerous was the 'Centre' tendency, which had on its side all those influential representatives of the Second International who were to come out frantically against a split. That is why when German Social-Democracy split, the Bolshevik Central Committee regarded this event as highly important since the former now appreciated that the idea of unity which had weighed upon the German working class had rendered impotent all those groups which had wished to stand up against the war.

Consequently, starting from the plenum of 1910, we were no longer dealing with the Mensheviks from within a united organization. We survived the whole of the 1914-1917 war as a separate party. The Mensheviks by and large supported the world-wide slaughter, approved of the activity of the Industrial War Committees, and formed a bloc with the Cadet bourgeoisie. Meanwhile the Bolsheviks pursued a line which had a dual character. On the one hand those of them who had been scattered abroad were gathering there the nucleus of the future representatives of the Zimmerwald Left and the future supporters of the Communist International, while those who were living in Russia were waging a war against the Industrial War Committees and the chauvinists and bringing together and uniting workers for the struggle for the proletarian revolution.

The prevalence of social-chauvinism

Chauvinism did not pass by Russian workers either. This is evident if only from the fact that in the first half of the February revolution the huge majority of workers of even such cities as Petrograd were on the side of the Mensheviks and S.R.s. When we look back we can be quite convinced what a powerful tool the war was in the hands of our opponents when, with the aid of the spurious slogan of 'the fatherland in danger' and resorting to such an incomparable instrument as the Second International, the bourgeoisie was able to infect the young Russian working class, then full of militant revolutionary ardour, with chauvinism. The Petrograd workers, who had built barricades against Tsarism two or three weeks before the war, stood behind the Mensheviks and the S.R.s for several months from the beginning of the February revolution, that is, behind social-chauvinists. That is why the harsh lessons of the imperialist war were so invaluable for the working class and that is why the contribution of the Bolshevik party during that war was so great, since, although representing a minority in the working class, it nevertheless did not roll up its banner but swam against the current, and so could bring the workers to their glorious victory in October.

The February revolution and our party's role in it —even more so the October revolution and our party's role in that—would require several dozen further lectures to provide any sort of detailed account. I cannot do this. I am taking my account, a very schematic and incomplete one at that, as far as February. I have said hardly anything about the economy of Russia during the epoch I have described. This is, of course, a huge omission. I have restricted myself to the history of the party in the narrowest sense of the word, and have not even given a detailed history of the revolution. My task has been only to assist you to *approach* the study of the party's history. The remainder you must do yourself.

The February revolution found our Central Committee in part abroad and in part in jail and exile. The party appeared not to exist, it was dispersed and broken. But,

LECTURE SIX

despite all this, the work undertaken over twenty-five years made itself felt. Our party was a genuinely revolutionary one and consequently it was at work not only when it existed as a hierarchical, closely-knit organization, but also when at first sight it did not exist at all and had gone completely underground. Such is the dialectic of the revolutionary process, and just such was our party. How many times during the long years of Tsarism did it seem that it was totally smashed, and amounted only to individual units, yet, as a result of the work it had undertaken, vital for the creation of the great all-Russian party of the working class, all those elements accumulated in the consciousness of the working masses. Thus our party arose like a Phoenix from the ashes. It did not play a decisive role in the February revolution, and could not, for the working class at that time leaned towards defencism; but a few months later, it was to realize the capital that it had invested in the workers' movement over 20 to 30 years, and guided by the beacon-like idea of the hegemony of the proletariat it liberated the working class from its captivity by the Mensheviks and S.R.s and led it to complete victory over the bourgeoisie.*

---

* When Zinoviev here says that the working class leaned towards defencism he again covers up the real nature of the inner Party struggle, Lenin's *April Theses* and his own role in these events.

First World War and the February Revolution 1917:
Disaster at Tannenburg
A Food Queue

Russian soldiers in retreat

Deserters from the Russian Army

The war-widows of Moscow protest

A meeting of one of the Soldiers' Committees

Fraternization at the front

The workers take up arms

News of the Revolution reaches the Front

APPENDICES

APPENDIX I

Manifesto of the Russian Social-Democratic Labour Party (1898)

Fifty years ago the life-giving storm of the 1848 revolution swept over Europe. For the first time the modern working class came on to the stage as a major historical force. By its efforts, the bourgeoisie succeeded in sweeping away many feudal-monarchic institutions and laws. However, it quickly saw in its new ally its most avowed enemy and betrayed itself, the latter and the cause of freedom into the hands of reaction. But it was already too late: the working class which was for a while pacified, ten to fifteen years later re-appeared on the historical scene, but with redoubled force and an adult self-consciousness, as a wholly mature fighter for its own final liberation.

All this while, Russia seemingly remained aside from the high road of historical development. There the struggle of classes was not apparent, yet it existed and what is more, matured and grew. The Russian government itself sowed the seeds of the class struggle with laudable zeal by dispossessing the peasants, patronizing the landowners, rearing and fattening the big capitalists at the expense of the labouring population. But a bourgeois-capitalist system is inconceivable without a proletariat or a working class. The latter is born along with capitalism, grows up with it, and becomes stronger, thereby increasingly coming into struggle with the bourgeoisie.

The Russian factory worker, whether free or a serf, has always waged both a hidden and an open struggle against his exploiters. As capitalism developed, this struggle took on greater dimensions and embraced wider and wider layers of the working population. The awakening of the class consciousness of the Russian proletariat and the growth of the spontaneous workers' movement coincided with the conclusive development of international social-democracy as the vehicle of the class struggle and the class ideal of conscious workers throughout the world. All the most recent Russian workers' organizations have undertaken their activity consciously or unconsciously in the spirit of social-democratic ideas. The strength and significance of the workers' movement and the social-democracy it supported has been most clearly displayed by the whole series of strikes in Russia and Poland in the past period, and especially the celebrated strikes of St. Petersburg textile workers in 1896 and 1897. These strikes compelled the government to promulgate the law of 2nd June 1897 on the length of working hours. However great its shortcomings, this law will forever remain memorable proof of the enormous pressure that the united efforts of workers can exert upon the legislative and other activity of the government. But in vain does the government suppose that it can pacify the workers with concessions. Everywhere, the more the working class is given, the more demanding it becomes. Likewise with the Russian proletariat. Until now it has been given only what it has demanded, and in the future it will be given only what it demands.

But what is it that the Russian working class needs before everything else? It is all of those things that its foreign comrades can freely and peacefully enjoy: participation in government, freedom of the spoken and written word, freedom of association and assembly; in short all those tools and means by which the western European and American proletariat improves its position, and at the same time fights for its own final liberation from private property and capitalism and for socialism. The Russian proletariat needs political liberty as healthy lungs need fresh air. It is a basic condition of its free development and successful struggle for partial improvements and final liberation.

But the Russian proletariat can only win the political liberty it needs by itself alone.

The further to the east of Europe (and Russia, as we know, is the east of Europe) the weaker, more cowardly and baser in its political attitude is the bourgeoisie, and the greater the cultural and political tasks that fall to the proletariat. The Russian working class must and will take upon its strong shoulders the task of winning political freedom. This is a vital, but merely an initial step towards realizing the great historical mission of the proletariat: namely the creation of a social system in which there will be no place for the exploitation of man by man. The Russian proletariat will cast off the yoke of autocracy in order to pursue more energetically the struggle against capitalism and the bourgeoisie until the total victory of socialism.

The first steps of the Russian workers' movement and Russian social-democracy could not escape being unco-ordinated, to a certain extent haphazard, and without unity or plan. Now the time has come to unite the local groups, circles and organizations of Russian social-democracy into a single 'Russian Social-Democratic Labour Party'. With this end in view, representatives of the 'Leagues of Struggle for the Liberation of the Working Class', the group publishing *Rabochaya Gazeta* and the 'General Jewish Workers' League in Russia and Poland' have organized the congress whose decisions are printed below.

The local groups which have united into the party are conscious of the great importance of this step and the whole meaning of the responsibility which flows from it. They have thereby finally consolidated the transition of the Russian revolutionary movement into the new epoch of conscious class struggle. As a movement and as a socialist tendency, the Russian Social-Democratic Labour Party carries forward the cause and traditions of the whole of the preceding revolutionary movement in Russia; by posing the conquest of political liberty as the principal of the party's immediate tasks, social-democracy is aiming at the same object which was clearly marked out by the ever-glorious figures of the old Narodnaya Volya. The means and paths which social-democracy selects are, however, different. Its choice is determined by the fact that it consciously wishes to be and remain the class movement of organized working masses. It is firmly convinced that 'the liberation of the working class is a matter for itself' and will unswervingly fit all its actions to conform with this basic principle of international social-democracy.

Long live Russian and long live international social-democracy!

APPENDIX II

The War and Russian Social-Democracy (1914)

The European war, which the governments and the bourgeois parties of all countries have been preparing for decades, has broken out. The growth of armaments, the extreme intensification of the struggle for markets in the latest—the imperialist—stage of capitalist development in the advanced countries, and the dynastic interests of the more backward East-European monarchies, were inevitably bound to bring about this war, and have done so. Seizure of territory and subjugation of other nations, the ruining of competing nations and the plunder of their wealth, distracting the attention of the working masses from the internal political crises in Russia, Germany, Britain and other countries, disunity and nationalist stultification of the workers, and the extermination of their vanguard so as to weaken the revolutionary movement of the proletariat—these comprise the sole actual content, importance and significance of the present war.

It is primarily on social-democracy that the duty rests of revealing the true meaning of the war, and of ruthlessly exposing the falsehood, sophistry and 'patriotic' phrase-mongering spread by the ruling classes, the landowners and the bourgeoisie, in defence of the war.

One group of belligerent nations is headed by the German bourgeoisie. It is hoodwinking the working class and the toiling masses by asserting that this is a war in defence of the fatherland, freedom and civilization, for the liberation of the peoples oppressed by Tsarism, and for the destruction of reactionary Tsarism. In actual fact, however, this bourgeoisie, which servilely grovels to the Prussian Junkers, headed by Wilhelm II, has always been a most faithful ally of Tsarism, and an enemy of the revolutionary movement of Russia's workers and peasants. In fact, whatever the outcome of the war, this bourgeoisie will, together with the Junkers, exert every effort to support the Tsarist monarchy against a revolution in Russia.

In fact, the German bourgeoisie has launched a robber campaign against Serbia, with the object of subjugating her and throttling the national revolution of the Southern Slavs, at the same time sending the bulk of its military forces against the freer countries, Belgium and France, so as to plunder richer competitors. In fact, the German bourgeoisie, which has been spreading the fable that it is waging a war of defence, chose the moment it thought most favourable for war, making use of its latest improvements in military technique and forestalling the rearmament already planned and decided upon by Russia and France.

The other group of belligerent nations is headed by the British and the French bourgeoisie, who are hoodwinking the working class and the toiling masses by asserting that they are waging a war for the defence of their countries, for freedom and civilization and against German militarism and despotism. In actual fact, this bourgeoisie has long been spending thousands of millions to hire the troops of Russian Tsarism, the most reactionary and barbarous monarchy in Europe, and prepare them for an attack on Germany.

In fact, the struggle of the British and the French bourgeoisie is aimed at the seizure of the German colonies, and the ruining of a rival nation whose economic development has been more rapid. In pursuit of this noble aim, the 'advanced' 'democratic' nations are helping the savage Tsarist regime to still more throttle Poland, the Ukraine, etc., and more thoroughly crush the revolution in Russia.

Neither group of belligerents is inferior to the other in despoliation, atrocities and the boundless brutality of war; however, to hoodwink the proletariat and distract its attention from the only genuine war of liberation, namely, a civil war against the bourgeoisie both of its 'own' and of 'foreign' countries—to achieve so lofty an aim—the bourgeoisie of each country is trying, with the help of false phrases about patriotism, to extol the significance of its 'own' national war, asserting that it is out to defeat the enemy, not for plunder and the seizure of territory, but for the 'liberation' of all other peoples except its own.

But the harder the governments and the bourgeoisie of all countries try to disunite the workers and pit them against one another, and the more savagely they enforce, for this lofty aim, martial law and the military censorship (measures which even now, in wartime, are applied against the 'internal' foe more harshly than against the external), the more pressingly is it the duty of the class-conscious proletariat to defend its class solidarity, its internationalism, and its socialist convictions against the unbridled chauvinism of the 'patriotic' bourgeois cliques in all countries. If class-conscious workers were to give up this aim, this would mean renunciation of their aspirations for freedom and democracy, to say nothing of their socialist aspirations.

It is with a feeling of the most bitter disappointment that we have to record that the socialist parties of the leading European countries have failed to discharge this duty, the behaviour of these parties' leaders, particularly in Germany, bordering on downright betrayal of the cause of socialism. At this time of supreme and historic importance, most of the leaders of the present Socialist International, the Second (1889-1914), are trying to substitute nationalism for socialism. As a result of their behaviour, the workers' parties of these countries did not oppose the governments' criminal conduct, but called upon the working class to *identify* its position with that of the imperialist governments. The leaders of the International committed an act of treachery against socialism by voting for war credits, by reiterating the chauvinist ('patriotic') slogans of the bourgeoisie of their 'own' countries, by justifying and defending the war, by joining the bourgeois governments of the belligerent countries, and so on and so forth. The most influential socialist leaders and the most influential organs of the socialist press of present-day Europe hold views that are chauvinist, bourgeois and liberal, and in no way socialist. The responsibility for thus disgracing socialism falls primarily on the German Social-Democrats, who were the strongest and most influential party in the Second International. But neither can one justify the French socialists, who have accepted ministerial posts in the government of that very bourgeoisie which betrayed its country and allied itself with Bismarck so as to crush the Commune.

The German and the Austrian Social-Democrats are attempting to justify their support for the war by arguing that they are thereby fighting against Russian Tsarism. We Russian Social-Democrats declare that we consider such justification sheer sophistry. In our country the revolutionary movement against Tsarism has again assumed tremendous proportions during the past few years. This movement has always been headed by the working class of Russia. The political strikes of the last few years, which have involved millions of workers, have had as their slogan the overthrow of Tsarism and the establishment of a democratic republic. During his visit to Nicholas II on the very eve of the war, Poincaré, President of the French Republic, could see for himself, in the streets of St. Petersburg, barricades put up by Russian workers. The Russian proletariat has not flinched from any sacrifice to rid humanity of the disgrace of the Tsarist monarchy. We must, however, say that if there is anything that, under certain conditions, can delay the downfall of Tsarism, anything that can help Tsarism in its struggle against the whole of Russia's democracy, then that is the present war, which has placed the purses of the British, the French and the Russian bourgeois at the disposal of Tsarism, to further the latter's reactionary aims. If there is anything that can hinder the revolutionary struggle of the Russia's working class against Tsarism, then that is the behaviour of the German and the Austrian Social-Democratic leaders, which the chauvinist press of Russia is continually holding up to us as an example.

Even assuming that German Social-Democracy was so weak that it was compelled to refrain from all revolutionary action, it should not have joined the chauvinist camp, or taken steps which gave the Italian socialists reason to say that the German Social-Democratic leaders were dishonouring the banner of the proletarian International.

Our Party, the Russian Social-Democratic Labour Party, has made, and will continue to make great sacrifices in connection with the war. The whole of our working-class legal press has been suppressed. Most working class associations have been disbanded, and a large number of our comrades have been arrested and exiled. Yet our parliamentary representatives—the Russian Social-Democratic Labour group in the Duma —considered it their imperative socialist duty not to vote for the war credits, and even to walk out of the Duma, so as to express their protest the more energetically; they considered it their duty to brand the European governments' policy as imperialist. Though the Tsar's government has increased its tyranny tenfold, the Social-Democratic workers of Russia are already publishing their first illegal manifestos against the war, thus doing their duty to democracy and to the International.

While the collapse of the Second International has given rise to a sense of burning shame in revolutionary social-democrats—as represented by the minority of German Social-Democrats and the finest social-democrats in the neutral countries; while socialists in both Britain and France have been speaking up against the chauvinism of most social-democratic parties; while the opportunists, as represented for instance by the German *Sozialistische Monatshefte*, which have long held a national-liberal stand, are with good reason celebrating their victory over European socialism—the worst possible service is being rendered to the proletariat by those who vacillate between opportunism and revolutionary social-democracy (like the 'Centre' in the German Social-Democratic Party), by those who are trying to hush up the collapse of the Second International or to disguise it with diplomatic phrases.

On the contrary, this collapse must be frankly recognized and its causes understood, so as to make it possible to build up a new and more lasting socialist unity of the workers of all countries.

The opportunists have wrecked the decisions of the Stuttgart, Copenhagen and Basle congresses, which made it binding on socialists of all countries to combat chauvinism in all and any conditions, made it binding on socialists to reply to any war begun by the bourgeoisie and governments with intensified propaganda of civil war and social revolution. The collapse of the Second International is the collapse of opportunism, which developed from the features of a now bygone (and so-called 'peaceful') period of history, and in recent years has come practically to dominate the International. The opportunists have long been preparing the ground for this collapse by denying the socialist revolution and substituting bourgeois reformism in its place; by rejecting the class struggle with its inevitable conversion at certain moments into civil war, and by preaching class collaboration; by preaching bourgeois chauvinism under the guise of patriotism and the defence of the fatherland, and ignoring or rejecting the fundamental truth of socialism, long ago set forth in the *Communist Manifesto*, that the workingmen have no country; by confining themselves, in the struggle against militarism, to a sentimental, philistine point of view, instead of recognizing the need for a revolutionary war by the proletarians of all countries against the bourgeoisie of all countries; by making a fetish of the necessary utilization of bourgeois parliamentarianism and bourgeois legality, and forgetting that illegal forms of organization and propaganda are imperative at times of crises. The natural 'appendage' to opportunism—one that is just as bourgeois and hostile to the proletarian, i.e. the Marxist, point of view—namely, the anarcho-syndicalist trend, has been marked by a no less shamefully smug reiteration of the slogans of chauvinism during the present crisis.

The aims of socialism at the present time cannot be fulfilled, and real international unity of the workers cannot be achieved, without a decisive break with opportunism, and without explaining its inevitable failure to the masses.

It must be the primary task of social-democrats in every country to combat that country's chauvinism. In Russia this chauvinism has overcome the bourgeois liberals (the 'Constitutional-Democrats'), and part of the Narodniks—down to the Socialist-Revolutionaries and the 'Right' social-democrats. (In particular, the chauvinist utterances of E. Smirnov, P. Maslov and G. Plekhanov, for example, should be branded; they have been taken up and widely used by the bourgeois 'patriotic' press.)

In the present situation, it is impossible to determine, from the standpoint of the international proletariat, whose defeat, of the two groups of belligerent nations, would be the lesser evil for socialism. But to us Russian Social-Democrats there cannot be the slightest doubt that, from the standpoint of the working class and of the toiling masses of all the nations of Russia, the defeat of the Tsarist monarchy, the most reactionary and barbarous of governments, which is oppressing the largest number of nations and the greatest mass of the population of Europe and Asia, would be the lesser evil.

The formation of a republican United States of Europe should be the immediate political slogan of Europe's social-democrats. In contrast with the bourgeoisie, which is ready to 'promise' anything in order to draw the proletariat into the mainstream of chauvinism, the social-democrats will explain that this slogan is absolutely false and meaningless without the revolutionary overthrow of the German, the Austrian and the Russian monarchies.

Since Russia is most backward and has not yet completed its bourgeois revolution, it still remains the task of social-democrats in that country to achieve the three fundamental conditions for consistent democratic reform, viz., a democratic republic (with complete equality and self-determination for all nations), confiscation of the landed estates, and an eight-hour working day. But in all the advanced countries the war has placed on the order of the day the slogan of socialist revolution, a slogan that is the more urgent, the more heavily the burden of war presses upon the shoulders of the proletariat, and the more active its future role must become in the re-creation of Europe, after the horrors of the present 'patriotic' barbarism in conditions of the tremendous technological progress of large-scale capitalism. The bourgeoisie's use of wartime laws to gag the proletariat makes it imperative for the latter to create illegal forms of agitation and organization. Let the opportunists 'preserve' the legal organizations at the price of treachery to their convictions — revolutionary social-democrats will utilize the organizational experience and links of the working class so as to create illegal forms of struggle for socialism, forms appropriate to a period of crisis, and to unite the workers, not with the chauvinist bourgeoisie of their respective countries, but with the workers of all countries. The proletarian International has not gone under and will not go under. Notwithstanding all obstacles, the masses of the workers will create a new International. Opportunism's present triumph will be short-lived. The greater the sacrifices imposed by the war the clearer will it become to the mass of the workers that the opportunists have betrayed the workers' cause and that the weapons must be turned against the government and the bourgeoisie of each country.

The conversion of the present imperialist war into a civil war is the only correct proletarian slogan, one that follows from the experience of the Commune and is outlined in the Basle resolution (1912); it has been dictated by all the conditions of an imperialist war between highly developed bourgeois countries. However difficult that transformation may seem at any given moment, socialists will never relinquish systematic, persistent and undeviating preparatory work in this direction now that war has become a fact.

It is only along this path that the proletariat will be able to shake off its dependence on the chauvinist bourgeoisie, and, in one form or another and more or less rapidly, take decisive steps towards genuine freedom for the nations and towards socialism.

Long live the international fraternity of the workers against the chauvinism and patriotism of the bourgeoisie of all countries!

Long live a proletarian International, freed from opportunism!

Central Committee
of the Russian Social-Democratic Labour
Party

APPENDIX III

To the Workers of the USSR (1923)
On the 25th anniversary of the Russian Communist Party (Bolsheviks)

Workers of the World, Unite!

The proletarian party in Russia has existed for a quarter of a century. But our party could quite justly reckon its existence from 1895, the year of the formation of the St. Petersburg League of Struggle for the Liberation of the Working Class which was founded by V.I. Lenin, or even from 1883, the year of the formation of the 'Emancipation of Labour' group, or again from 1878, the year of the formation of the North Russian Workers' League (by Stepan Khalturin), or from 1877, the year of the formation of the South Russian Workers' League (by Zaslavsky). The working class of Russia and its communist party are the sole legitimate heirs to the best that there was in the heroic era of Zemlya i Volya and Narodnaya Volya. The names of Stepan Khalturin, Petr Alexeev, Andrei Zhelyabov, Sofiya Perovskaya, and Alexandr Ulyanov on the one hand, and Ivan Babushkin, Shelgunov, Nikolai Bauman, Jakov Sverdlov, Dubrovinsky (Innokenti), Schanzer, Uritsky and Volodarksy on the other, are all equally dear to the conscious workers of Russia. The theoretical heritage of the revolutionary Plekhanov is regarded by communist workers as the finest page of its own past.

On the day of the twenty-fifth anniversary of the existence of its party the advanced workers of Russia will, with their caps doffed, mentally file past the countless graves containing the mortal part of the tens and hundreds of thousands of our fighters who have perished for the cause of the party, the cause of the Russian proletariat, and the tens if not hundreds of thousands of years of hard labour and imprisonment that Russian workers have paid with in order to destroy the Tsarist autocracy and erect the dictatorship of the proletariat. Whole generations of revolutionaries have perished in the struggle for the liberation of the country from the yoke of autocracy. Whole armies of exiles, countless tens and hundreds of thousands have trodden the remote trails into the infernal regions of Tsarist exile, where a good half of them were to perish while, until the last, retaining their confidence in the working class. Before the graves of our fallen predecessors and leaders and before the memory of the tens and hundreds of thousands of nameless heroes and fighters who sprung from the depths of the masses, the workers of Russia today dip the victorious banners.

The Russian Communist Party (Bolsheviks) was born in the working class districts. Small workers' propagandist circles, persecuted by the fire and sword of the Tsarist autocracy in the 1890s, have now turned into the most powerful proletarian party in the world, which governs a mighty proletarian state whose territory covers one sixth of the earth.

In the middle of the 1890s our party, in the form of the League of Struggle for the Liberation of the Working Class, organized for the first time a mass struggle of workers around their economic demands. At the end of 1900 the party organized the all-Russian newspaper *Iskra*, which illuminated for Russian workers the thorny but glorious road of political struggle against autocracy and the bourgeoisie. In 1905 the party led workers in the first great revolution which formed an overture to the proletarian victory to come in 1917. In December 1905 the party stood at the head of the Moscow proletarians who mounted that armed uprising of the oppressed class which played no less a role in the history of the liberation struggle of the proletariat than the uprising of the Paris Communards of 1871.

Dedication to the party of the working class can be tested more during its defeats than during its victories. After the defeat of the 1905 revolution in the harsh and dark days of the counterrevolution the Bolshevik party did not divorce itself for a moment from the working class. Under the crossfire of innumerable blows from the Tsarist autocracy and the counter-revolutionary bourgeoisie, the party upheld the banner of the proletariat and the revolution. In the tough struggle against Menshevism—which by this time had become open betrayal of the working class and the revolution, i.e. 'liquidationism'—the Bolsheviks alone fought to the end for the party. In 1912 the Bolsheviks finally broke off all connections with Menshevism, which hung like a ball and chain on the feet of the proletarian vanguard. *Zvezda* and *Pravda* reared a new generation of Russian workers, whose best representatives are today carrying great responsibilities. In 1914, on the eve of the imperialist war, the St. Petersburg workers built the first barricades against the Tsarist autocracy since 1905, and once again standing at the head of this newly emerging armed uprising was the Bolshevik party. From the start of the imperialist war all the Mensheviks and S.R.s, with isolated exceptions, went wholly over to the side of the bourgeoisie, and called the workers to defend the Tsarist-landlord 'fatherland' in the imperialist slaughter. The Bolshevik deputies were thrown into hard labour camps. All the unbridled fury of the rabid autocracy and chauvinist bourgeoisie hurled interminable repressions on the Bolsheviks who alone had remained true to the proletarian international and who alone throughout Russia had taken on the struggle against the imperialist war. In 1917 our party was in a minority for a time in the working class, which had fallen under the influence of defencism. But the party knew how to explain insistently to its class what it still did not understand. As soon as the majority of workers in Russia realized the fraud of defencism and as soon as the mirage of bourgeois democracy and an S.R.-Menshevik 'coalition' dispersed, the Bolshevik party led the working class of Russia into its decisive battle and secured its victory over the bourgeoisie.

Soviet power has entered the sixth year of its existence, with its hardest time now behind it. Consolidating the victory proved to be far more difficult than to tear it from bourgeois hands in the first place. The best worker members of our party cemented the Red Army with the blood of their hearts. From the first combat group which fought in December 1905 in Krasnaya Presnya, and the first Red Guard detachment which rebuffed the S.R. Kerensky's march on Petrograd in 1917, until the bloodiest battles of the Red Army on the Perekop the Russian Communist Party was in the front ranks. Always in the most dangerous spot. Always in the heat of events. Always under the fire of the cruellest foe. Together with the working class its party learnt *by experience*, committing frequent mistakes and blunders. But one mistake it did not make—it did not surrender power to the bourgeoisie.

In a backward, largely illiterate country, which only a few years ago was groaning under the yoke of the most savage landlord autocracy, the Russian Communist Party proved able to raise the lowest layers of workers and help them to learn to govern the state. In the difficult years of 1920 and 1921 when the hardships and anguish of the first proletarian revolution, surrounded on all sides by enemies, reached their highest point, the party of the Bolsheviks proved able to stand out fearlessly against the vacillations within its own class, vacillations which, with the slightest weakness in the vanguard, could turn into an unprecedented defeat for the proletariat.

Russian workers were to prove in one respect more fortunate than their predecessors, the French proletarians, who were the first to win power for a short time in 1871 in Paris. One of the principal causes of the fall of the Paris communards was the absence of a single, closely-knit proletarian party with a clear revolutionary programme and tactics. The Paris Communards *lacked a communist party* to head the working class which was rising up in insurrection. The Russian workers created such a party themselves. By harsh experience they reached the conviction that without such a party, effecting the dictatorship of the class is impossible.

The fundamental idea of Russian revolutionary Marxism, which began in the 1890s, consists in that the working class of Russia must become the *hegemonic class*, the main driving force of the revolution, the *leader class* which will take on the reconstruction of the whole country and effect its dictatorship for this purpose. *Soviet power, workers' power is in fact the hegemony of the working class in the revolution, invested in flesh and blood*. Only Bolshevism defended the idea of the hegemony of the proletariat to the end and carried it forward for decades through all the stages of Russia's political history to make it a living reality today. But the hegemony of the proletariat is impossible without the hegemony of the communist party. The dictatorship of the working class finds its expression in the dictatorship of the party created by it and standing at its head. The history of the R.C.P is the history of the Russian working class. This history shows what the proletariat is capable of when it dares to create its own independent proletarian party, not turning from its path and fearlessly realizing its historical mission.

The communist party created by the Russian proletariat was able to become the guiding spirit and chief force of the international community of workers, the Communist International. The example of the Russian workers shines like a bright star on the proletarians of all countries. The Russian Communist Party has linked its fate indissolubly with the fate of the working class of Russia and the advanced detachments of the proletariat of the whole world. This is a life-and-death link. The worker of Russia today sees the truth of the Russian Communist Party. Even those layers of non-party working people who in the hardest times of the proletarian revolution stood aside and regarded the work of our party with mistrust, are today convinced that the only correct road was the one followed by the advanced section of Russian workers organized in the Russian Communist Party. The workers are with us. And this is the finest proof of the correctness of our tactics. The workers are with us, and non-party proletarians look upon the R.C.P. as *their* party. For the whole proletariat of Russia the R.C.P. is 'our' party. The time will come, moreover, when the overwhelming majority of workers will be organizationally connected with the Russian Communist Party and when only isolated workers will not be party members, and in working-class districts the days when a worker might not have been a member of his communist party will be recalled with wonder. But already today the working class and its R.C.P. are a single entity.

You, old workers who remember the yoke of Tsarism, who have passed through hundreds of Tsarist jails and places of exile, who have not forgotten the shootings of January 9th, who remember the December Rising of 1905 and the massacre on the Lena, who have not forgotten what it meant to be unemployed under the power of the bourgeoisie and have tasted the regime of capitalist hard labour, must teach the younger generation of workers that *there is no higher task and greater honour than to live and die for the party of the proletariat, the Russian Communist Party*, which has already given our working class its first victories and is leading it to the final victory over the bourgeois world.

Let anyone tell us another name anywhere in the world which is as close and as dear to millions of workers throughout the world as the name of the leader and teacher of *our* party, Vladimir Ilyich Lenin. Let anyone tell us another party in the world which is so linked to the working masses of its country as *our* party.

Long stubborn years of struggle to build our proletarian state, to reconstruct our economy, to eliminate illiteracy and poverty in our country, to raise the culture of the working class and the peasantry following it, and to create a genuinely socialist state apparatus in the socialist fatherland are still ahead. But we know that we will manage these tasks. As one of the detachments of the international army of labour, and following the behests of the great teachers of the international proletariat, Marx and Engels, we shall triumph.

Workers of Russia! Close ranks to the last man around the Russian Communist Party!

Long live the working class of Russia and its advance guard, the Russian Communist Party!

Long live the international communist party, the Communist International!

Central Committee
of the Russian Communist Party
(Bolsheviks).

APPENDIX IV

The Bolsheviks and the Hegemony of the Proletariat (1923)

An article by G. Zinoviev

If we had to express the essence of Bolshevism and its role in the Russian revolutionary movement in a phrase, and to name the main regulating idea of Bolshevism, we would say that this idea is the *hegemony of the proletariat*. The real watershed between revolutionary Marxism and populism in all its shades and varieties, and subsequently the difference between the tendencies within so-called 'Legal Marxism', between 'Economism' and '*Iskra*-ism' and between '*Pravda*-ism' and 'liquidationism', is the question of the hegemony of the proletariat. This is the basic divergence from which springs all the remaining differences which, however major in themselves, are nevertheless relatively secondary. This is the nodal point of all differences. The question of the hegemony of the proletariat is the problem of all problems.

The formula we use today says: *democracy or dictatorship*. But this formula in essence flows wholly from the problem of the hegemony of the proletariat, and in fact forms the converse side of this problem.

The founders of the idea of the hegemony of the proletariat in the Russian revolution were Plekhanov and Lenin. The 'little difference' between Plekhanov and Lenin consists only in the fact that Plekhanov emerged on to the political arena earlier than Lenin and was the first to proclaim theoretically the idea of the hegemony of the proletariat in the Russian revolution (if only to *betray* politically this idea at the most critical points of Russia's political history), while Lenin remained true to this basic idea for over 30 years, carried it forward through all the most difficult stages of the Russian liberation movement, and created a party which put this idea into practice.

As is known, at the Paris International Congress of the Second International in 1889, Plekhanov, who then was the undisputed leader of all revolutionary Marxists in Russia and the dominant influence among the Marxist intellectuals of that time, spoke the historical truth: 'The Russian revolution will triumph either as a revolution of the *working class* or it will not triumph at all'.

This was in fact one of the tersest and most concise political formulations of the idea of the hegemony of the proletariat. To today's generation of Bolsheviks and today's workers' party Plekhanov's phrase might seem to be a simple truism. For what conscious revolutionary does not now understand that only the working class could have become the main force which carried out the victorious revolution in Russia? However, at the end of the 1880s what Plekhanov said was a discovery not only for international socialism but also for the Russian workers' movement of that time. Plekhanov 'discovered' the working class in Russia just as Marx and Engels 'discovered' the working class in all the capitalist countries in Europe. In the era which preceded Plekhanov's historic statement at the Paris Congress, the revolutionary, or rather Narodnik intellectuals of the day based themselves on the 'people', that is, on the *peasantry*. The working class existed for the Narodniks only at best as a subsidiary force, as one group within the population which could also be of help to the victory over autocracy. As a great concession, one of the principal leaders of Narodnaya Volya, Lev Tikhomirov, when at the zenith of his fame and no one could suspect that he would descend to the steps of the Tsar's throne, agreed that the working class was very important 'for the revolution'. Plekhanov had to prove exhaustively that for this formula to be true it had to be stood upon its head, that is, one should say that *the revolution is very important for the working class* and not the reverse.

Plekhanov remained true to the idea of the hegemony of the proletariat in 1903 also; he betrayed it for the first time about 1905, that is, immediately the first great revolution which was to serve as a rehearsal for the events of 1917 was at hand, and when the idea of the hegemony of the proletariat had for the first time to be put to a historical test and pass through the crucible of a real revolution.

The discussion which took place over the programme at the Second Congress of our party in 1903 deserves that all conscious workers be acquainted with it in detail. It was none other than Plekhanov with typical brilliance and talent who at the Second Congress ridiculed the fetishistic attitude towards the principles of 'democracy'. The duration of parliament, universal suffrage—these all depend on circumstances. If a particular parliament (as it was with the Constituent Assembly) is hostile to the interests of the working class, then we have an interest in its term of existence being short, and if possible dissolving it in two days rather than endure it for two years. An instance is theoretically possible where a victorious proletariat would deprive its class opponents of the franchise. All this was said by none other than Plekhanov. Abolition of the death penalty? But what about Nikolai the Bloody? Surely it would be needed here? Everything depends on circumstances, time and place. The interest of the revolution is the highest law. So said Plekhanov, thus causing hissing from the future Mensheviks. One section of the congress stormily applauded Plekhanov, while a couple of delegates began to catcall. 'If such speeches meet approval at a congress of social-democracy then we are obliged to catcall', these delegates declared. Among these latter was also the Menshevik leader Rozanov who had to be put on trial by the Soviet authorities in 1920 for belonging to a landlord counter-revolutionary party.

V.I. Lenin for the first time formulated in sufficient detail the idea of the hegemony of the proletariat in the Russian revolution in 1894. Quite recently the comrades who were working on the publication of the complete collected works of Comrade Lenin had the good fortune to unearth (for this we are indebted to the comrades) a remarkable work by Comrade Lenin of 1894 which had not seen the light of day called *What the 'Friends of the People' are and How They Fight the Social-Democrats*. This work will probably soon be published and then of course every thinking worker can study it diligently.

Lenin's *Collected Works*, Vol. 1, pp. 129-326.

The following quotations are to be found on pages 299-300.

This work consists of a reply to articles by N.K. Mikhailovsky and S. Krivenko in the Narodnik *Russkoe Bogatstvo* opposing the Marxists, which appeared at the end of 1893 and the beginning of 1894. The reader will not complain of the following lengthy extract from this remarkable work of Vladimir Ilyich which formulates with a classic clarity and simplicity the idea of the hegemony of the proletariat:

'The worker cannot fail to see that he is oppressed by capital, that his struggle has to be waged against the bourgeois class. And this struggle, aimed at satisfying his immediate economic needs, at improving his material conditions, inevitably demands that the workers organize, and inevitably becomes a war not against individuals, but against a class, the class which *oppresses and crushes the working people not only in the factories, but everywhere*. (my emphasis—G.Z.) That is why the factory worker is none other than the *foremost representative of the entire exploited population*. (my emphasis—G.Z.) And in order that he may fulfil his function of representative in an organized, sustained struggle ... all

APPENDIX IV

that is needed is simply to make him understand his position, to make him understand the political and economic structure of the system that oppresses him, and the necessity and inevitability of class antagonisms under this system'.

The bourgeoisie is the class which presses down not only on the factories and plants but everywhere. The working class, the proletariat in the factories and plants, is none other than the foremost representative of all exploited people, that is of the landless peasants too. The conclusion is that the working class must stand at the head of all the exploited, i.e. become hegemonic in the struggle for liberation. Further on Vladimir Ilyich provides an even more precise substantiation of the idea of the hegemony of the proletariat. He writes:

> 'This position of the factory worker in the general system of capitalist relations makes him the sole fighter for the emancipation of the working class, for only the higher stage of development of capitalism, large-scale machine industry, creates the material conditions and the social forces necessary for this struggle. Everywhere else, where the forms of capitalist development are low, these material conditions are absent; production is scattered among thousands of tiny enterprises (and they do not cease to be scattered enterprises even under the most equalitarian forms of communal landownership); for the most part the exploited still possess tiny enterprises and are thus tied to the very bourgeois system they should be fighting ....Scattered individual petty exploitation ties the working people to one locality, divides them, prevents them from becoming conscious of class solidarity, prevents them from uniting once they have understood that oppression is not caused by some particular individual but by the whole economic system. Large-scale capitalism, on the contrary, inevitably severs all the workers' ties with the old society, with a particular locality and a particular exploiter; it unites them and compels them to commence an organized struggle'.

And in conclusion the following political final chord:

> 'When its advanced representatives (of the working class) have mastered the ideas of scientific socialism, the idea of the historical role of the Russian workers, when these ideas become widespread, and when stable organizations are formed among the workers to transform the workers' present

sporadic economic war into conscious class struggle, then the Russian worker, rising at the head of all the democratic elements, will overthrow absolutism and lead the Russian proletariat (side by side with the proletariat of all countries) along the straight road of open political struggle to the victorious communist revolution'.*

Neither more nor less. The words, written almost 30 years ago, sound as if they had been written today. Mastery of Marxist theory, deep dedication to the working class and individual genius enabled Comrade Lenin to make a statement 30 years ago which was to become directly prophetic.

'Russia's man of the future is the muzhik — thought the representatives of peasant socialism, the Narodniks in the broadest sense of the word. Russia's man of the future is the worker, think the social-democrats. That is how the Marxist view was formulated in a certain manuscript'.

In this brief footnote inserted in this work of Vladimir Ilyich the gist of the question was grasped perfectly. In order to express the present-day views of the Bolsheviks and to formulate exhaustively the idea of the hegemony of the proletariat, one has possibly only to modify the formula in this fashion: 'Russia's man of the future is the worker *leading the peasantry behind him*'.

The whole history of Bolshevism is nothing other than the struggle for the realization of the idea of the hegemony of the proletariat. Starting with the *Friends of the People* (1894), continuing with the old *Iskra* (1900), through *Vpered* and *Proletarii* (1905-1906), and followed by *Zvezda* and *Pravda* (1911-1914) and until our time, Bolshevism has conducted the same struggle. And the perpetual leader of this struggle was V.I. Lenin. *Kornilov or Lenin* was the title of an entire volume of the history of the second Russian revolution by the eminent leader of the party which fought against the hegemony of the proletariat and for the hegemony of the bourgeoisie in the revolution. We are speaking of P.N. Milyukov, and he was right. The whole essence

---

*In *What the 'Friends of the People' Are* V.I. Lenin differed widely from the then Marxist P. Struve, but they still remained ostensibly in the same camp in 1894 until as late as the end of the 1890s. The two poles in the 'single' camp of so-called Legal Marxism are best of all characterized by the concluding note of the notorious P. Struve's *Critical Notes* and on the other hand the above-quoted closing words from *What the 'Friends of the People' Are*. 'Let us learn from capitalism' pronounced Struve. 'Let us lead the Russian proletariat to the communist revolution' pronounced Lenin. Two classes and two worlds. G.Z.

of 1917, which decided the fate of Russia, could not be more succintly and sharply expressed than by those three words: *Kornilov or Lenin*.

Whoever really desires the hegemony of the proletariat in the revolutionary movement, that is, the leading role of the working class during the struggle, must naturally strive for the dictatorship of the proletariat after the victory which terminates the struggle. Menshevism did not put two and two together over this. At the moment of the high point of the movement in the second half of 1905, Menshevism was sometimes, under the pressure of events, not far from recognizing in words the necessity for the hegemony of the working class in the struggle against autocracy. Yet it did not for a moment doubt, and this was an axiom for them, that on the day after victory the working class must put the power in the hands of the liberal bourgeoisie. Why? Because, you see, the revolution can only be bourgeois. Power must belong to the bourgeoisie, and the working class must content itself with being allowed to burn its fingers pulling chestnuts out of the fire for others. The notorious five-volume Menshevik work (the Menshevik history of the 1905 revolution), compiled by the main pillars of Menshevism after the defeat of the first revolution, held on this score a quite definite 'philosophy of history'. The 1905 revolution was smashed because the workers, without prior arrangement, introduced the demand for the eight-hour working day and went in general further than was acceptable to the liberal bourgeoisie. Moreover, one could say that the whole 'tactic' of the Mensheviks in the first period of the February revolution of 1917 was dictated by the same philosophy: you, worker, can take on the struggle on the streets and barricades, but when you've won, immediately take that power along to Milyukov and Guchkov. For the revolution is a bourgeois one ...

The idea of the hegemony of the proletariat in the liberation movement is the sister of the idea of the dictatorship of the proletariat in the period of transition to the abolition of a state of any kind. It is the soul of revolutionary Marxism and thus of Bolshevism.

It has befallen our party to embark practically upon the realization of this great idea. A considerable part of the hard road has been covered. Let us close our ranks firmly!

Over all obstacles, all the complexity of the transitional period, through all the diversions and dead-ends of NEP we will carry onwards the idea of the hegemony of the proletariat. For the proletariat is the only class capable of ending capitalism and creating a socialist system.

APPENDIX V

Trotskyism

[Footnote added by the author to the 2nd (1924) edition]

This footnote was written in the year following 1923, when the Lectures were given, and clearly reveals the extent to which the campaign against 'Trotskyism' had developed in such a short space of time. Zinoviev is clearly attempting to confuse the growing differences within the Russian Communist Party and the International with references to the period before 1917, as he was later to admit. Second, his distortions of the theory of Permanent Revolution, Trotsky's great contribution to Marxism, are even more serious than in the lectures themselves. Trotsky's 'Lessons of October' is his reply to these growing attacks and his 'Permanent Revolution' should be read against Zinoviev's 'account' of this theory. (Ed.)

Trotskyism became a more or less clearly defined tendency in the Russian workers' movement over a period of some years.

At the Second Congress in 1903 Comrade Trotsky immediately joined the Mensheviks. In 1904 his pamphlet *Our Political Tasks* was published by the Mensheviks and was directed against the old *Iskra*, and in particular against Lenin's *What is to be Done?* as well as Comrade Lenin's contemporary pamphlet *One Step Forward Two Steps Back*. Comrade Trotsky's statement in this pamphlet, that between the old (Leninist) *Iskra* and the new *Iskra* (from which Comrade Lenin had resigned and which had fallen into the hands of the Menshevik 'Staff') 'there lies an abyss', did a great service to the Bolsheviks through its revisionist candour.

In 1905 Comrade Trotsky, along with Parvus, formed a left group within Menshevism which took issue with the main core of the Mensheviks over the question of the bourgeoisie. Nevertheless, both in the Menshevik newspaper *Nachalo* (which was published in St. Petersburg) and in the St. Petersburg Soviet of Workers' Deputies Comrade Trotsky continued to work alongside the Mensheviks, although still defending his own particular views. His theory of the 'permanent revolution' had in common

APPENDIX V

with Menshevism that it denied the revolutionary role of the peasantry in our country. The Achilles heel of this whole theory lay in its underestimation of the peasantry.

During 1906 Comrade Trotsky collaborated on several Bolshevik publications.

In 1907 at the London Party Congress, Comrade Trotsky spoke on certain questions as a non-factional social-democrat, though he remained on the whole in a bloc with the Mensheviks. At this congress Comrade Trotsky defended the view that Prokopovich could and should become a member of the party.

From 1910-1911 onwards Comrade Trotsky began to draw closer to the liquidator Mensheviks. He maintained the view that the workers' party must be the sum of different trends, different factions, different groups and different tendencies. At this point Comrade Lenin, who had come out very sharply against such a concept of the role of the party, coined the jocular term 'tendency-ite'. At the beginning of the controversies between the Bolsheviks and the liquidators, Comrade Trotsky did not openly defend the liquidators and acknowledged that in many respects the liquidators were incorrect. But he considered liquidationism to be a 'legitimate trend' in the workers' party. 'Live and let live' was his attitude. This amounted objectively to the party being not an organization cast in one mould but a conglomeration of separate factions and tendencies.

In 1910-1911 Comrade Trotsky published the popular workers' paper *Pravda* in Vienna, which attempted to occupy a non-factional position but it in practice aided the liquidator Mensheviks.

In 1911-1913, Comrade Trotsky was one of the principal organizers of the so-called 'August Bloc'—a bloc of liquidators and Mensheviks which in August 1911 called its liquidator Menshevik conference and declared the most malicious and irreconcilable struggle against the Bolshevisk. When the two daily legal newspapers, *Luch*, the liquidators' organ, and *Pravda*, the organ of the Bolsheviks, began to appear in St. Petersburg, Comrade Trotsky became one of the leading contributors to the former. At the same time he worked on the theoretical journal of the liquidators, published by Potresov, *Nasha Zarya*.

Important re-groupings occurred at the beginning of the imperialist war and Comrade Trotsky took a clear stand against the imperialist war and the leaders of the Second International as a whole. He declined however to collaborate on the Bolshevik journal *Kommunist*, but embarked on the publication of the paper *Nashe Slovo* in Paris jointly with Martov and several conciliator Bolsheviks. Despite its internationalist character and its critical attitude to the Second International, the paper *Nashe Slovo* continued to defend Chkheidze's (Duma) faction against Comrade Lenin and the Leninists.

After the February revolution, Comrade Trotsky at first participated in the Petrograd Inter-District organization, but in June-July 1917 Comrade Trotsky joined the ranks of our Bolshevik party.

Glossary

Names and Organizations

AXELROD, P.B. (1850-1928) — Social-Democrat. In 1883 helped form the Emancipation of Labour group and became a member of the *Iskra* editorial board in 1900. After the 1903 Congress became a prominent leader of Russian Menshevism.

BLACK HUNDREDS — Counter-revolutionary terrorist organization used repeatedly against the Russian working class and democratic movements.

BREST-LITOVSK PEACE (1918) — concluded the war between Revolutionary Russia and Imperial Germany. Although the peace terms were resisted by more than half the delegates of the All-Russian Soviet Congress, Lenin's policy eventually prevailed and the German terms were accepted. Russia had to concede a huge indemnity and relinquish a large amount of territory. Within the Russian Communist Party the negotiations precipitated a sharp crisis because of the opposition of the 'Left Communists' led by Bukharin who opposed the peace on the grounds of principle. Trotsky, who led the Soviet delegation, protracted the negotiations as long as possible in order to give the strike movement in Germany a chance to develop to revolutionary proportions, but the German social democrats stifled the insurgent movement. In the circumstances, said Lenin, Russia was in no position to wage a revolutionary war, but needed a breathing space to consolidate itself and create its own armed forces. Lenin carried the day because of the assistance rendered to him by Trotsky. Later the Stalinists tried to make use of the disputes over Brest-Litovsk as part of their campaign against Trotsky. (See Trotsky's *My Life* for further details of this campaign).

CADETS — Constitutional-Democratic Party. The principal party of the Russian imperial bourgeoisie, founded in October 1905. Cadets called themselves the party of 'people's freedom' but their aim was to preserve Tsarism in the form of a constitutional monarchy. In World War One, Cadets were zealous 'defencists' (q.v.) and after the February Revolution, with the consent of the Socialist-Revolutionary and Menshevik leaders of the Petrograd Soviet, they dominated the capitalist Provisional government and directed its counter-revolutionary policies. After the October Revolution the Cadets organized counter-revolutionary conspiracies against the Soviet Republic, acting as agents and mercenaries of foreign imperialism.

CHERNOV V.M. (1876-1952) — One of the leaders and theoreticians of the Social Revolutionaries. From May to July 1917 he was Minister of Agriculture in the Provisional government and sanctioned severe repressions against peasants who seized landed estates. After the Revolution he organized anti-Soviet risings and emigrated in 1920.

DECEMBRISTS — The first revolutionary movement in Russia, formed after the end of the Napoleonic Wars (1815) chiefly by aristocratic officers. The movement aimed for the abolition of serfdom and the introduction of a liberal constitution. A badly organized revolt in 1825 resulted in the hanging of five of the participants and the exiling of many others to Siberia.

DEFENCISM — was the name given to the view that the Russian army must continue the war so long as the German army still supported the Kaiser. It was opposed by the 'defeatism' of Lenin who proclaimed that 'the defeat of Russia is the lesser evil'. Before Lenin's arrival back in Russia in 1917, the Bolshevik paper *Pravda* supported a 'defencist' position through its policy of 'pressure' on the Provisional government. Lenin, against the line of 'old Bolsheviks' like Zinoviev denounced the Provisional government as capitalist and the policy of patriotically 'defending' it as a betrayal of socialism and internationalism.

DENIKIN, A.I. (1872-1947) — Leading Tsarist General and prominent counter-revolutionary whose troops almost reached Tula in the autumn of 1919. After his defeat he departed for Europe.

ECONOMISM — an opportunist trend among Russian Social-Democrats at the turn of the century. According to the Economists the sole aim of the working class was to wage the economic struggle for higher wages, better conditions etc. Political struggle, they argued, should be left to the liberal capitalist class; they denied the leading role of the working class and its party. Their belief in the spontaneity of the workers' movement led them to belittle the importance of revolutionary theory (Marxism). Lenin's *What is to be Done?* is directed against this trend.

ENGELS' INTRODUCTION (1895) to Marx's *Class struggles in France* — this introduction of Engels was subjected at the time to gross distortion by the opportunist leadership of the Chairman of the Social Democratic Party. In March 1895, Wilhelm Liebknecht printed in *Vorwärts*, the Party's central organ, a number of arbitrarily chosen excerpts from this introduction *'which serve to defend the tactics of peace at all costs and of the abhorrence of force'* . . . as Engels wrote in a letter to Lafargue. Despite Engels' strenuous objections to Kautsky, the German party refused to print the introduction in full and Engels was compelled to agree to the deletion of certain passages where mention was made of the forthcoming armed struggle, because of the threat of the new Anti-Socialist Law in Germany.

ISKRA — was a newspaper founded by Lenin in 1900 as the organ of the RSDLP. It played a decisive role in the foundation of the revolutionary Marxist movement in Russia. After the Second Congress of the RSDLP the Mensheviks gained control of *Iskra* and in October of that year it became a Menshevik mouthpiece.

KOLCHAK, A.V. (1873-1920) — Russian Tsarist admiral, monarchist and one of the main leaders of the 1918-1919 counter-revolution against the Soviet Republic. After the October revolution, with the support of British, Fench and American imperialism he proclaimed himself Supreme Ruler of Russia and headed the military-bourgeois-landowners' dictatorship in the Urals, Siberia and the Far East. The Red Army, built, by Trotsky, eventually brought about Kolchak's defeat.

KRASNAYA NOV — Literary journal founded in Petrograd in April 1921 and subsequently a publishing house.

LASSALLE, F. (1825-64) — German petty bourgeois writer and lawyer; in 1848-49 he took part in the democratic movement in the Rhenish Province; early in the 1860s he joined the German working class movement and became one of the founders of the General Association of German Workers (1863). He stood for the unification of Germany from above under Prussian hegemony. He laid the foundations for the opportunist trend in the leadership of the German working class movement.

LEAGUE OF STRUGGLE FOR THE EMANCIPATION (LIBERATION) OF THE WORKING CLASS — was formed by Lenin in the autumn of 1895 and united all the Marxist workers circles in St. Petersburg. It was the first organization which led the struggle to combine socialism with the labour movement. Its influence spread far beyond St. Petersburg and it gave a powerful impulse to the amalgamation into similar Leagues of workers' circles in other areas of Russia.

LUNACHARSKY, A.V. (1875-1933) — Soviet writer and playwright, wrote a number of important works on literature and art. Joined the Bolsheviks in 1903 but in the period of reaction following the 1905 defeat he turned away from Marxism and advocated the reconciliation of Marxism with religion. In 1917 became a member of the Bolshevik Party and became Commissar for Education until 1929.

MARTOV, Y.O. (1873-1923) — Social-Democrat since 1900 and member of *Iskra* editorial board. After 1903 RSDLP Congress a leader of the Mensheviks. Following the October Revolution an opponent of the Soviet power and emigrated in 1920.

MENSHEVISM — refers to the reformist wing of the Russian Social Democratic movement. They split with the Bolsheviks in 1903 over the questions of Party organization and revolutionary policy. The Mensheviks opposed Lenin's conception of a revolutionary party as the vanguard of the proletariat, built on the basis of democratic centralization. They favoured a looser form of organization, akin to that of Western European Social Democracy. Considering the character of the Russian Revolution to be bourgeois-democratic, the Mensheviks advocated a coalition with the liberal bourgeoisie. They supported the Provisional Government in 1917 and strenuously opposed the October insurrection on the grounds that Russia 'was not ripe for socialism'.

MIKHAILOVSKY, N.K. (1842-1904) — Russian sociologist and publicist, leader of liberal populism, determined opponent of Marxism. For Plekhanov's polemic against him see the latter's *The Development of the Monist View of History*.

MILLERAND, A. (1859-1943) — opportunist member of French Socialist Party who in 1899 joined a bourgeois government in France.

MILYUKOV, P.N. (1859-1943) — Leader of the Cadet Party, historian and writer. Active White guard émigré.

MONTAGNE AND GIRONDE — Political trends during the French bourgeois revolution. The Montagnards, or Jacobins, was the name given to the more resolute representatives of the revolutionary bourgeoisie who advocated the destruction of absolutism and feudalism. They were bitterly opposed by the Girondists who vacillated between revolution and counter-revolution. Their policy was one of a deal with the Monarchy, and after 1793 they went over to the counter-revolutionary forces.

NARODNAYA VOLYA (People's Will) — a secret Narodnik society founded in 1879. It regarded the political struggle as a conspiracy to be organized by small groups of intellectuals. The Narodnaya Volya was smashed by the Tsarist government soon after the assassination of Alexander II by members of the society in March 1881. After that most of its members deserted the revolutionary struggle and preached reconciliation with the autocracy.

NARODNIKS — Followers of a petty bourgeois trend in the Russian revolutionary movement which arose in the 1860s. The Narodniks stood for the abolition of the autocracy and the transfer of landed estates to the peasantry. At the same time they believed capitalism in Russia to be a temporary phenomenon with no future, and they therefore considered the peasantry, not the working class, to be the main revolutionary force. They regarded the village commune (*mir*) as the embryo of socialism. With the object of rousing the peasantry to struggle against Tsarism the Narodniks 'went amongst the people' to the villages, but found little support.

PEROVSKAYA, Sophia Lvovna (1853-1881) — Russian revolutionary and member of Narodnaya Volya; took an active part in the assassination of Alexander II.

PETROVSKY, G.I. (1878-1958) — Later became a functionary in the Stalin period. From 1919 to 1938 Chairman of the All-Ukraine Central Executive Committee, Deputy Chairman of the USSR Central Executive Committee.

PLEKHANOV, G.V. (1856-1918) — Leader of the Russian and international working class movement who laid the basis for the Marxist movement in Russia. He founded the Emancipation of Labour Group in Geneva in 1883. After the Second Congress of the Russian Social Democratic Labour Party (1903) he adopted a conciliatory attitude towards revisionism and later joined the Mensheviks. During The First World War he was a social-chauvinist.

RABOCHAYA MYSL (Workers' Thought) — a newspaper published by a group of Economists (q.v.) in Russia from 1897-1902. A critique of the paper's policy is to be found in Lenin's *What is to be Done?*

ROBESPIERRE, M.F., (1758-1794) — outstanding French revolutionary leader of the Jacobins (q.v.) during the French Revolution at the end of the 18th century, and head of the Revolutionary government (1793-94).

SOCIALIST-REVOLUTIONARIES (S.R.s) — Russian petty-bourgeois party founded in 1902 through the merger of various Narodnik groups and circles. The S.R.s made no distinction within the peasantry and repudiated the leading role of the working class in the revolutionary movement. Their chief demand was for the socialization of land under capitalism. They subscribed to the theory of 'active heroes' as against the 'passive mob' and regarded individual terror as the prime weapon of struggle.

STOLYPIN, P.A. (1862-1911) — Headed the Tsarist cabinet following the period of reaction in the wake of the 1905 defeat. His favourite formula was: 'first pacification, then reform'. 'Pacification' meant the entrenchment of autocratic rule through organized terror. His 'reforms' amounted to an attempt to stabilize Russian society through the fostering of 'strong peasant economies' (kulaks) in the country.

GLOSSARY

STRUVE, P.B., (1870-1944) — Russian bourgeois economist and writer who underwent an evolution from Marxism to monarchism.

THE EMANCIPATION OF LABOUR GROUP — was founded by Plekhanov with other Russian refugees, including Axelrod (q.v.) Zasulich (q.v.) after the break with Populism. It was the first definitely Marxist organization in Russia and was dissolved when the united Social Democratic party was formed.

TUGAN-BARANOVSKY, M.I., (1865-1919) — Prominent Russian bourgeois economist and 'Legal Marxist' who tried to use parts of Marx's writings in *Capital* to 'prove' that there could be a smooth, crisis-free development of capitalism in Russia.

WEBB, S. (1859-1947) and Beatrice (1858-1943) — were leading members of the Fabian Society, established in 1884. The Webbs repudiated working class struggle as the vehicle for achieving socialism and advocated the possibility of a peaceful, gradual, transition to socialism through Parliament.

WRANGEL, P.N. — Was elected Commander-in-Chief of the White forces attempting to overthrow the young Soviet Republic. For most of 1920 he succeeded in remaining in the Crimea and only after heroic efforts by the Red Army was he forced to flee with the remnants of his troops to Turkey and then to the Balkans.

ZASULICH, Vera (1849-1919) — a prominent member of the Narodniks and later of the Social-Democratic movement in Russia; became a leader of the Mensheviks following the 1903 Congress of the RSDLP.

ZEMSTVOS — The Zemstvo was a form of local government introduced in the central Russian provinces in 1864 and dominated by the nobility. The Zemstvos had jurisdiction over purely local affairs — hospitals, roads, etc. Their activities were under the ultimate control of the Ministry of the Interior who could cancel any decisions of which he did not approve.

ZHELYABOV, A.I. (1850-1881) — Prominent Narodnik revolutionary and initiator of Narodnaya Volya organization. Executed for his part in the assassination of Alexander II.

ZIMMERWALD LEFT — was formed at Lenin's initiative at the International Socialist Conference in Zimmerwald (Switzerland) in September 1915. It brought together left Social-Democrats from various European countries and its Manifesto condemned the war, exposed the social-chauvinists and called for a determined revolutionary struggle against the war. Lenin and Zinoviev were amongst the members of the Bureau which the Conference elected.